2

Self-Directed Behavior

Self-Modification for
Personal Adjustment

Self-Directed Behavior

Self-Modification for Personal Adjustment

David L. Watson and Roland G. Tharp

University of Hawaii

Brooks/Cole Publishing Company
Monterey, California

A Division of Wadsworth Publishing Company, Inc.
Belmont, California

ISBN: 0-8185-0035-2
L.C. Catalog Card No: 78-178891
Printed in the United States of America
5 6 7 8 9 10—77 76 75 74

This book was edited by Phyllis London and designed by Linda Marcetti. It was typeset by Datagraphics, Inc., Phoenix, Arizona, and printed and bound by Kingsport Press, Kingsport, Tennessee.

For our parents

Preface

There are many books about personal adjustment but almost none about how to achieve it. Many books exhort us to become better every day, but few tell us how. This state of affairs is no longer necessary, because a general theory explaining human behavior has been developed, and techniques for applying it to problems of behavior are available. This book is designed to acquaint you with the general theory of behavior, to guide you through exercises for developing skills in self-analysis, and to provide concrete information about how to achieve the goals you hold for yourself. The most important goal of this volume is to help you, the reader, achieve more self-determination, more "willpower," more control over your own life.

The book can serve as a textbook in psychology courses, but it does not depend on a formal course structure. Any reader can use it for self-instruction; no "prerequisites" are necessary. Clients of therapists or counselors can use it as an adjunct in planning their own self-change.

You should be warned about one possible unexpected side effect: you may become interested in the science of behavior. A startling number of people do find themselves delving deeper into the subject as a result of studying this material. This interest may be partly in response to the current rage for relevance—few things are more immediately interesting to us than ourselves. But it is also in response to the genuine experiential learning that can result from the self-change process.

The vehicle for learning will be your own self-analysis, your own programs for implementing your values. After reading a discussion of the individual nature of values, you will become acquainted with a few basic theoretical concepts of behavior analysis, and you will then move quickly through a series of topics that constitute the several steps toward achieving greater self-determination. Next is a discussion of the kinds of professional help available for those whose problems do not yield to self-help. Finally, you will find a theoretical and philosophical discussion of will and self-control. Throughout, you are urged to accompany each chapter with your own self-improvement project. In a sense, your daily life will become the laboratory in which you will study and develop your own behavior.

Acknowledgements

It is difficult to acknowledge all those individuals without whom this work could not have been done. We are particularly indebted for the excellent critical analyses provided by Leonard Ullmann, Donna Gelfand, and John Peters. Joyce Watson helped at every stage in the project, most particularly in reading the manuscript for clarity.

Financial support was provided, in part, by grants from the University of Hawaii Research Council and the National Institute of Mental Health (Grant #MH 17747.01).

This book grew primarily from our experiences with students and colleagues at the University of Hawaii. Hours of patient conversation with Jack Annon, Richard Dubanoski, Ian Evans, Ronald Johnson, Scott MacDonald, and Gisele Speidel provided significant contributions. Several students have worked closely with us from the beginning, helping in many ways to develop ideas: Barbara Brown, Janice Kaya, Linda Mahoe, Chantis Stinson, Kathleen Westropp, and Brian Young. A number of students participated in our first seminars, and we are happy to acknowledge their contributions: Gale Ashby, Jim Bell, Steven Brown, Diana Chang, Pamela Dominy, Catherine Frost, Sandra Gatz, Velma Hata, Liana Higa, Nancy Hunter, Alice Johnson, Ellen Kaguni, Lynette Kajiwara, Jane Krisberg, Janice Ledoux, Anne Leung, Sylvia Lum, Lynette Mizuno, Tomoko Nagado, Abdul Halim Othman, Ron Pickus, Lanette Shizuru, Walter Skiba, Clarence Steadman, Loxy Strahle, Eta Yee, Ernie Yoshimoto, and Gwen Young.

Roberta Fong, Catherine Frost, and Irene Ohashi prepared the manuscript; Janet Sall assisted in proofreading.

Lastly, we acknowledge the help of some 500 students enrolled through several semesters in the Psychology 110 course at the University of Hawaii. They studied self-modification by undertaking self-change projects, thereby helping both themselves and us. The book could not have been written without their cheerful cooperation.

Foreword for the professional

Self-modification is an effort to link self-change strategies to a general theory of behavior. The systematic study of self-modification probably began with Skinner's 1953 work, *Science and Human Behavior,* in which he listed eight ways of achieving self-control. In 1965, Ferster distinguished three such forms (following the Ferster, Nurnberger, and Levitt study of 1962), and Goldiamond published his well-known case-studies paper (Ferster; 1965, Goldiamond, 1965). At least five years earlier, Kanfer, with his associates, began his pioneering work on self-reinforcement (Kanfer and Marston, 1963a; 1963b; Marston and Kanfer, 1963). There followed Kanfer and Phillips' (1966) "instigation therapy" paper, which outlines aims and techniques for the clinical teaching of self-regulation. An excellent example of instigation-therapy research and treatment soon appeared (Rehm and Marston, 1968). In 1966, Cautela had published his covert sensitization technique. The gradual exploration of self-control adaptations of standard behavior therapy techniques began—first with aversion therapy (McGuire and Vallance, 1964) and with desensitization (Migler and Wolpe, 1967). From 1967 to the present, case reports, parametric studies, and technique suggestions have burgeoned. A representative list would include Stuart, 1967; Tooley and Pratt, 1967; Kolb, Winter, and Berlew, 1968; Kahn and Baker, 1968; Davison, 1968; Nolan, 1968; Bergin, 1969; Harris, 1969; Rardin, 1969; Rutner and Bugle, 1969; Nurnberger and Zimmerman, 1970; Reppucci and Baker, 1969; Stuart, 1971; and Marston and McFall, 1971.

Self-modification procedures are based on a substantial body of laboratory experimentation, much of which is discussed in Chapter Fourteen. Excellent reviews of theory and research in this area are available in Kanfer (1970), Kanfer and Phillips (1970), and Bandura (1969).

Two very promising lines of self-modification theory are not included in this present edition. Both have been well reviewed by Cautela (1970). One is the use of verbal, or subvocal, or coverant self-reinforcement, as suggested by Homme (1965). While this procedure may be one of great power, we have elected to await further experimental and clinical evidence for the most effective methods of managing it. The second theory deals with methods of covert sensitization—counterconditioning by use of noxious imagery (Cautela, 1966). While this technique has demonstrated clinical utility, there are reasons to be wary of its inappropriate use. In our experience, many individuals are prone to let their images drift into fantasy while on "take-home" covert sensitization instructions. The guiding of imagery by a therapist protects against this, but self-directed fantasizing can produce unfortunate, unintended sensitizations. By contrast, it is difficult to see a destructive outcome for self-desensitization, even if it is unsuccessful.

These two techniques, coverant conditioning and covert sensitization, which rely on the manipulation of mental events in accordance with behavioral ones, deserve vigorous research. Subsequent treatments of self-modification may well include them.

David L. Watson
Roland G. Tharp

Contents

Chapter Five
Specifying the Problem 59

Chapter Six
Gathering Baseline Data 79

Chapter Seven
Analyzing Reinforcers 101

Chapter Eight
The Basic Form of Intervention 115

Chapter Thirteen
Professional Help 215

Chapter Fourteen
Self-Modification and Willpower 239

Self-Directed Behavior

Self-Modification for
Personal Adjustment

Chapter One
Overview

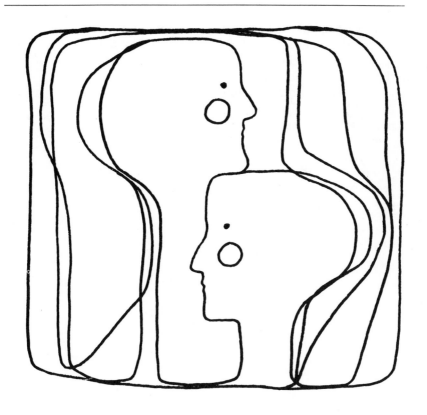

1. The purpose of the book is to teach the reader how to self-direct, or self-modify, his behavior. The principles recommended are derived from the science of behavior, psychology.
2. The ideas presented in each chapter of the book are noted briefly.
3. An example of a self-modification project is given, in which a young man modifies his relations with his parents.
4. Step one in choosing a self-modification project of your own is specified.

This book is written for the reader who wants to improve the quality of his personal relationship to the world around him. If you are such a person, then you should find the book useful in your efforts to establish greater harmony between yourself and your environment.

The material in this volume is based on principles discovered in the psychological laboratories of the world during the last hundred years. These principles of psychology have been extended more widely than ever during the last decade. Human problems—from mental illness to criminology, from marital disorder to public education—have been usefully analyzed in terms of psychological principles. Some solutions have led to new techniques. One of these techniques is *behavior modification.* Using this technique, psychological principles are systematically applied to human problems for the purpose of changing behavior.

This book is a guide to the self-use of behavior modification. The procedures recommended are derived from the self-modification projects of hundreds of our students.

You will absorb some principles of psychology from this reading— at times we will ask you to think about principles rather carefully—but the basic aim is to help you learn to do something about your own dissatisfactions.

Of course, shelves are filled with instructions about how to have a better life, better friends, better sex, and better children. You can read about how to stop smoking, lose weight, quit gambling, and attract dates. Not all these advice manuals are worthless; many have sound ideas. *But their ideas are sound only to the extent that they are in accord with the general principles of human behavior.* This book is different in that the procedures and techniques recommended are all derived from the science of psychology and therefore are known to be in accord with these principles of human behavior.

To learn easily, it usually helps to have an advance idea of what you are going to learn. For this reason, each chapter in the book is preceded by an outline. Look over the outline and ask yourself questions about the ideas presented before beginning to read the chapter. You will also be more likely to remember what you have read if you examine the outline again after completing the chapter (Fox, 1966).

Outline of the book

This principle, that an overview of ideas to come will aid in the learning process, may be applied to all the material presented in this book. For that reason, an outline of the entire book follows. It will acquaint you with the order in which ideas are presented and some of the relationships between the ideas.

In Chapter Two, we present a viewpoint on adjustment in which adjustment is seen to be the quality of the relationship between a person's behavior and his environment. These relationships are the product of learning experiences. Therefore, in Chapter Three, we examine the principles of learning: to improve your adjustment to your environment, you must be able to direct your own learning experiences.

Chapter Four is an overview of the principles and procedures involved in self-directing behavior change. Briefly, self-direction involves observing your own behavior, identifying areas where change or improvement is needed, arranging your life so that appropriate learning experiences can occur, and then carrying out a plan to obtain those learning experiences. Such plans must be carefully worked out and then maintained and adjusted until the preset goal is achieved. Chapters Five through Twelve deal with these procedures in detail.

The last two chapters deal with issues that some might think should come first: the willpower required to be self-directing and the role of professional help in self-direction. We have dealt with these issues at the end because we feel that it is very important that you actually have the experience of becoming self-directing as you read this book, and because we want to introduce you to the necessary techniques as soon as possible. After you have actually attempted self-direction, you will be able to apply the ideas presented in these last chapters to your own experience. If the book is to be an actual guide to self-modification, or self-direction, as well as a text, *it is very important that you carry out the practices we recommend as you read the book.*

A case history in self-modification

When we teach the college course in which the procedures presented in this book were developed, each of our students carries out a self-modification project of his own choice as a part of the course requirement. Later, we will discuss how you can choose a problem of your own to work on as you read.

The book is full of case histories. Care has been taken to protect the privacy of the people whose case material we use. Sometimes we present cases as they actually happened, with enough changes to disguise the persons involved, while at other times we present a composite of several cases blended together to make a point while disguising individuals. All case material comes from the self-modification projects of our students. An actual case history of a complete project in self-modification follows.

Case #1 was a twenty-year-old male student, Ted, who lived at home with his parents and attended the University full time. Ted reported that over a period of several months his relationship with his parents had become so bad that they were now having major blow-ups over very trivial incidents. There were few real reasons for disagreement, and many times Ted himself saw his own behavior as the major source of the conflict. He would ignore questions from his parents, "talk back" to them, or say something sarcastic; the usual result was that his parents became angry and retaliated in kind. He then felt both angry and guilty. The problem had been developing over a three-year period and seemed to be getting worse. Ted had reached the point where he was rarely able to engage in simple pleasant conversation at home.

When he enrolled in our course, Ted chose to work on the problem of his poor relationship with his parents as his self-modification project. He decided that he would try to *increase* the number of times he said something pleasant to his parents. First he had to determine how often he made pleasant remarks, so for three weeks, he simply made a mark on a piece of paper whenever he said something pleasant. Over the three-week period, his total output of pleasant remarks to them was four. Just over once per week, on the average, he said something like "Mother, that was a really great meal!" or "Dad, that's very kind of you to offer to help." He decided that it would be reasonable to start by trying to say something pleasant once every three days. This would be an improvement, a first small step.

Ted looked for a way to increase the frequency of his pleasantries. Because shooting pool was a favorite hobby, which he engaged in at least once every three days, he set a rule that he would not allow himself to shoot pool unless he had said something pleasant to his parents first.

At the end of three weeks, Ted had successfully met his goal for each three-day period so he decided to increase his expressions of pleasantness to his parents to once every two days. If he was able to accomplish that goal, he intended to try a gradual increase to at least one pleasant remark every day. He gave himself points for each pleasantry and did not play pool until he had accumulated a certain number of points. As time went on, he gradually increased the number of points required.

Eight weeks after he had begun his plan, Ted was saying something pleasant once every day. His parents were very pleased. The number of arguments had decreased noticeably and this, coupled with his increased pleasantness, made the home situation much nicer. What Ted had done was to use the principles of psychology to direct a change in his own behavior in dealing with a problem in his life.

Ted's is an excellent plan for self-direction. What makes it so? What are the principles involved? What are the essential elements in the plan? These questions are the central issues of this book.

Your own self-modification project: Step one

We strongly suggest that the reader accompany this book with his own self-modification project. You should be thinking about dissatisfactions in your own life that you might like to modify. The first step in choosing one problem to work on is to *make a list of these dissatisfactions.*

Chapter Two
Adjustment: Behavior
and the Environment

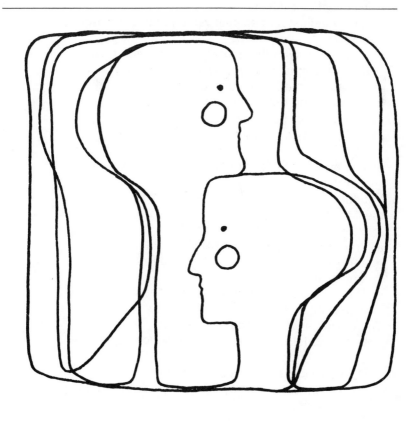

1. Adjustment is defined.
   a. It may indicate a personal value judgment about behavior.
   b. It may deal with the question of behavior in specific situations: behavior changes from one situation to another, so adjustment might be good in one situation but not in another.
2. Two sources of personal problems are specified.
   a. You may perform some behavior but wish that you didn't.
   b. You may fail to perform some behavior but wish that you did.
3. Your behavior in a situation is learned. Your environment teaches you new behaviors and evokes behaviors that you have already learned.
   a. You can self-modify your behavior, then, by deliberately setting out to teach yourself new behaviors in specific circumstances.
   b. This way of looking at adjustment is called the behavioristic model.
4. There is an alternate idea: the medical model.
   a. In this model, inner problems are thought to cause outer symptoms.
      (1) Behavior is seen as a symptom.
      (2) The inner cause may be conflict, or disturbed emotions.
   b. Throughout history, there have been other models as well.
   c. Each model has certain different implications about what you should do about problems in adjustment.
5. Conclusion: adjustment is a value judgment about

the relationship between a person's behavior and his environment. These relationships are learned. In self-modification, you try to analyze the relationships, modify the environment, and produce new learning.

To arrange, compose, harmonize; to come to terms; to arrange the parts suitably to themselves and to something else; and to do this according to the laws which govern this harmony: that is the definition of adjustment.

Ordinarily, we think of self-adjustment as meaning harmony among the various parts of the self—that is, harmony among our thoughts, our feelings, our actions. The person who is racked by internal contradictions, who is indecisive, confused, self-contradictory, is not considered happy or balanced. In common language, such a person may be called mentally ill, disturbed, or badly adjusted. Significantly, a synonym for mental illness is unbalanced.

There is another aspect of adjustment which we often consider—the adjustment of the self to the environment. An individual may be out-of-phase with the world around him. He may be called out-of-touch, flipped, spaced, gone, 'way out. These terms colorfully express our awareness that the maladjusted individual is out-of-tune with his environment.

How can the individual adjust to his environment harmoniously? Too often, the idea of adjustment has been used to mean conformity. Thus, many people believe that the well-adjusted individual must not be in conflict with his environment. Particularly, he must not be opposed to his social environment: he must be like the others around him. Given such a view, the rebel, the artist, the protestor, the hermit, and the individualist are all maladjusted. But this view will not stand scrutiny. A completely conforming society would not be able to adapt to changing circumstances, to meet new challenges with new harmonies. For this reason, both conservatives and radicals can agree that the best form of adjustment an individual can make to his environment is dynamic interaction. The pattern of the adjustment must be responsive and changing if the individual is to maintain a chosen course. Like the rudder of a ship, behavior must be changed to adjust to the changing currents and tides of the environment. These adjustments may be in the service of a harmonious and well-charted voyage or they may be chosen to seek out the tempestuous course, the route of adventure. In either event, the pilot is in a constant and dynamic interplay with his environment.

Adjustment and values

A value judgment is a personal decision that something is good or bad. If we say that someone is "badly adjusted," we are making a value judgment. It means *we do not think he should be engaging in a particular behavior* or *we think he should be engaging in some other behavior.* We may even make these judgments about ourselves.

The point is this: different people assign different values to the same behavior. Behavior we think good may seem bad, or at least neutral, to someone else. Behavior we think bad may seem good to others.

There are many people and groups who insist that their values are *true.* Yet if one makes observations around the world, it is easy to see that for any particular behavior thought to be good in one society, it is almost always possible to find another society where the same behavior is thought to be bad. Within each of those groups, what is said to be "good behavior" is defined as the behavior of a well-adjusted person. Thus, opposite behaviors may be defined as "adjusted" in different societies. This is even true within a given society. In America, for example, there are people who think that those who work hard for success and strive to get ahead are well adjusted; there are others who think that to do those very things represents maladjustment.

It is not always obvious that our own values are relative because, for one thing, we are usually taught that the values of *our* group are *true.* This acceptance of a value system seems to occur whatever the group is to which we belong. Also, most of the people around us share our values and their social support makes our jointly held values seem universal. Yet, because there are so many different values, held fervently by different people, *many thoughtful persons have concluded that the values attached to most specific behaviors are indeed relative to one's society and one's time in history.*

The philosophical discipline of ethics seeks to discover regularities in values; many thinkers contend that certain values are not relative but are common to all men at all times. Values such as life, liberty, and the pursuit of happiness—as stated by the early American revolutionaries —are among those which appear repeatedly in many societies. However, to say that to live, feel free, and pursue one's own chosen happiness is a value shared by all men does not specify the exact acts which are permissable. The conditions under which one should forego his own happiness-seeking—or indeed his life—for the benefit of other community members differs sharply across time and societies. Thus, even though there may be universal values, the value assigned to specific acts is highly relative.

The values behind this book

The values the authors hold do influence the specific ideas that follow. Specifically, we value the self-determination of behavior: it is better to design one's own life than to be a passive victim of things that happen. That is our general value-definition of adjustment. We believe that people should be free to pursue their own happiness to the greatest degree that it does not harm others. We believe that society should define its limits of tolerance as widely as possible, to maximize these freedoms for everyone.

The teaching and learning of self-determined behavior seems to us to fall squarely within the value system that allows maximum individual freedom. But of the values of specific acts, or behaviors which one might self-determine, we will speak very little. This, too, is consistent with our argument for freedom and tolerance. There is always the theoretical possibility that someone will teach himself, through self-determination, to be an oppressor of others. This is a risk we run, but a slight one. People who experience their lives as self-determined seem to us more likely to grant self-determination to others.

Values and goals of the individual

A partial list of some of the goals assigned value by a student during one day might look like this: First, he wanted to run a mile, because it would help him stay in shape. Then he wanted to be nice to his mother, to make her day a little brighter. When he went to school, he wanted to study for two hours. At lunch he wanted to appear to be a nice interesting person so that a new friend would accept his invitation to go on a date. During the afternoon, he thought about his future career as an engineer and wanted to be a good one. That night on a date, he thought about his future career as a husband and father and wanted to be good at that too.

Each of us goes through every day with a long list of goals like this. If we can accomplish them, or at least move toward them, we are likely to consider ourselves well adjusted.

Of course, we never accomplish every goal we set. We have inherent limitations, and our environment imposes other limitations upon us. But when we are not achieving our goals because our own behavior is getting in the way or because we don't know how to achieve them, then the question of "maladjustment" may arise. In such situations, we are not at harmony with our environment, or we are not at harmony within our own values.

Adjustment is a question of behavior in specific situations

Often when people ask "Am I well-adjusted?" they imply that there is a single answer to this question. The assumption behind such a question is that adjustment is a unitary characteristic, and that one either has it or he doesn't, just as one is sick or he isn't. For example, if you are sick and the illness is defined by the presence of a fever, then you are feverish, and consequently sick, in all situations until your fever goes away. In this situation it would make sense to ask "Am I sick or healthy?" There is one answer to that question; you are either sick or you are not. This is not true of a characteristic such as adjustment.

Adjustment is a question of feelings and behavior, both of which occur in specific situations. Thus *a person might be well adjusted in that he can do what he wants to do in one type of situation, but badly adjusted in that he cannot do what he wants to do in another situation.* For example, a young man might be able to deal with women quite well and happily but make a miserable botch of his attempts to do well in his career. Or a woman might be able to control her life very adequately when she is functioning as a student but be very unhappy about the lack of control she has over her behavior when she is functioning as a mother.

One of the best ways to understand an abstract point is to have a concrete example. The following case history serves as a specific example of the general issues presented above. It illustrates very well this general point: *Adjustment is a question of behavior and emotion in specific situations.*

Case #2 concerns John S., a nineteen-year-old student. When John came to the office, he looked tired, and his eyes were red and nearly full of tears. He had spent a sleepless night, he said, worrying that he was no good, a fool, probably neurotic, definitely very unhappy. His life was in crisis. He was asked if he had any idea what had set off these terrible feelings.

"Well," he reported, "I know what happened last night. I went to a party by myself, and was having a pretty good time talking to some of the guys, when Ed came in with this terrific chick. I'd seen her on campus before. Really nice. When they came to my group, I tried to talk to her. Man, it was a disaster. I really liked that girl. But after about twenty minutes, she started blasting me.

"The terrible thing is, she said these things about me, and I think they're true. She said I was aloof, that I must think I am a very superior person, and that it hurt her feelings to keep on talking to someone who was so egocentric.

"Every time I try to talk to a nice girl, the same thing happens: disaster. I don't seem to be able to relate to people. The reason this one time upset me so much is that it is so damned typical. I can't get along with people. The ridiculous thing is, I don't feel superior at all. Just the opposite. I feel foolish and stupid."

John was angry and hurt. After he had talked awhile, he was asked to come back to see us the next day, in the afternoon.

The next day, John appeared different. He came into the office with a slight smile. He looked rested; his eyes were dry. "John, you look like a changed man. What happened?" he was asked.

"Nothing much," he replied. "Yesterday when I left here I felt a little better, so I went down to the gym to shoot baskets. I used to play basketball in high school. It was pretty good. Got up a game with a bunch of guys. I always enjoy that."

"What else has been happening?" he was asked.

"Nothing. This morning I spent about two hours talking to Alice. She's too fat for me to get serious about, but she's alright. We have a sort of brother and sister relationship. I like to talk to her.

"Uh, look," he continued, "have you figured out what's wrong with me? I guess I'm just maladjusted. I mean, I feel okay now, but sooner or later, probably sooner, the miseries are going to come back. I think I'm neurotic. For all I know, I'm going crazy."

The reply at this point is crucial to John's understanding of the problem.

"John, you don't seem crazy right now, or even neurotic. You don't even seem maladjusted. Why not?"

"I don't know, Professor. Maybe you have a calming effect on me."

"When you were playing basketball with the guys, do you think you were being neurotic, crazy, or maladjusted?"

"No."

"When you were talking to Alice, do you think you were being any of those things?"

"No."

"Then it looks like we're on the way to understanding your problem."

"We are? Can you help me?"

"Maybe you can help yourself. This is probably what your problem is: you do the wrong things when you are talking to attractive girls. Maybe you withdraw from talking very much, because you feel uncomfortable, because attractive girls make you feel a bit nervous. So you cover up your nervousness with aloofness, you withdraw, and they think you feel superior to them."

"Yeah, okay. But that means I'm neurotic, doesn't it?"

"Not if you mean that you act in a maladjusted manner in every situation you encounter. In most situations, in fact, you're pretty comfortable, and you are happy with the way you act. When you're talking here, or playing basketball, or talking to a girl who's like your sister, you're okay. Your problem in adjustment seems to be about your behavior in one particular situation: talking to pretty girls." (We will return to John's strategy for self-improvement in Chapter Three.)

There is no single answer to a question like "Am I well-adjusted?" Adjustment is specific to the situation. This is another way of saying that we do not operate within a unitary environment. For John we can identify many environments: talking with his professor; talking with his friend, Alice; playing basketball; talking with male friends at a party; talking with an attractive girl at a party. *Each of these sub-environments may be called a situation.*

Each of us is differently adjusted to the many situations in which we regularly find ourselves; in some we will consider ourselves well adjusted, while in others we may feel that we fail miserably.

The self-modification of behavior

If we define our problems as particular behaviors in situations, we can profit from understanding the ways in which behavior and the environment interrelate. There are regular observable patterns that emerge in the interrelationships between behavior and environmental situations. These patterns are described by certain laws or principles governing human behavior. We can use these laws, or principles of behavior, to correct, modify, or improve our adjustments.

The techniques of self-modification can be used either to decrease undesirable behavior or to increase desirable behavior. To modify your own behavior—to bring it under control, or to determine its course—means that you will learn new behaviors for particular situations.

Sometimes the problem will be that you are presently behaving in a way you wish you were not. You may become nervous every time you take a test, and this nervousness or anxiety is actually interfering with how well you perform on the test. If you were calm, you could remember more information, think more clearly, and generally perform at a higher level. In that case, you would want to eliminate the behavior of getting nervous while taking tests.

Sometimes the problem will be that you are not behaving in a way you wish you were. You might not be studying enough, and you know that you're not doing well in school for that reason. In that case, you would want to learn to increase the behavior of studying.

Behavior is a function of the environment

What we do in a particular situation—how we behave—is determined by the nature of the situation. That is, behavior is a function of the environment. The concept, *functional relationship,* here applied to behavior, is borrowed from mathematics. It means that in a two-part relationship, as one part changes, the other changes also: changes in our environment will produce changes in our behavior.

For example, suppose you are at home. There are certain things you will do there that you would not do in other physical surroundings, such as school. You might take a nap at home, but you would not do so in a classroom. Or suppose you are on a picnic. You would do things there that you would not do at a formal dinner. Or suppose your girl friend or boy friend has just kissed you. That behavior will affect what you do next. If you had just been punched in the nose, you would react differently.

Because behavior is a function of the environment, changes in your physical surroundings or in your social circumstances or in the behavior of others will produce changes in your behavior. Of course, this is not a simple one-way relationship. Our behavior can affect our environment as well as be affected by it. The changes that result in the environment in turn affect our later behavior.

Recall John S., the young man who was so upset by the reaction of the attractive girl. When he first began talking to her, he was talking to a pretty, interested stranger. His problem was that he found it very difficult to talk to such people. His difficulties gave him the appearance of being too aloof, too superior, which tended to make people angry. His apparently superior behavior actually produced a change in his environment: at first John was talking to a pretty, *interested* person, but after several minutes of unfortunate behavior he had changed her into a pretty, *irritated* person. In this very different environment that resulted from his earlier actions, John's subsequent behavior also changed. When the girl was interested, John tried to talk; as she grew increasingly angry, he became hurt and puzzled. His behavior changed his situation, which in turn produced his new behavior.

All of us are constantly involved in interactions like this, interactions in which an environmental situation evokes behavior from us that in turn affects our situation. This kind of process is continuous in our lives and works not only for the reactions of specific others but for any kind of social or physical environment. Therefore, adjusting always involves changing the way our environment and our behavior in that environment relate to each other. The changes may come quickly, minute to minute, or extend over very lengthy periods.

Behavior is learned

In any particular situation—some combination of physical setting, social circumstances, and the behavior of others—not everyone will behave in the same way. How then does it make any sense to say that behavior is a function of the environment? *The particular behavior that one person shows in a particular situation is influenced by the learning experiences that person has had in similar situations.* Different learning experiences produce different behavior.

John S., later in his self-modification program, told us that he had profited from observing the behavior of a friend who was not at all nervous or backward in approaching a new girl for a date. John was struck by the great difference between their two behaviors in the same situation. Their two learning histories had been very different, and each behaved and felt in his own learned way in a specific environment.

The behavior produced in a particular situation had to be learned. The effect of the environment is to evoke this or that set of behaviors that we have learned in the past.

The fact that behavior has to be learned does not imply that, once you are an adult, all you do is produce behaviors that you learned as you were growing up. New or changed situations may produce new behavior. For example, a young woman who has just become a mother finds herself in a relatively novel situation—she has a real breathing baby to cope with, and she will learn new ways of behaving as she deals with the novel situation. Some of her behavior, however, will have been learned in the past. She did not come to motherhood completely naive. She probably already had developed certain ideas, attitudes, and specific ways for dealing with babies; for example, she may have had practice in caring for someone else's baby, she may have observed others caring for theirs, or she may have read books about child care.

The effect of the environment, then, is to evoke behaviors already learned and to teach new behaviors. The implication is clear. If adjustment reflects learned behavior in specific situations, then dealing with your problems in adjustment is accomplished by dealing with what you have learned, or not learned, to do in a particular situation. *Therefore, in the process of self-modification, you set out to produce new learning for yourself in specific situations.*

To modify your own behavior—to bring it under control or determine its course—means that you will seek to learn new behaviors for particular situations in which your current behavior is unsatisfactory.

The medical model of human behavior: An alternative view

Historically, the most popular view of adjustment has been quite different from the behavioral model. This view, called the medical model, is taken from psychoanalysis, from psychiatry, and from medicine. In this system, problems in adjustment are considered analogous to problems in physical health and are viewed as being similar to *diseases.*

The rationale underlying the medical model

How does this model work in medicine? Its basic characteristics are the ideas of *inner cause* and *outer symptom.* For example, if you had a fever of 102 degrees, you might very well go to a physician. The doctor has a particular way of thinking about your fever. He regards it as a symptom, or signal, that there is something wrong inside you. He would not try to eliminate just the fever, for that would be treating the symptom and leaving the inner illness untreated. The physician's approach will be to try to discover the inner problem and then eliminate it through drugs, rest, or some other treatment. If he can get rid of the inner problem, the outer symptom—the fever—will cease. That is the medical model: *inner problems cause outer symptoms,* and the proper course of treatment is to eliminate the inner problem. Of course, physicians do sometimes give symptomatic relief but, whenever possible, they seek to eliminate the basic problem.

How does this model shape the thought of people who deal with issues of adjustment? First, what is the analog of the fever? "Adjustment" deals with issues of behavior. Thus, some problem in behavior will take the form of the "symptom." For example, you might be unable to concentrate while studying, and this could be serious enough to interfere with your work in school. You might talk with someone—a friend, a counselor—about your problems. If this person took the medical model as his point of departure in thinking about your problem, he might view the lack of concentration as *a symptom of some inner problem.* He would attempt to discover this "inner problem" and then "treat" it. This is perhaps the most common point of view in traditional psychology and psychiatry.

The medical model in action

The traditional medical approach attempts to discover and remedy some condition *within* the person which is producing the outer problem in behavior. Different theories have held that there are different kinds of inner problems, but some have stressed the idea that *inner conflicts* are the source of symptomatic behavior. Common to many theories is the idea that in order to get rid of a problem in behavior it is necessary to change the inner mental or emotional process causing it.

This point of view has become so widely accepted that our language reflects the concept of mental problems as comparable to physical illness. We commonly speak of "mental health" and "mental illness," and of course health and illness are words borrowed from medicine. We speak of "treatment" or "psychotherapy," and therapy is a medical word. People who have serious problems in adjustment—those who are "insane"—are sent to "hospitals." This point of view is so common that it is sometimes accepted as the only one.

Conflict as the inner cause. If the outer behavior—such as drinking to excess or disturbing a class at school or always feeling depressed—is the symptom, what is the inner cause? Sigmund Freud, and many subsequent theorists, viewed behavioral problems as symptoms of *inner conflicts* or *frustrations.*

An "inner conflict" means that a person wants two or more mutually exclusive things. For example, a boy might want to masturbate while at the same time believing that masturbation is evil. Thus, he wants something but also does not want it. Such conflict produces frustration: one cannot have both. And the frustration itself produces additional upset and disappointment.

In such a view, all outer behavior is an indication of our inner mental state. If the inner state is in conflict, then the outer behavior will reflect the inner stress. If we are frustrated inside, our outer lives will be maladjusted.

Different theorists have specified different kinds of internal conflict or frustration as the cause of disturbed behavior. Freud, the most famous theoretician of human conflict, believed that conflicts over *sexual* and *aggressive* impulses were at the heart of almost every inner frustration. Later theorists have emphasized various other kinds of inner conflicts. Some have focused on *self-regard* versus *self-devaluation,* some on *ascendance* versus *dependence,* others on *security* versus *anxiety.* Some recent writers have said that there is no one common source of conflict but that any inner conflict or unresolved problem can lead to outer problems in behavior.

Other models

Throughout human history, there has always been some theory to explain problems in adjustment. In every civilization there is some explanation, and this explanation is always consistent with the general beliefs of that society.

The "possession" model has been a common idea. It is not at all unusual in preliterate societies. It was almost universal in Western European civilization during the Middle Ages. Serious forms of maladjusted, bizarre, "crazy" behaviors occurred because the person was "possessed" or occupied by a spirit, a devil, an evil presence. This was entirely consistent with the general view of a world rich with spirits, both good and evil. Both adjusted and maladjusted behaviors were believed to be influenced by these supernatural beings. And, naturally, a prescribed form of treatment followed from the explanation. If one were possessed by a devil, the way to achieve better adjustment was to drive the devil out.

In different societies, different rituals have been developed for driving out devils: sometimes the medicine man imitates the devil and tries to trick or lure the spirit into coming out; sometimes the devil is driven away by obnoxious odors or discordant music. In medieval Christianity, the rites of *exorcism,* performed by the priest, invoked the power of the heavens against the possessing evil spirit in the body of the maladjusted sufferer. The disruptive child in the monastery school might thus need praying over. Or one might decide to "beat the devil out" of the child —a phrase, incidentally, that derives from just such a practice. In either event, when the spirit leaves, so does the problem behavior.

Another model that has had wide usage in the history of thought could be called the "sinner model." The theory explaining man as a "sinner" is complex but, since we are using it only as an example, we present a simplified version: people behaving in maladjusted ways are doing so because they are being punished by God for some sin they committed. Fully extended, the "sinner model" allows children to be punished for the sins of their fathers. In the past it has been argued that we should do nothing for unhappy people because their unhappiness is clearly a sign that they are being punished by God, and it would be an antireligious act to interfere with their punishment. Therefore, if a person acted really crazy, he was likely to be locked away and forgotten.

As with the devil model, once the initial assumption underlying the sinner model is made, the behavior accorded the person with the problem proceeds in a relatively logical fashion. Similarly, the assumption underlying the medical model and the behavior-modification model also dictate the behavior of those holding each point of view.

Implications of the medical model

Whenever a theorist adopts a particular model or theoretical approach, it implies certain things. What are the implications of the medical model? We have named some: behavior problems are like diseases. Treatment should be in the hands of physicians, or under their direction. People with such problems should be put into hospitals and/or given treatment. Society should care for them as it does for others who are sick. The "sick" person is excused from responsibility for his illness, and because of it, is not required to carry out usual activities.

Some of these implications seem clearly desirable. For example, before the medical model was widely adopted, "insane" people were treated in abominable ways, locked away in stinking, repressive, filthy institutions. The medical model makes it easier to forgive those people who have been acting in unhappy or even crazy ways: disease, after all, can often be cured, and the person who is well again need not be feared, ostracized, punished. Finally, because of these changing attitudes, society has sponsored research into the causes of behavioral problems.

Perhaps the major advantage of the medical model is that physicians have discovered medical reasons for some behavior problems—for example, in extreme mental retardation or diseases of the nervous system. Further, physicians have discovered symptomatic treatments, such as drugs to reduce anxiety or depression, that are effective in alleviating the suffering that so often accompanies an adjustment problem.

Problems with the medical model

Recently the medical model has been reexamined because the mental-health movement, which has been advanced by physicians, psychologists, social workers, counselors, educators, and ministers, has been scientific enough to attempt to evaluate its effectiveness. Many social scientists feel that these evaluations demonstrate that treated individuals have not improved more than those who have had no treatment. Others feel that improvements have been demonstrated and that there are problems with the evaluations. Some have argued that the research indicates that treatment is effective for only a small percentage of individuals. These differences of opinion show that *there is no general agreement on the effectiveness of treatment that derives from the medical model.*

Perhaps an even greater problem is the fact that most treatments require considerable expertise. Because there are so many people who have problems in adjustment, a vast army of expert professionals would be required to offer treatment to all—an army so large that a society could not possibly make the necessary investment in manpower.

One of the greatest failures of the medical model has been that it makes no provision for the individual who wishes to achieve, for himself, greater personal adjustment: the medical model clearly implies the necessity for professional treatment. Attempts have been made to provide the individual with information about mental illness in the hope that he will never develop the disease in the first place. However, since most individuals have problems they would like to correct, it would be far preferable to make available a model that can offer guidance to the individual in regulating his own behaviors and relationships to his environment.

For these reasons, the past decade has seen discontent with the helping professions. This discontent has led to the exploration of new models and new treatment philosophies, which in turn have led to a real revolution in the basic assumptions and techniques surrounding issues of adjustment.

To work within a different model does not imply that the medical model is untrue. The medical model has certain internal consistencies and accurately predicts certain outcomes. It has a number of advantages along with its disadvantages. But the desirability of the medical model for helping individuals with problems in adjustment must be judged by comparing its effectiveness and utility with the effectiveness and utility of alternative models.

Conclusion

In the behavioristic model, adjustment is seen as a value judgment that people make when observing a relationship between a person's behavior and his environment. The kinds of relationships between behavior and environment that people exhibit are learned relationships. This implies that new desirable relationships can be learned, to replace undesirable ones. It further implies that people can guide their own learning. Thus, each person can, to some degree, affect his own adjustment by deliberately altering the environment so that he will learn new behaviors. Directing your own behavior is a process of directing the relationships between your environment and your behavior. In order to do this effectively, you must understand some of the basic principles that regulate this behavior-environment relationship. That is the subject of the next chapter.

Your own self-modification project: Step two

You should continue to think about various aspects of your behavior, trying to select some particular problem as the target for your self-modification project. The crucial question is this: *Can you state your problem in terms of your behavior in particular situations?*

From the list of personal dissatisfactions that you constructed after Chapter One, choose one or more. Write a one-paragraph analysis of each, in which your problem behavior is linked to the particular situation in which it occurs (or does not occur).

Chapter Three
Behavior-Environment
Relationships

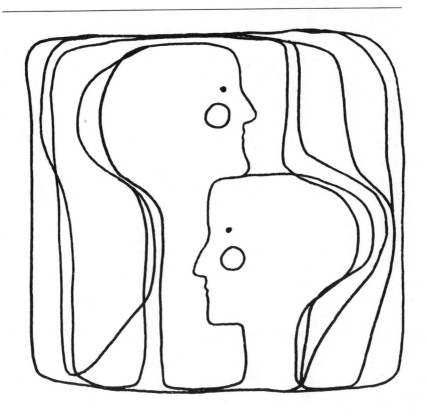

1. Learning is defined as any change in behavior due to prior experience with the environment; even inherited patterns are modified by environmental interaction.
2. Principles of behavior are specified.
   a. Behavior occurs in a sequence of events: antecedent—behavior—consequence.
   b. Respondent behaviors are almost automatically controlled by their antecedents.
   c. Operant behaviors have an effect upon the environment and are usually controlled by their consequences.
3. Basic principles of operant behaviors:
   I. Operant behavior is a function of its consequences.
   II. Some consequences strengthen behavior.
      a. Any consequence that strengthens (increases the likelihood of) behavior is called a reinforcer.
      b. A positive reinforcer has its effect by being added to the situation.
      c. A negative reinforcer has its effect by being subtracted from the situation.
   III. Withholding reinforcers will weaken (decrease the likelihood of) behavior. Extinction is the name for this process.
   IV. Intermittent reinforcement increases resistance to extinction.
   V. Behavior that is punished will occur less frequently.
   VI. Punishment alone does not teach new behaviors.

VII. Punishment leads to escape or avoidance behaviors.
   a. Avoidance behavior may come under antecedent-stimulus control.
   b. Avoidance behavior is highly resistant to extinction.
VIII. Most operant behavior eventually comes under the influence of antecedent stimuli, or signals. A cue may then come to evoke behavior.

Chapter Two has suggested that adjustment—however defined—must be a dynamic thing, ever changing. Furthermore, behavior itself is specific to situations: there is no "one" environment but rather a continuous flow of situations—mini-environments—which affect our behavior and to which we must adjust.

The science of psychology has attempted to discover the basic principles underlying those limitless ways in which people think, feel, and act. Recently, this effort has concentrated on the principles that relate behavior to its situational setting.

A few of these well-established principles form the basis for this volume. During the reading of this chapter, you should master those principles thoroughly. In chapters to come, we will examine the way they may be applied to the achievement of personal adjustment.

Learning

These principles are often called laws of learning. In the science of behavior, "learning" refers to far more than memorizing multiplication tables, mastering a foreign language, or reciting the alphabet. *Learning refers to any changes in our acts or capacities that develop as a result of interaction with the environment.* Thus, the vast majority of our actions, thoughts, and feelings are learned. Even our inherited tendencies are modified by environmental interaction, so that *learning*—as psychologists mean it—is quite a comprehensive term. Indeed, it is hard to discover any of our behaviors that are not influenced by the experiences we have—by interaction with our environments.

Inherited behavior patterns

Does our biological make-up influence our behavioral characteristics? To a degree, the answer is clearly yes. No matter what experiences or environment they may have, a gorilla will not fly nor a chicken swim like a fish. All people, in spite of their many differences, are more like each other than they are like kangaroos.

Here we are interested in examining biological differences between individuals of our own species. Are Spaniards hot tempered? If they are, is this due to their biological differences, inherited from their European cousins? Are other human characteristics—motherliness, humor, friendliness—explained by genetic differences between people?

Research in the field of behavior genetics generally indicates that some behavioral tendencies are indeed inherited. Such general tendencies as intelligence, activity level, and excitability appear to be heavily influenced by inheritance. There is almost overwhelming evidence, for example, that heredity contributes significantly to intelligence. But there is also overwhelming evidence that each individual inherits a wide band of intellectual potential. His environment and his history of learning determine his actual intellectual performance.

Certainly other inherited characteristics influence our behaviors. Short or fat people behave differently than tall or thin ones, beautiful people behave differently than those who are not beautiful. The physical characteristics may be genetically determined, but the effects on behaviors are indirect because they are mediated by learning. The behaviors that emerge from these physical characteristics will be due to environmental circumstances.

Skin color serves as an excellent example. For decades in America, dark skin pigmentation (genetically determined) has been roughly correlated with undesirability. Even among Afro-Americans, light color has previously been considered more attractive than dark. The very dark-skinned individual inevitably developed behaviors as a result of the "punishment" administered by other people—the punishment of disregard or disdain. In the 1960s, however, with its "black-is-beautiful" movement, such an individual found himself more "rewarded"—admired—by the people around him. Thus, when the environment changed, the inherited characteristic that had previously elicited negative responses now served to evoke behavior characteristic of beautiful people: pride, self-confidence, and social ease. The learning that took place as a result of the changed environment would probably be transferred to other situations, and other new behaviors would be learned as a consequence.

In general, then, inherited biological characteristics interact with the environment to produce specific learned behaviors. The effects of learning are pervasive; learning is one of the most fundamental processes affecting human lives.

The principles of behavior

The effect of the environment on behavior is profound as well as lawful and regular. Certain principles of behavior explain these behavior-environment relationships. A study of the principles helps us understand how behaviors become linked to particular situations. These principles can guide us when we want to develop new behaviors or modify old ones: that is, they guide our efforts to achieve a harmonious adjustment to our life situations.

Antecedents and consequences

Situations, or mini-environments, may be arbitrarily divided into two parts: those that come *before* a behavior and those that come *after* it. For our purposes, we can refer to these as the *antecedent* events and the *consequent* events. The antecedents and the consequences may sometimes be the same, but they have a different effect on subsequent behavior depending upon whether they come before or after it.

Psychologists refer to the antecedents and consequences as *stimuli* because they *stimulate* behavior. This is a familiar concept to all of us. We say that an insult, for example, stimulates us to anger, or that music stimulates us to dance, or that a particular light stimulates our vision to register "red." In less obvious ways, consequent events also influence our behaviors. A behavior that produces praise as a consequence is apt to be repeated: the consequent event has affected later behavior. We all know of times when the punch-line of a joke has been repeated again (and sometimes again!) after the consequence of audience laughter. Thus, both types of stimuli, antecedent and consequent, affect the behaviors that they surround. This entire book is an analysis of the effects of antecedent and consequent stimuli on our behaviors: it is through these relationships that behavior and the environment become adjusted to one another.

Respondent behaviors

Some behaviors are "automatically" controlled by antecedent stimuli. When the knee tendon is struck lightly, the behavior of leg extension follows automatically. The antecedent stimulus of striking has control over this reflex. A fleck on the eyeball is a controlling antecedent for eye blinking. Milk in the mouth produces salivation automatically from the earliest hours of life. Behaviors for which there are original, controlling, antecedent stimuli are sometimes called reflexes. Man has fewer of these automatic behaviors than organisms with less complicated nervous systems, but even for us, they are numerous.

Here is a small experiment that will illustrate one of your reflexive responses. Have someone agree to surprise you with a sudden loud noise. For example, ask a friend to slam a book onto a table sometime within a fifteen-minute period, but when you seem to expect it least. Observe your reactions: you will tense, whip around, blink. This is reflexive; the stimulus is sufficient to cause it. Only repeated familiarity with the stimulus will allow the behavior to fade. But notice too that there is an *emotional* component to your reaction. There is a feeling of arousal and emotional fullness, a discomfort that is much like a small fear reaction that reaches its peak a second or two after the stimulus and then gradually subsides.

This experiment is useful because it illustrates the control of the antecedent stimulus over emotional reactions. Indeed, the class of behaviors we are now discussing—the automatic ones that are controlled by antecedents—also includes many emotional reactions. The behaviors in this class have certain properties; for example, they are largely controlled by the autonomic nervous system, they involve smooth muscles, and they are highly similar among individuals of the same species. These behaviors are sometimes called *respondent* behaviors because they occur originally in *response* to the antecedent stimulus.

For our purposes, the most important characteristic common to all respondent behaviors is that there are original antecedent stimuli adequate to produce the behavior. The laws which govern the *learning* of this class of behaviors describe relationships among the antecedent stimuli.

While an unexpected loud noise is an adequate stimulus for fear reactions from the earliest days of our lives, we certainly learn to be afraid of many other things that are not originally controlling stimuli: tests or examinations, walking into a crowded room, snakes, spiders, being embarrassed. How do these new stimuli gain control over our reactions? The process is one that psychologists call *respondent conditioning*. It involves a pairing of the original stimulus with the new one, so that they occur together: the individual reacts automatically to the original stimulus in the presence of the new (or *conditioned*) stimulus. After a number of these occurrences, he will react to the new conditioned stimulus alone in nearly the same way he reacts to the original stimulus. In this way, the automatic reactions can be transferred to many new conditioned stimuli, according to the way that antecedent stimuli happen to occur together.

We will return to this topic in detail in Chapter Ten, where we will discuss the laws that govern the learning of emotional responses, which are apparently the same as the laws controlling automatic antecedent-controlled behaviors.

For the present, we will examine a second class of behaviors—behaviors that are quite different in form and are learned differently.

Operant behaviors

The classification of behaviors is based on whether or not the behavior has an original, controlling, antecedent stimulus. Respondent behaviors do: they are called "respondent" just because they occur in response to some stimulus. Those that do not have an original, controlling antecedent are called *operant* behaviors. They are called "operant" because their role is to operate on our environment—to do things to it or in it.

The dictionary defines "to operate" as "to perform an act, to function, to produce an effect." *Through operant behaviors we function, act, and produce effects in our environment.*

Operant behaviors usually involve the striped muscles and the central nervous system. They vary widely from individual to individual, even within the same species. Operants are behaviors for which we generally assume conscious control; they are not automatic. Operant behaviors are felt to be "free," subject to our own volition. We generally think "can't help it" if we are afraid, angry, sexually aroused, or startled. But we feel that we can choose to walk, to talk, perhaps to think, to engage in most of the complicated behaviors that are the fabric of our daily lives.

The distinction between respondents and operants is not as clear and precise as this discussion seems to indicate. Indeed, psychologists are now studying the interrelationships between respondent and operant behaviors and finding that they are most intimately connected (Miller, 1969; Di Cara, 1970; Staats, 1968). But the distinction remains very useful because it points up two quite different relationships to situations. *Operants are learned and maintained primarily by consequent stimuli rather than by antecedents.* A set of principles describing how operant behaviors are acquired follows. First, however, a brief summary of the points covered so far will help you remember the meaning of the terms used and the relationships between the ideas they represent.

Remember that the principles discussed in the rest of this chapter refer to *operant behaviors.* Respondent behaviors will be covered in more detail in Chapter Ten, "Emotional Problems."

Summary

Learning means any change in our behavior that develops due to interaction with the environment. Even inherited behavior patterns are affected by interactions with the environment.

Behavior is embedded in a sequence: it is preceded by antecedents and followed by consequences. *Respondent* behaviors are almost "automatically" stimulated by antecedents. Emotional responses can fall in this category and will be considered in detail later. *Operant* behaviors are affected by their consequences. Now follows a series of principles for operant behaviors.

Principle I: Operant behavior is a function of its consequences

---

Operant behaviors are strengthened or weakened depending upon what follows them. While this may appear to be a "common-sense" statement—naturally we persist in those acts that succeed and we stop when we get no satisfaction—the principle involved is quite complicated. Let us take a simple example. A boy and a girl are under a tree; he offers a kiss. What determines whether or not this behavior will reoccur? The consequences. We can all agree that the probability of his future kissing behavior will differ, depending on whether she gives him her lips or a karate chop. While this example is obvious, we rarely extend this basic principle to less dramatic, more obscure examples, even though the principle applies equally well.

Whether we are learning to kiss, type, speak, write, study, smoke, or compose a string quartet, our behaviors will be strengthened or weakened—made more or less probable—according to the events that follow them. A child learning to speak will become more verbal if he is praised than he will if he is scolded. A composer will be more or less likely to attempt a second quartet depending on the consequences that follow the first one.

Will the consequence make a behavior *more* or *less* likely? That depends on the quality of the consequence. The next principle describes how consequences make behavior more likely to occur.

Principle II: Some consequences strengthen behavior

Understanding this principle will require first understanding three definitions.

Definition 1: Behavioral "strength," as used here, refers to the *likelihood* that a particular behavior will be performed. Behavior is "stronger" if it is more probable. The best practical index for gauging the probability of behavior is its *frequency.* In behavior analysis, we usually infer the strength of a behavior from its rate—we count the number of times the behavior occurs during a given period of time.

Now we can turn to a discussion of Principle II—Some consequences strengthen behavior. Of course, not every consequence strengthens. Many elements of situations that follow a behavior have no functional relationship to it. If we return to our couple under the tree, we might find a plane flying overhead just as the boy offers the kiss. Indeed, the plane might happen to fly overhead several times as he is kissing. We can assume that the plane would not strengthen his kissing tendencies, but, that whether or not the girl kisses back would have a marked effect on them. Her kissing back would no doubt result in his kissing behavior becoming more probable, more frequent.* This example illustrates *positive reinforcement,* an important term that we can now define.

Definition 2: A positive reinforcer is a consequence that strengthens behavior by its added presence.

Positive reinforcers may be many things—kisses or food or money or praise or the chance to ride a motorcycle. The list is inexhaustible and highly individualized.

A positive reinforcer *adds* something to the situation. The young man kissed the girl and by doing so produced a new, added consequence: her kissing back. Before he had offered, she was not kissing him, so we can say that her kiss has been added. A positive reinforcer is anything which, when added to the situation, makes the behavior that preceded it more likely to recur.

The composer is more likely to attempt a second string quartet, then, if his first composing behavior is positively reinforced. This positive reinforcement might consist of one or more of a variety of conse-

---

*His kissing will become more probable with that girl and, only to a lesser extent, with other girls. The way in which behavior probabilities *generalize*—spread to similar situations—will be discussed in Chapter Nine.

quences: praise from his audience, the pleasure of hearing his work performed, or the sense of satisfaction in knowing it met his own standards.

Definition 3: A negative reinforcer is a consequence that strengthens behavior by being subtracted from the situation.

We will immediately go back under the tree for an example. The boy and girl were having a lovers' quarrel. Before he kissed her, she was frowning and appeared distressed. But his friendly kiss made her feel better, and her face relaxed. We could say that the frowning and distress were negative reinforcers, in this case, because they strengthened the behavior that led to their subtraction—that is, kissing. *A negative reinforcer is any consequence that has the power to increase a rate of behavior by its removal.*

Of course, the girl might add a positive reinforcer—smiling, or saying she feels better. But this is not a necessary condition; the negative reinforcer alone—by its removal—will increase his kissing probability.

Although there are exceptions, usually your own positive reinforcers will be anything that you feel to be pleasant, and negative reinforcers will be anything that you feel to be unpleasant. Each individual could list many negative reinforcers as well as many positive ones, and each list would be different. The saying "One man's meat is another man's poison" reminds us that the same thing or event can have an opposite function for different people. Of course, reinforcement need not be some external thing or event. There is clearly such a thing as "self-reinforcement," in which we praise or encourage ourselves (see Chapter Fourteen). There are good and bad feelings that follow our own behavior, and these have reinforcing properties.

Furthermore, the reinforcement of behavior does not have to follow our own actions for learning to occur. We learn much of our complicated repertoires by simply observing other people and the consequences that follow *their* behaviors. Learning can occur by watching the behavior of others, whether or not that behavior is reinforced for them. But the *performance* of what we have learned—the behavior itself—depends on the reinforcement, either to the model, or to us when we actually imitate the behavior.

Although the distinction between learning and performance is a real one, it is a most difficult one to make because we can never judge learning unless there is some performance, some behavior. We can't tell if someone has learned something unless he shows some difference in his behavior. A person might secretly learn to speak Spanish, for example, but if we never observe any change in his behavior, we will not be able to tell what he has learned. It is for that reason that *behavior science* emphasizes behavior and that principles of behavior are really principles of performance.

Principle III: Withholding reinforcers will weaken behavior

The first two principles concerned the performance of new behaviors. Now let us examine behavior that has already been learned—that is, previously reinforced. Under this condition, the withholding of reinforcement will make that behavior less likely. We can all imagine instances when reinforcement is discontinued. When it is, previously performed behavior will not be maintained. This process is called *extinction.*

Suppose our couple under the tree has acquired the habit of going there on Saturdays, and they kiss a lot. The boy's kissing behavior has been reinforced sufficiently to become highly probable. But life, alas, changes: the environment may discontinue reinforcement. Let us adopt the girl's point of view for this example. Suppose she feels that they are kissing too much and engaging in conversation too little. She wants to reduce his frequency of kissing. She has many strategies available, of course, one of which is to stop kissing back—to withhold the reinforcement. His kissing behavior will *extinguish;* that is, it will gradually discontinue. If she really wants him to stay with her under the tree but increase conversation, she must reinforce conversation while simultaneously extinguishing kissing. If she doesn't care whether he stays or not, she can just not respond. In either event, the kissing behavior will diminish.

Extinction occurs all around us, continuously. It is the process by which we adjust our behaviors to a changing environment. Behaviors that are no longer productive are gradually dropped and new ones learned according to the ways they are reinforced in new situations. Extinction is an adaptive, active process. Behaviors always cost an expenditure of energy, and we generally avoid waste.

Principle IV: Intermittent reinforcement increases resistance to extinction

---

If reinforcement follows each instance of a behavior, it is said to be under *continuous reinforcement.* This could be described as a 100% schedule of reinforcement. Most naturally occurring behaviors, in the real

world, are not reinforced for each instance. Sometimes they are reinforced, sometimes not. This is called *intermittent reinforcement.*

As you might expect, continuous reinforcement provides for more
rapid new learning. But *intermittent reinforcement* has a most interesting
effect: *it makes behaviors more resistant to extinction.* A behavior which has
been reinforced randomly, but on the average of every other time (a
50% schedule), will persist longer when reinforcement is withdrawn
than if it had been reinforced continuously.

Let us go back under the tree for a minute. Suppose the girl has
kissed back on the average of every other time. Then on the first extinction day, when she is no longer interested, the boy would probably keep
trying, even though there was no response. (These are called extinction
trials.) The *intermittent* reinforcement schedule would require more trials
before final extinction of the behavior. If nonreinforcement continued,
of course, extinction would eventually occur. But *the number of trials to
extinction is affected by the previous reinforcement schedule.* If she had always
kissed back, and then stopped altogether, kissing behavior would extinguish faster than if she had kissed back on an irregular schedule.

Schedules that are intermittent, and especially those that are unpredictable, are particularly effective in producing resistance to extinction. The extinction effects of schedules are rather close to a
common-sense view of *expectations.* That is, if we *expect* that sometimes
she will and sometimes she won't, we will not know as readily that we
are on an extinction schedule. We may well think that we're still on the
previous intermittent schedule and, thus, persist until we do see that a
new arrangement is in force. If we have been kissed back only once in
twenty efforts (a one-to-twenty ratio), we will "expect" to have to wait
for the twenty-first. If we never knew exactly when reinforcement
would be forthcoming, as on a high-ratio, random schedule, it would
be reasonable that we would not know what to expect and would
continue a long time before "getting the message." Extinction effects are
consistent with common-sense "expectations," but we do not need the
concept of expectation to explain it; even the lowly laboratory mouse
extinguishes on about the same patterns.

Intermittent reinforcement and maladaptive behavior. These effects of intermittent reinforcement are significant for our purposes because they
help explain the persistence of some maladaptive behaviors. In fact,
many of our persistent complex behaviors are on intermittent schedules
of reinforcement. Perhaps we are reinforced irregularly but, on the
average, once every hundred times we perform a given act. First of all,
think how very resistant to extinction that behavior would be. The

casual observer might label our behavior "stubborn" or "foolish" since
it would persist for so long after reinforcement had been withdrawn.
Besides, the observer might well not see the rare reinforcement when
it did occur, and thus our behavior would seem very paradoxical to him.
Many maladjusted behaviors that we see in other people are reinforced
on schedules like this.

Summary

So far we have covered four principles. *Operant behavior* is a function of its effects, or its consequences. *Positive reinforcement* increases the
chances that the behavior will occur again by adding something to the
situation. *Negative reinforcement* has the same effect by subtracting something. If reinforcement is discontinued, the process of *extinction* occurs,
and the behavior declines in frequency. Behaviors are made resistant to
extinction by intermittent reinforcement.

Principle V: Behavior that is punished will occur less often

Remember that a negative reinforcer is a stimulus that, if withdrawn, increases the preceding behavior. *But what if this same unpleasant
stimulus is added, following a behavior? This is one form of punishment.* After
all, a negative reinforcer is most often something painful, distasteful,
undesirable, something toward which we feel an *aversion.* Negative
reinforcers are often called *aversive stimuli.* They may be anything from
electric shock, to embarrassment, to mowing the lawn, depending upon
the individual. *To take such a thing away, as in negative reinforcement, would
be rewarding. To add it to a situation is punishing.*

Punishment has several effects. *One is to reduce the probability or
frequency of the behavior that it follows.* We all know that we can suppress
behavior by punishing it, and this is, again, a way in which behavior
becomes adjusted to the environment. Parents spank their children to
get them to stop doing something. But this form of punishment—the
application of an aversive stimulus—also has other effects that need to
be understood. Punishment does more than simply suppress behavior.

What happens to you when you are punished? Think back to the
last time the world punished you severely for something. Maybe you
were physically pained, or embarrassed, or just psychologically "hurt."
You will remember that you may have stopped doing the behavior in
question, but you also experienced several unpleasant "side effects." For

example, you experienced feelings of unhappiness—perhaps fear, perhaps a more vague feeling of general discomfort. You may have felt angry and possibly behaved more aggressively toward the punisher. In addition, you probably experienced some minor disorganization of your thoughts and feelings—probably nothing serious, perhaps only a brief moment of confusion and less effective activity. *These are typical effects of punishment: emotional arousal, unpleasant feelings, sometimes counteraggressive behaviors, and disruption of previously organized behavior sequences.*

Our girl under the tree can stop the boy's kissing behavior by slapping him, but she will also produce these side effects. However, the kissing will stop quickly. The biggest advantage to using punishment for systematic teaching is that inhibition of the unwanted behavior occurs very rapidly. For this reason, even the kindest parents use punishment with their children if a behavior, particularly one dangerous to the child, must be quickly terminated.

Another form of punishment, *the withdrawal of a positive reinforcer,* is slower in its effects and less emotionally disrupting. Suppose you are engaging in a regular learned behavior such as surfing. During the whole season, the waves have been high with good form. The environment has reinforced a whole sequence of events—getting out of bed, carrying the board to the beach, paddling out—by the outcome of good rides. Suppose the surf suddenly goes flat and stays without waves for days or weeks. Carrying the board to the beach would certainly decrease in frequency under this condition. We ordinarily do not think of the environment as "punishing" our behaviors in this way, but such an event does have a punishing effect. *The behavior is punished by the withdrawal of previously present positive reinforcement.* The suddenly cold girl can punish the boy's kissing by withdrawing the previous reinforcement—her affectionate responses.

Imagine the last time such a withdrawal of reinforcement happened to you. You were probably not so upset, angry, or disorganized as if you had been slapped, or otherwise punished by an aversive stimulus. Your feeling was probably nearer to disappointment—still not pleasant, but not so emotionally arousing. Recall, too, that your behavior did not stop so rapidly as it would have, given a painful stimulus. *These are characteristics of punishment by withdrawal of positive reinforcement: less emotionality, less unpleasantness, and less rapid decrease of the behavior.*

Parents often use these techniques. A teenager may be "grounded" or lose previous privileges such as use of the car when he misbehaves. Similarly, the little child is not allowed to go out to play. As adults, we use these reactions in our daily lives: from the friend who becomes cantankerous we withdraw our previously friendly responses.

The thoughtful reader will have noticed that this second form of punishment is similar to *extinction* procedures: both involve withdrawal of positive reinforcement. This is important to remember because, when you begin to modify your own maladjustive behavior, you will want to know that extinction, like withdrawal of positive reinforcement, brings some unpleasant side effects.

Principle VI: Punishment alone does not teach new behaviors

The next principle, that punishment does not teach new behaviors, is often overlooked by people trying to teach others. In childrearing or in friendships or in formal teaching, we are often content to stop undesirable behavior. But if we do only that, the development of new desirable behaviors is left to chance. In achieving your own improved self-adjustment, there are some things that you will want to stop doing: smoking, being shy, studying poorly, or taking drugs. But you will also want to develop new, desirable, *alternative* behaviors to use in these situations. To stop the old ones is only half of the problem, and punishment can help only with that half. In self-modification, one tries to learn new behaviors, not simply suppress old ones.

Principle VII: Punishment leads to escape or avoidance behaviors

What you do learn by punishment is to get away from the punishment. Exactly *how* you will get away, or what you will do when you have gotten away, is not determined by the punishment itself. Rather, these getting-away behaviors are learned according to the patterns of reinforcement that follow them. If you learn to jump over the fence to avoid a thrashing, you will jump (head-first or scissors-style, for example) in the way most reinforced—that is, you will jump in the way that has allowed you to jump the fastest and most effectively.

Of course, *emotional* reactions are learned, as discussed under the previous principles, because emotionality is a by-product of punishment. This is especially true of *escape learning*. Technically, escape learning refers to behaviors that terminate punishment. *Avoidance learning,* on the other hand, refers to *behaviors that remove the possibility of punishment.* In other words, in escape learning the punishment is actually delivered, but in avoidance learning, the punishment is avoided. This difference is very important because the attendant emotional patterns are quite different.

In the escape pattern, the emotional unpleasantness continues because the punishment is always there. Our young man kissing would be upset every time he was slapped and then had to escape. On the other hand, suppose he learns to *avoid* the punishment—for example, by staying away from the girl. The emotional reaction will not have to be experienced.

A history of avoidance learning may help explain many behaviors that do not seem to be positively reinforced. People can learn to avoid each other, not because they are positively reinforced for doing so, but because they are avoiding situations that have been punishing in the past.

When you begin to analyze your own behavior, you may discover that you do things for which there is no apparent reward. People sometimes think of these behaviors as being "unmotivated," but they are often avoidance behaviors. For example, you may sometimes go off by yourself rather than to a place frequented by your friends, even though being by yourself is not reinforcing. You might ask "What am I responding to?" The answer may lie in your learning history—you may have been punished in the past for going to the popular meeting place. You have learned an avoidance behavior. An important characteristic of avoidance behaviors is that they can often be performed in an unemotional, even blasé, way. People are not particularly uncomfortable about avoidance behaviors; such behaviors are evidently not motivated by anxiety. Until someone calls it to your attention, you may be totally unaware that some of your behaviors are based on the avoidance of discomfort.

Avoidance behavior eventually comes under antecedent stimulus control, even though it is not elicited as in respondent conditioning. *People perform avoidance behaviors in response to antecedents, not consequences.* In order to avoid a punishment, you have to know that the punishment is about to occur. You learn to avoid the situation when you get a *signal* that the punishment is imminent.

A young man who has been punished by his girl for kissing her at inappropriate times will learn which signals indicate that a particular time is not appropriate. For example, he may be punished for kissing his girl when her parents are present. He would learn to suppress kissing behavior, as a way of avoiding punishment, when he sees the signal: parents. Thus we can say that his kissing behavior is under antecedent-stimulus control. It is the presence of the parents (signal) that controls his behavior, not the punishment he might receive from his girl.

Because it is the signal and not the punishment that is a cue to avoidance behaviors, avoidance behaviors persist even though punishment would no longer occur. Suppose the girl, now engaged to the young man, feels that it is permissible for him to kiss her in front of her parents. If she does not happen to tell her fiancé that the situation has changed, he may continue to suppress kissing at those times, even after the possibility of punishment has been removed.

Avoidance learning is highly resistant to extinction because the antecedent stimulus evokes the avoidance behavior, and the person who has learned the avoidance response will not have an opportunity to learn that the old punishment has been removed.

A common occurrence in our society can serve as an example. Children and teenagers are often punished for sexual behavior, and this punishment is likely to produce various kinds of avoidance behavior. Some will simply learn to avoid being caught, but others may learn to avoid sex altogether. As the children grow older and marry, the situation changes: the parents are very unlikely to punish sexual behavior in their married children. What was formerly punishable behavior is now permissible. Even so, the person who has learned to avoid making love as a way of avoiding the earlier punishment may continue to avoid—even though the situation has changed and the punishment is no longer a threat.

In this way, much "neurotic" or maladjusted behavior is learned. Because you were once punished in the presence of a particular stimulus —in childhood, for example—you continue to engage in old habits of avoidance which might seem "foolish" to someone else. Such avoidance behaviors may be truly foolish: you may avoid situations that could be pleasant for you, because the signals that control your behavior continue. One of the techniques of self-modification is to gradually make yourself engage in previously avoided behaviors and situations that seem to be desirable. In this way, you can learn whether or not the old punishment will occur.

Summary

One form of punishment is *the addition of a negative reinforcer following some behavior.* A second form is *the withdrawal of a positive reinforcer* that has usually occurred. Each kind of punishment will reduce the chances that the behavior which led to the punishment will occur again, but the addition of a negative reinforcer is more unpleasant.

A major characteristic of punishment as a means of changing behavior is that it does not, by itself, teach new behaviors but only teaches to escape or avoid the punishment. This is a problem often not recognized.

Punishment may lead to avoidance behavior, which removes the possibility of the punishment. Avoidance behavior eventually comes under the control of an antecedent stimulus so that when the cue or signal occurs, the person performs the avoidance behavior and the dreaded punishment is avoided. This kind of behavior is very resistant to extinction. It may explain the presence of behaviors that are not adaptive and have no obvious reinforcement.

Principle VIII: Most operant behavior eventually comes under the control of antecedent stimuli, or signals

---

Signals, or antecedent conditions, eventually control not only avoidance behavior but *most* learned behavior.

How does this come about? In avoidance learning, a person learns to avoid certain punishments—being reprimanded by a girl, for example —by paying attention to the signals' which indicate that he should avoid. Thus, the behavior comes under the control of the *antecedent* stimulus.

This is also what happens with behaviors that are learned by other patterns—even those learned by positive reinforcement. In ordinary language, we speak of this situation as a *cue* to behavior. In real life, most of our actions are controlled by cues. For example, when the bell rings, or the lecturer says "That's all for today," students get out of their seats and move toward the door. Each student knows perfectly well how to leave a classroom, but ordinarily no one does so until the cue is given. Our kissing couple can serve as another example. The boy will eventually offer a kiss only when the girl is "ready." She will give some cue —a way of looking at him, a pause in the conversation, a movement of her head. If she does not give the cue—if she is looking away or down, or busy talking or studying—he is much less likely to try a kiss. So after the original learning has taken place, the cue will evoke the behavior. His offering a kiss will have come under antecedent-stimulus control.

The interesting question in the science of psychology, and in the effort to modify our behaviors, is *How do we learn the cues?* In any hour of our lives, there are thousands of cues provided by the environment. The world is rich with stimuli—conversations, sounds, sights, events, smells—and our behaviors are orchestrated into this complexity.

Cues that evoke a particular action are called *discriminative stimuli.* This technical term is useful because it helps us understand how a cue works; that is, *a cue identifies the conditions under which an action will be reinforced or not reinforced.* It is a stimulus that helps us to *discriminate* between appropriate and inappropriate conditions for an action. *"Appropriate," in this context, means that the behavior will be followed by reinforcement; "inappropriate" means that the behavior will not be reinforced or that it will be punished.* In college, when the lecturer says "That's all," you soon learn that it is appropriate to leave. In the absence of that statement, you learn that it may not be so appropriate. In the earlier example of the kissing couple, when the girl shows that she is "ready," the boy has learned to kiss; when she doesn't, perhaps he should refrain.

The learning of complicated cues follows rather simple principles. When the girl looks up through her eyelashes, the boy has learned that a kiss will be reinforced. You learn that if you leave the classroom after the correct cue, the instructor will be reinforcing, but that if you leave at some random moment, he will not.

A stimulus becomes a cue to a behavior when that behavior has been previously reinforced in the presence of that stimulus and not reinforced in the absence of that stimulus. That sentence is a complicated one, but the idea behind it is really very simple: when a stimulus and a behavior occur, and the behavior is followed by reinforcement *only* when they occur together, the stimulus will become a cue for the behavior.

In the laboratory, this process may be studied by reinforcing a hungry mouse for pressing a lever only when a light is on and not giving food reinforcement for pressing it when the light is off. The mouse will learn to press only in the presence of the light. In our everyday lives, this process occurs continually. For example, couples who date regularly can "tell" when it is time to leave a party. A girl has learned that when her date gives certain cues—perhaps getting quieter or acting edgy—she will be reinforced for preparing to leave. In the absence of that cue, he is not nearly so likely to reinforce her leaving. Of course, if the relationship is a good one he will have learned her cues too and will have a higher probability of taking her home when she gives them.

You can see that human relationships are composed of these exquisitely balanced sensitivities and that much of our complex behavior is learned according to these simple principles. Our lives are made up of this network of cues and responses and, in this way, our adjustment to the environment can be seen as a continuous interplay between behaviors and situations.

Your own self-modification project: Step three

This chapter presents background material that is necessary for success in your attempts at self-modification. It is very important that you understand the principles governing your behavior. Can you answer these questions?

1. What is a positive reinforcer?
2. What is a negative reinforcer?
3. What is extinction?
4. What is the effect of intermittent reinforcement on extinction?
5. What effect does punishment have on the frequency of behavior?
6. Does punishment alone teach new behaviors?
7. What is avoidance behavior?
8. How does avoidance behavior come under antecedent-stimulus control?
9. Why is avoidance behavior so resistant to extinction?
10. How does most operant behavior eventually come under antecedent-stimulus control?
11. What is the role played by the "cue"?

If you can answer all the questions, then you have a good grasp of the principles that explain your behavior. The following task, which is the third step in choosing your own self-modification project, will help you develop some skill in applying these principles to your own situation.

Select one of the problems-in-a-situation paragraphs that you wrote for Chapter Two. Write an analysis of that problem, using as many principles of behavior as you can. Of course, much of what you write will be speculation but, for the moment, that is appropriate. The purpose of the assignment is to develop facility in handling the concepts. In later chapters we will discuss methods for testing your hypotheses.

The case of John in Chapter Two can serve as an example of this analyzing process. His problem-behavior-in-a-situation was that he acted "aloof" when he met an attractive woman. If John were to analyze this problem using the principles in Chapter Three, his speculations might proceed like this:

"I withdraw from active conversation to *escape* the *punishment* of my own anxiety. The withdrawal is maintained by *negative reinforcement.* The 'aloofness' must be other people's interpretation of my silence. This pattern has happened so often that meeting a girl I like has become a *discriminative stimulus,* a cue, for withdrawing from the conversation. Because of this I never gain *positive reinforcement* for conversing with her, and if I ever did know how to talk to attractive girls, it was *extinguished* long ago."

Recommended readings

Reynolds, G. S. *A primer of operant conditioning.* Glenview, Ill.: Scott, Foresman, 1968. This book comprises concise explanations of basic concepts and vocabulary.

Ferster, C. B., & Perrott, M. C. *Behavior principles.* New York: Appleton-Century-Crofts, 1968. This reference is designed to teach proficiency in analyzing man's behavior in his natural environment, through the study of basic behavior processes and through the refinement of skills in observation. It is thorough, entertaining, and useful.

Skinner, B. F. *Science and human behavior.* New York: Macmillan, 1953. The fundamental scientific and social philosophy of behaviorism is covered in this book.

Chapter Four
Self-Modification of
Behavior

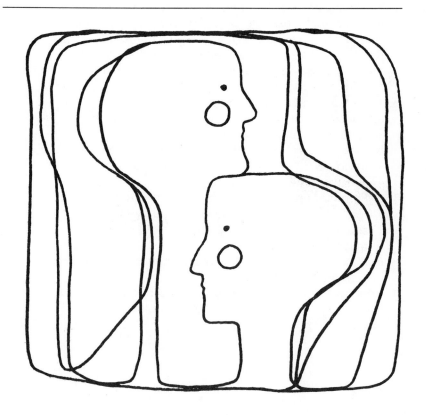

1. The basic idea in self-modification is to arrange situations so that desirable behavior is positively reinforced and unwanted behavior is not reinforced.
2. Reinforcement is made contingent, which means that it is gained only if some particular behavior (the target) is performed.
3. The steps in self-modification are:
   a. Specifying the target in terms of behavior in a specific situation.
   b. Making observations on how often the target behavior occurs, the antecedents that precede it, and the consequences that follow it.
   c. Forming a plan to intervene by contingently reinforcing some desirable behavior and by arranging situations to increase the chances of performing that behavior.
   d. Maintaining, adjusting, and terminating the intervention program.
4. Your own self-modification project: Step four. Points to consider in selecting a target problem are discussed.

The principles of learning describe the ways that behaviors change —the ways that new behaviors are acquired, old ones lost, and current ones modified. These principles are stated in terms of relationships between the environment and the person. They are some of the laws that govern our adjustment to our environments.

These principles were discovered through research by scientists seeking to *understand* why people behave as they do. For over a hundred years, scientific curiosity has led researchers to conduct careful experimentation on different behaviors. Today we can use the knowledge gained about these principles to arrange, to harmonize, the relationship between our own behavior and our environment. *Self-modification,* the process through which these principles are applied to behavior, is an attempt to achieve improved personal adjustment.

Most problems of adjustment can be viewed as difficulties with behaviors. Here are typical statements of students who have engaged in self-modification:

"I want to lose weight—to stop overeating. I look at myself in the mirror and get nauseated."
"I guess the problem is that I'm lonely. I try not to think about it much, but I wish I wouldn't get so uptight with new people, so I can't even talk. I haven't made a new friend in two months. The truth is that I run every time a boy gets near me. No wonder I don't get any dates."
"If I don't start studying better, I'm going to bust out of this school and straight into the army."
"I gotta get off dope before I get spaced."
"Cigarettes are a disgusting, filthy habit and I smoke thirty of them every day."
"I don't know what's the matter. I just don't do anything. Lie around. Sleep a lot. I guess I don't want to do anything. I don't know."

Each of these complaints—these problems of adjustment—are problems of behavior: too much smoking, too much sleeping, avoiding people, infrequent studying, overeating. Because they are behaviors, they can be understood in terms of the principles of behavior. Some may continue because of positive *reinforcement;* others may have been learned by *avoidance.* Some problems may occur because adequate learning has never been acquired at all.

Characteristics of self-modification

Self-modification has these characteristics:

1. It concentrates on behaviors.
2. It applies the laws of learning.
3. There is a heavy emphasis on positive reinforcement.
4. If possible, the project is planned so that the new learning occurs in real-life situations.
5. The person attempting self-modification designs and executes his own program.

One of the most effective self-modification techniques uses the principle of *positive reinforcement.* This technique involves *arranging situations so that desirable behavior is positively reinforced and unwanted behavior is not reinforced.* In this way, the desirable behaviors are increased and the undesirable ones are decreased.

The person engaging in self-modification works out a plan to change the course of events in his life. This is called an *intervention plan.* Recall that certain situations act as cues, or signals, for behavior. *An intervention plan calls for reinforcing desirable behaviors in the presence of our real-life cues.* This allows the cues and the behaviors to become closely associated with one another, thus solidifying their relationship.

Contingent reinforcement in self-modification

How do we use positive reinforcement in self-modification? *The basic principle is that the positive reinforcer is made contingent on the desired behavior.* The idea of *contingency* is very important. A contingent reinforcer is one that is delivered after, and only after, a specified response. *The response leads to the reinforcer. A reinforcer can be expected to bring about improvement only if it is made contingent on an improved response.*

If you gain a positive reinforcer whether or not you perform some desirable behavior, then that reinforcer will not affect the behavior. If you can gain the reinforcer only by first performing some behavior, then the behavior will be strengthened—that is, it will be more likely to occur again. Thus, *it is the contingent relationship that is important, not the positive reinforcer itself.*

Steps in self-modification

The behavior that you choose to modify is often called the *target behavior*. The target behavior can be some undesirable behavior that you want to eliminate, or some desirable behavior that you want to increase.

There is a definite sequence in self-modification. Most self-modification projects can be divided into four phases. These are:

1. Defining the problem in terms of behavior in specific situations.
2. Making observations on how often the target behavior occurs, the antecedents that precede it, and the consequences that follow it.
3. Forming a plan to intervene by contingently reinforcing some desirable behavior and by arranging situations to increase your chances of performing desirable behaviors.
4. Maintaining, adjusting, and finally terminating the intervention program. In Chapters Five through Twelve, each of the stages will be discussed in detail.

The basic procedures of self-modification

Because active practice facilitates learning, each student taking a course in the psychology of adjustment at a particular university was asked to complete at least one self-modification plan. The case presented below illustrates a project typical of those carried out by these students.

Case #3 concerns a twenty-year-old male college senior, Steve C. His report follows with comments interjected at various points.

Specifying the target behavior

Steve wrote: "I am the oldest child in a family with six other children. So far, I'm the only one in college. My problem is that I am constantly arguing with, or yelling at, my younger brothers and sisters. We don't get along nearly as well as I would like. Particularly now that I am about to move out of the family, I would like to leave with good feelings. After thinking about the arguments I have with the others, I decided that one area in which we seem to have constant trouble centers around the requests the others make for me to help them with their school work. With six of them, it seems like I get about a hundred requests per day, and it drives me crazy. Worse, I have developed a usual way of replying to them which, I'm ashamed to admit, is pretty bad.

"One of them will come up and make some kind of request, and my usual response is to start yelling at them. 'Leave me alone!' Or 'I'm too busy!' Or, 'Do it yourself, lazy!' Naturally, this sets off an argument. Sometimes my parents get involved and start yelling at me for being so selfish. But what can I do? If I helped each one of them only one time each day, I'd spend a lot of time doing it, and besides, lots of times they are just being lazy and really could figure out the school-work problem by themselves. Nevertheless, I feel bad, because sometimes the kid really does need my help, and I shouldn't be so rude to my own brothers and sisters, anyway."

Most cases start with some sort of self-dissatisfaction. There is some behavior that you are performing but wish you were not—such as always yelling at brothers and sisters—or there is some behavior you are not performing but wish that you were—such as, helping them when they really need it. Steve was able to start off with a clear idea of his problem. *The first job in self-modification is, always, to translate abstract, vague statements of our problems into words that stand for behavior.*

Counting how often the behavior occurs

For his first self-modification project, Steve decided that he would like to give more help when he felt that it was actually needed. He hoped that doing so would decrease the arguments. Therefore, his next step was to find out how often he actually gave his brothers and sisters needed help.

"For two weeks, I counted how often I performed any behavior that might fall in the general category of helping my brothers and sisters. My total for the first week was two; for the second week, one. Average: one and a half."

Thus, *you begin by making observations.* This is a critical step, but one of the hardest to accomplish, because once you have decided to do something, it is tempting to change immediately. Yet, it is critically important to observe the target behavior as it now occurs, without the effects of an intervention plan. You will need to know three things about the behavior: (1) its frequency, (2) its antecedents, and (3) its consequences.

The first thing the person engaged in self-modification needs to know is the frequency of the behavior. In order to find out, he gathers observations on how often the target behavior is occurring. This information is called the *baseline* and is needed whether you are trying to increase some desirable behavior or decrease some undesirable behavior. *It is important to get accurate information about how frequently the target behavior is occurring, because that is the only way you can see if your attempts at influencing that behavior are having any effect.*

The intervention plan

Steve continued, "My first goal is to be helpful, when I am asked, at least one time each day. I have chosen three reinforcers. Each evening, I will allow myself to watch TV, call my girl friend, or go out for the evening only if I have been helpful at least one time. Many evenings I would like to do one of those things but, for one reason or another, I don't. All three are pretty strong reinforcers for me, so the rule will be: if I'm helpful, I definitely will do one of those three things. If I do not give somebody help at least once, I will not engage in any of these behaviors. The only catch would be if no one asks me to help (that seems unlikely!); then, I can go ahead and do what I want. But if I am asked, I have to help one time."

The important thing about this plan is that the reinforcer is *contingent.* He intends to allow himself to engage in his favorite evening activities only *following* performance of the target behavior. Doing so will reinforce the target behavior and increase the probability that it will recur. Making reinforcement contingent upon performance is the essence of the intervention plan.

Steve's was a good plan, though probably not a perfect one. It was reasonably successful. His helping behavior increased substantially over the baseline rate and, although he did not reach the criterion every day, he was able to increase his weekly average considerably. It had a very nice side-effect for the number of arguments in other areas dropped quite a bit also. At the end of the project he reported that he was feeling better about himself—feeling like a better big brother—and finding it easier to get along at home.

Applying principles

What makes an "intervention plan" different from any New Year's Resolution? What does self-modification mean but just "resolutions to be better"?

In general, we can say that Steve devised a plan that systematically applied principles of human behavior—the laws of learning—and techniques for accurate observation. While we know that strong resolutions can have very real effects in changing our own behavior, we also know that they are often insufficient. If we could change ourselves at will— and by the use of our will alone—there would be only self-satisfied people in the world. Since very few of us are completely pleased with our behaviors, we can readily see that something more than good intentions is often necessary.

That "something more" is a correct application of the principles of behavior. Devising correct applications requires some knowledge of the principles, some experience in the process, and ability to use techniques that will maximize success. Self-modification is, itself, a behavior that must be learned.

As a further test of your grasp of these principles and procedures, evaluate the following report, which is another student's first effort in self-modification. Is it a good plan? What is your judgment: Does it follow principles of behavior? Does it make sense to you?

Case #4, Bryan W., a twenty-year-old male college junior, writes: "I'm a nail-biter, but I wish I weren't. It's embarrassing, sometimes it's painful, and it seems childish to me—something that is o.k. when you're a kid, but not now. It doesn't seem very masculine to me either.

"Target Behavior: reduce nail-biting to zero.

"Baseline: I took a baseline count for three weeks. The frequency of nail-biting ranged from one to eight times a day, with the average about four or five at first, but during the last week it's down to two times a day. I think counting the biting makes me more aware of it, and sometimes I stop where I would have gone ahead and bitten them before.

"The situations that seem to produce more biting are (1) watching TV, (2) being bored, almost anywhere, and (3) listening to lectures. I don't see any way I can change these situations, since I don't want to give up TV, I have to go to lectures, and how can anybody completely avoid being bored?

"Intervention plan: I have signed the following contract and put it up on the mirror where I see it every morning. 'I promise not to bite my nails at all each day. If I do not bite my nails all day, then (1) I get to eat dinner, and (2) I get to see my girl friend that night. If I refrain from biting my nails all week, I get to go out Saturday night, which I usually do. Otherwise, I must stay home. Signed, Bryan W."

In our opinion, this case has some good points and several bad ones. The good points are that he had an accurate count of how often he bit his nails, and that he knew the situations in which he was likely to bite them. The major bad points are that he is requiring himself to stop completely—"cold turkey"—in a manner that may be too rapid, and that he intends to punish himself if he does not succeed. Such heavy demands are bad simply because they decrease his chances of success. By the end of the book, you will be better able to judge the quality of possible plans. Even now, it is a good learning technique to begin thinking critically about the many cases that will be included as examples. Doing so will help you devise a better intervention plan of your own when you have selected the problem for your self-modification project.

Willpower and professional help

Two questions may arise at this point. First, how can you know whether or not a self-modification project should be under professional guidance? Second, how can you determine whether or not you will have the "willpower" to carry through a self-modification project? These are important questions to which there are no simple answers. Willpower, for example, is not an either/or thing. Many techniques discussed in future chapters will actually increase "willpower." Chapter Thirteen deals with professional help—where and when to get it—and Chapter Fourteen discusses "willpower" in detail. These chapters may be read at any time by readers who have a particular interest in these issues.

Choosing a project

What kind of self-modification project should you choose? The two cases we have presented concern minor problems in adjustment experienced by essentially "normal" college students. Even these modest problems of dissatisfaction often will not yield to good intentions alone. The principles of behavior control may be applied to mild problems as well as serious ones.

The problems chosen by our students for their self-modification projects have varied considerably. To illustrate the range, a partial list of problems that have been attempted follows:

stopping smoking
losing weight
increasing studying
decreasing fights with roommates or spouse
stopping "nervous habits" such as nail-biting
decreasing anxiety
learning how to be more attractive to the opposite sex
decreasing stage fright
decreasing nervousness when meeting other people
preventing feelings of depression
eliminating irrational fears (birds, water, girls, professors, and so on)
increasing various desirable behaviors, such as good grooming, reading, etc.
being pleasant to parents
smiling

A very wide range of problems and interests has been represented. In general, any problem in adjustment that can be expressed as behavior-in-a-situation may respond to self-modification techniques.

The behavior that you will initially choose for a self-modification project will depend on your value judgments about what is desirable or undesirable and the ease or difficulty of the project.

We can think again about some of the definitions of adjustment discussed in the first chapter. The seriousness of a problem, or even whether a behavior is labeled as a problem, depends on the values of the individual and the environment (particularly the social environment) in which the behavior occurs. For that reason, we have avoided and will continue to avoid stating what kind of behaviors any reader *should* have. For the same reason, we will not recommend particular problems for the initial project of the reader.

The fact that we do not make recommendations does not mean that we have no values. We have advised against some projects that were repulsive to us, or that seemed unwise or badly thought out. Some of these judgments would not be the same as yours. In self-modification, it is always the individual himself who must make the value judgments. When you choose your own project, you will be making such a value judgment.

Even though the choice depends on the values of a particular individual, some general guidelines should be observed when considering alternatives. For example, you would be wise to choose a plan that will work rather than one that will fail. It would be wise to avoid a very complex project for your first experience. It would also be better to devise a program for change that includes most of the steps of self-modification rather than one using only one or two principles.

It is difficult to make those judgments in advance. Some projects that seem to tackle the simplest problems turn out, in practice, to be the most complicated, while seemingly complex problems are sometimes simple to deal with.

Therefore, our advice is to remain very flexible. Change plans if your first choice is not being instructive. Change again if you are not getting the learning experiences you want.

Research has indicated that the chances of success in a self-modification project are increased if the student chooses a project that is personally important to him, rather than something that he really does not care very much about (Mahoe, 1970; Kolb, Winter, and Berlew, 1968). This suggests that *you should select some behavior that you care about,* one that is important to you, because doing so will increase your chances of success and success is usually a reinforcer: if you are successful in your first self-modification attempt, you will be more likely to try self-modification again. Self-modification, as a learned behavior, is strengthened by the reinforcing effect of success.

Most important, consider your first project as an experience *for learning self-modification. The most important issue in choosing a project is not its content but is that the course of the project will require you to perform each of the behaviors in the self-modification process.* For that reason, it is better to change plans—even more than once—than to miss some part of the self-modification sequence.

Summary

It is important that you understand the basic steps in self-modification. The first step is to be able to state the problem in terms of a specific behavior. The second step is to gather baseline data—to make observations—on the frequency of the target behavior. The third step is to devise an intervention plan so that you reinforce desirable behavior and do not reinforce undesirable behavior. The fourth step is to carry out the plan to its eventual termination.

The first step, expressing your problem in behavioral terms, is the subject of Chapter Five.

Your own self-modification project: Step four

From the list of problems you have prepared, select a problem that seems to be the best choice for a good learning experience. Attempt to phrase the problem in terms as precise as possible, describing your behaviors or your emotional feelings and the situations in which they occur.

Note where you are unable to do so. Bear these points in mind as you read the next chapter.

Chapter Five
Specifying the Problem

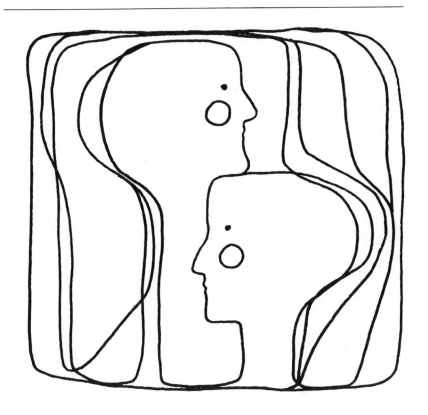

1. Obstacles to avoid in specifying the problem.
2. Tactics for specifying the problem.
   a. Using examples from your own life.
   b. Observing your behavior.
   c. Searching for antecedents.
3. More tactics: When the problem is that you are not doing something.
   a. Observing behaviors that interfere with some desirable behavior.
   b. Translating your problem into desirable behaviors to increase.
   c. Specifying the chain of events that will lead to some goal.
   d. Seeking advice from others.
   e. Using others as models.
   f. What to do when the goal is not explicitly or immediately behavioral.
4. Deciding how to categorize your behavior.

The first step in a self-modification program is to specify the problem in terms of behavior in specific situations.

Language patterns that detract from problem specification

Our language is full of abstract words such as aggressive, hostile, feminine, masculine, dependent, independent that stand for classes of behavior. For purposes of self-modification, words of this kind pose two dangers: they do not specify the situations in which the behaviors may occur, and they do not specify particular behaviors. Furthermore, these words seem to imply that certain behaviors exist independently of their environmental setting.

The use of such words in psychology comes from the belief that people possess *traits,* or habits of behaving, that are not dependent upon the environment. In this system, one might say "I am an independent person" or "I am not very sociable." For the purposes of describing specific behavior, this kind of language is misleading because you may act quite "independently" in one situation and "dependently" in another. A young woman, for example, might be emotionally dependent on her father but rather independent in interactions with her dates.

It is necessary to think of your behavior in combination with the situation in which that behavior occurs, something that is not always easy to do. The use of general class words for behavior, such as dependent and independent, interferes with thinking of behavior-in-a-situation.

A second pattern of thought, concentrating on motives rather than behaviors, can also interfere with associating particular behaviors with specific situations. In describing our lives, the use of words that emphasize motive has great appeal. For example, you may sometimes say to yourself "I guess I just don't want to study," or "My problem is that I'm not motivated enough to get a part-time job." If you use explanations of this kind, you will see self-modification as a problem in changing motives and will believe that inner motives must be changed before behaviors will change.

From the point of view of behavioral psychology, statements about motives are likely to be statements about classes of reinforcers. If someone says "I'm not motivated to study," we would understand him to mean that study behaviors are not usually followed by reinforcement sufficient to maintain the behavior. If someone says he is "not motivated to get a job," his statement would translate into these behavioral terms: "I am currently not receiving reinforcement for job-seeking" or, perhaps, "I am being reinforced for non-job-seeking!"

Analyzing the motives for your behavior is not necessarily inaccurate. Even for purposes of self-modification, such motive analysis can be very helpful, particularly when you come to the task of analyzing reinforcers. But motive analysis can detract from the task of specifying behaviors. Often you may think that you have completed an analysis if you can say "I am not motivated to study" when all you have done is label the problem. Actually, labeling the problem is only the beginning of an analysis. You must also know exactly what kind of behaviors you mean by "studying," and you must know the situations in which this behavior does or does not occur.

Even if your problem is that you have undesirable or uncomfortable attitudes or emotions, this problem can be specified as emotional-behaviors-in-specific-situations: for example, "In a particular situation, I become afraid." No matter what the type of problem, you must have well-defined objectives that are specified in terms of particular behaviors in particular situations. There are several tactics that will enable you to specify problems in this way.

Tactics for specifying the problem

Writing examples

Very often, just providing two or more examples of the behavior in question will show the situations in which it occurs. A young woman who says "I am too aggressive" is telling us nothing about the circumstances of her aggressiveness nor even what she means by "aggressive." When this young woman was asked "What situations, what antecedents, tend to turn on this aggressiveness?" she replied "I don't know."

This is a common response, because often we have not thought about the situations in which behaviors occur.

The next question to the girl was "Well, can you give us an example of aggressive behavior?"

"Sure. Yesterday my friend Martha asked to borrow my pen. It was my best pen, and I was afraid I wouldn't get it back. I'm afraid I said 'No!' rather rudely."

"Okay. Can you give us another example?"

She paused. "A boy who lives down the street also goes to the University. Two days ago he called and asked if he could have a ride to school. But I didn't want to come in so early. So I just turned him down with no explanation."

The point of this dialogue is to illustrate a process. The woman began with a vague, abstract statement, "I am too aggressive," but gave examples that were quite specific: when people asked her for a favor, she tended to respond rather ungraciously.

The first thing to do, if you are unclear about your problem, is to find examples from your real life. Write down at least two examples—three or four will be better—of times when you have shown the undesirable behavior in question. Then try to discover what they have in common.

Giving yourself examples will also serve to specify the circumstances under which the problem behavior occurs. It may be that it occurs in several situations. The point of giving yourself examples is not necessarily to specify only one situation; the point is to describe fully those situations in which it *does* occur. If the behavior occurs in several situations, it may be that these situations have some element in common. In the example above, a general class of situations could be identified: people asking for favors. When such a generalization can be made accurately, you have *one* behavior-in-a-situation unit. If no such general class can be identified, you merely have *several* behavior-in-a-situation units constituting separate problems. In such cases, you would want to treat each of these several units separately, perhaps one at a time. Whether there are several problem units or only one, you proceed by dealing with each in the same way.

Devising descriptive units for behaviors-in-situations

A second tactic that will make it easier to specify situations in which behaviors occur involves phrasing the problem in hyphenated units. The woman in the example above began by describing her problem with one term: aggressiveness. By collecting examples and examining them for some similarities, she was able to make her problem description much more useful. She could have phrased it as "aggressiveness-when-people-ask-me-for-a-favor." That description is a great improvement because it labels the behavior-in-a-situation as a single unit.

Is "aggressiveness-when-people-ask-me-a-favor" a completely adequate statement of the problem? Probably not, because it still contains a trait term (aggressiveness) as the behavioral description. Now it might be that this student will ultimately retain "aggressiveness" as a good summary statement of her various behaviors, but this decision should not be made until the several kinds of behavior actually performed in that situation have been considered. Then, perhaps she will call them "aggressive," or perhaps she will change the word to "ungracious." She might decide the best general word is "ungenerous." This decision is not critical because it is the specific behaviors that matter, but choosing the better term may enable you to observe the specific behaviors more accurately.

Becoming an observer

It is very true that you often *begin* with a vague trait term when you consider your own behaviors. You somehow feel that you are aggressive or dependent without knowing exactly which behaviors you mean when you use the term. In such cases, you need to become an observer of yourself.

A critical step in specifying the problem is to stop speculating about your behavior and start actually observing it. Your thoughts about your problem will probably remain overly vague until you begin to *actually watch yourself* behaving in various situations.

Not only should you actually observe your own behavior, you should keep notes on your observations. You might keep a narrative account of your daily life or simply note instances of behavior that seem related to the problem. Your goal is to gather enough observations of your behavior in various situations so that, when you sit down to read over your notes, it will be possible to see some pattern emerging.

The best way to make these observations is to write down your behaviors and the situations in which they occur as soon as you think you have an example of the problem.

Suppose, in the example above, the woman had not been able to specify situations in which she was too aggressive and decided to follow our advice and begin actually observing her behavior. When the student who lived down the street called to ask for a ride to the University and she responded with her rude "No!" she would have asked herself "Was that an instance of being too aggressive or not?" If she had decided that it was, she would have observed that her overaggressiveness had occurred when someone asked for a ride to school. The next day when her friend Martha asked to borrow her pen and she had responded ungraciously, she might have asked again "Was that another example of being too aggressive?" She would set out to observe all instances of aggressive behavior but would in time come to realize that her problem was more specific.

Another woman began by stating that her problem was overdependence on men. She couldn't think of any examples, so she started off by making observations and writing down instances that fit the problem. On a date a few days later, her escort asked her if she wanted to go to see a particular movie. It happened that she did not want to go but went anyway. Then she asked herself if that was an instance of being too dependent. A few days later another escort took her bowling, something that, she confided to us, she hates to do. She counted that as another instance of overdependence. Soon afterward she reported that she realized what her problem was: she tended to do whatever her escorts wanted to do, for fear of contradicting their wishes, even though she sometimes didn't want to do it. From a vague statement of "overdependency," she came to realize that her problem could be expressed as behavior in a particular situation: too often going along with her dates' wishes even when she did not want to.

Thus, *one of the best ways to make an unclear problem clearer is to start making careful observations of your behavior.* This has the advantage of getting you out of the armchair, where you often engage in nonproductive speculation, and into the real world, where your behavior occurs.

Searching for antecedents

A young man, Bruce, complained that he just didn't feel right. Things were not going well, but there was nothing he could put his finger on. That vague problem statement is not very helpful in working out some plan for self-modification of behavior, because it doesn't point to any particular behavior as the problem.

It was suggested that Bruce observe and write down the antecedents of "not feeling right"—in other words, define the situations that produced the vague state of unhappiness. It turned out that he usually felt bad the day after he had smoked marijuana. At first, he couldn't believe the implication and kept searching for other antecedents. Time after time, the vague feeling of uneasiness came over him after pot parties, which, in his case, were frequent.

"But marijuana doesn't cause hangovers," he complained.

"No, but it could cause worry or maybe feelings of guilt. Are you a little nervous about how often you smoke pot?" He admitted that he was. The pot smoking was the antecedent of the uneasy feeling.

Remember from Chapter Three that antecedents eventually have the power to evoke given behaviors. In well-rehearsed sequences, like most of the problem units of our lives, the antecedents (or cues, signals, or discriminative stimuli) are more important determinants of our behaviors than the reinforcers that follow the behavior.

For this reason, when you observe your behavior you should also observe the antecedents of the behavior. A complete description of the situation will ordinarily contain a specification of the antecedents.

In the examples above, the students began with the aim of observing instances of their problem behaviors. If you also focus on discovering the cues to your behaviors, you will increase the chances of accurately specifying the environmental settings in which they occur. We could diagram our examples like this:

Antecedents	Behaviors
people asking for a favor	aggressiveness
escort making suggestions	compliance
smoking marijuana	feeling bad

These antecedents and behaviors can be understood as hyphenated statements of problems—that is, as behavior-in-situations. As you will soon see, a full description of your problems will often involve longer chains of events. But before we discuss analyzing chains of events, we must treat an interesting kind of problem: that of a behavior which does *not* occur.

When the problem is not doing something

In all of the examples used so far the problem has been one of engaging in some undesirable behavior. Often, however, the problem will be that you are *not* doing something. For example, a student might realize that he is failing in college because he is *not* studying.

For behaviors that you value, and know how to perform, but that are *not* occurring, the same general strategy for specifying the problem still applies. That is, you should specify the situations in which you *want* the behavior to occur. A student who had such a problem might keep a journal to record these situations. In it he might have entries like this: "Wednesday. Roommate went out. Room quiet. Got out the history text and turned to the assignment. Remembered baseball game was on TV.

Started watching it. Tried to study between innings, but gave it up. Studied about five minutes the whole afternoon. Thursday. Went to the library to study. Saw Karen. Didn't study."

These observations do specify two situations in which studying would have been desirable: "room quiet in the afternoon" and "being in library." But his journal also contains other valuable information: it tells him what he did instead of studying.

This student was not simply "not studying." He was actively performing behaviors that were *incompatible alternatives* to studying. Behaviors *are* being performed, but they are the "wrong" behaviors. So his task of problem specification is not really different from the ones already discussed. He will want to specify the situation in question—for example, *"room is quiet"*—and then specify the behavior in question—for example, "watching TV instead of studying."

Later, we will discuss in detail the problem of increasing desirable, incompatible, alternative responses. For our purposes in this chapter—to specify the problem accurately—it is enough to remember that you should specify not only the *situation* and the fact that the desirable behavior is not occurring, but also the behaviors that do occur instead of the ones you want. Thus, our nonstudying student should first specify the situation in which he wants the behavior to occur—when he is alone in his room—and then observe what occurs instead of the desired behavior.

The problem of avoidance learning

Avoidance learning was discussed on page 40. You know from that discussion that many of your undesirable behaviors have been learned under aversive conditions; that is, you learned to do something in order to avoid some unpleasant consequence. By behaving in a particular way, you succeed in avoiding the punisher; thus, the reinforcing consequence can only be inferred. Trying to discover the reinforcer is exceedingly difficult because you are trying to discover something that is *not* occurring. Your own behavior may seem very paradoxical to you, for you seem to be doing undesirable things for little or no reason.

When you are not performing some behavior, but wish that you were, the reason for your lack of performance may be that some aspect of the stimulus situation has acquired aversive control over your behavior.

An example illustrating behavior under aversive control might be a young woman who wants to be friendly toward men but is somehow not able to bring herself to do it. She just shyly hangs around the edges of social gatherings and avoids the men who are there.

It is not always easy to notice when you are not doing something enough. It is easy to notice when you do something to excess: if you overeat, you know it; if you always argue with friends, you probably know it. But the woman who avoids interaction with men at social gatherings may not realize that she is failing to act in a way that men find socially attractive. Therefore, she might never identify her problem, much less solve it. When you are *not* doing something that you think would be desirable, your nonbehavior may be because of lack of reinforcement for performing the behavior or because of some part of the stimulus situation that has aversive control over the behavior. There are two tactics useful in coping with this problem. Neither require that you know the original pattern of learning. You can make useful behavior-in-a-situation observations, even when avoidance learning has taken place and even when nonperformance is the problem. The first tactic is to translate the problem into desirable behaviors. The second involves the use of chain-of-events analysis.

Translating the problem into desirable behaviors

In the example above, the woman who is afraid of men has two choices. She can seek to decrease her fear of men, which she may or may not realize is the problem, or she can set out to increase some desirable behavior. In this case, the desirable behavior to increase would be socially attractive actions.

Self-modification programs can be designed for both decreasing undesirable behaviors or increasing desirable ones. The girl could choose either tactic. Social-approach behaviors are desirable to the girl herself; fear responses to men are undesirable. If she were to define her problem in terms of the undesirable reaction (fear), then she must use the intervention strategy of *decreasing that undesirable behavior.* If she defines the problem more positively, in terms of desirable behaviors, then she will use the strategy of *increasing desirable behaviors.* Because it is better to state problems positively, the second choice would usually be the better one.

Behavior modification is more likely to succeed if you attempt to increase positive behaviors because you can probably use positive reinforcement rather than some kind of punishment. Even more important, simply decreasing some behavior does not automatically teach a new desirable alternative. It is for this reason that behavior modification uses the strategy of increasing desirable responses. We will return to this topic in detail when we discuss intervention plans in self-modification.

For the time being, remember that you should *specify desirable alternative behavior,* even when the problem is that you perform some undesirable behavior.

In the example of the student who does not study, specifying a desirable alternative is easy. By making records of his behavior, he saw that when he was alone in his room, he watched TV, and that when he went to the library, he talked with Karen. For each of those two situations, he could name the desirable alternative behavior: he should have studied. His intervention plan would *not* be to decrease directly the undesirable behavior of watching-TV-when-alone-in-room or talking-with-Karen-in-library but, instead, to *increase the desirable behavior* of studying-when-alone-in-room and studying-when-in-library.

It is always best to attempt to specify your problem in terms of some desirable behavior that you would like to increase.

A young woman came to one of us complaining that she was bothered by frequent feelings of depression. She had begun searching for the antecedents for these upsetting feelings but found that a great variety of things seemed to produce depression. A boy friend would mildly criticize her, her cat would briefly disappear, her new dress would be slightly soiled—many relatively meaningless antecedents seemed sufficient to set off hours of unpleasant feelings. It seemed that it would take a lifetime just to specify all the antecedents leading to depression, much less to do anything about them. When asked to specify a desirable alternative, she replied that feeling good would be such an alternative. It was suggested that she begin to search for antecedents leading to feeling good, and that she keep in mind the goal of attempting to increase them.

For these examples—not studying and not feeling good—specifying desirable alternatives is easy. But sometimes a person with a problem may not know what the desirable alternatives are.

We often continue old habits partly because we don't know what we *should* be doing. In such a case, you must begin to examine systematically the behavioral chains which, if carried out, would lead to certain of your goals. This will often reveal new behavioral possibilities.

Specifying the chain of behaviors
that will produce some goal

The things that happen to you—the outcomes you encounter or the goals you attain—are the result of a series of causes. They follow from a chain of behaviors. Although you may feel that, once set in motion, this chain of events leads inexorably to its conclusion, whether you like it or not, very often the chain of events is under your control. It is important that you understand that things happening to you are caused and that you can gain control over the causes. Obviously you are not going to succeed in controlling the events in your life if you do not believe that you can.

How does examining chains of events apply to self-modification of behavior?

Whenever there is some goal that you wish you were obtaining, but are not, figure out the chain of behaviors that must necessarily precede the goal.

A female student complained that no one ever asked her for a date.

"When was the last time you went to the student lounge, or to the dining room, or anywhere that young men tend to congregate?" asked her advisor.

"A long time," she replied.

"How can they ask you for dates if they don't even know you exist? If you want men to ask you for dates, you have to take the step of showing them that you are interested in being asked, and you do this by going where they are."

In this simple example, the chain of behavior necessary to the desired outcome is specified: if you want to meet men, you have to go where men are.

Suppose the girl now adds "But it scares me to go to these places. I hate to go around where there are a lot of people I don't know. They would all just ignore me, and that would be terrible." This statement represents a significant step forward in specifying the behavior that should be modified. She needs to work on her fear of going to social gathering places. Notice that when she started, she felt that her problem was that no one asked her for dates. After further examination of the situation, the problem in her behavior became clear: she failed to engage in the behavior necessary to start the chain of events that would produce the desired outcome.

Whenever there is some desired outcome that is not occurring, ask yourself what chain of behaviors has to happen before the chances that the goal will occur are increased. The location of your problem is the point in the chain at which you are not producing the behavior necessary to move to the next link.

In the example above, the chain should go like this: (1) the girl goes to a social gathering place; (2) she is noticed by some men who talk with her; (3) she behaves in a way that they think is attractive; (4) one or more of them—either immediately or, more likely, at a later time—acts on the basis of her attractiveness and asks her for a date.

The problem could occur at any stage of the chain. It might have been that the girl did go to social gatherings but failed to act in an attractive manner when she was there. She might have discovered this problem by listing the chain of events and identifying the point in the chain where the breakdown occurred.

In a process like this, you may be able to specify the problem in terms of your own behavior by gradually enlarging a brief general statement into increasingly specific statements of the behavior involved.

A young man complained that he was about to be flunked out of college.

"I'll bet you're not studying enough," suggested his cynical advisor.

"I knew you were going to say that," countered the student. "Well, you're wrong. I spend two hours a day in the library, studying."

At this point the advisor had to make a decision. Perhaps the young man really did study two hours daily and was still failing. If that were true and two hours a day should have been enough for his course of study, then the kindest thing might be to suggest that he consider not finishing college, on the assumption that he simply did not have the intellect to do college work. But the advisor decided the student was intelligent enough. Thus, he reasoned, the problem must be that the student did not study properly during his two-hour daily sessions.

"Tell me what you do when you are studying."

"Well, I sit and read the textbooks."

The advisor now asked the student to make some observations. Of the total time that he spent "studying" how much of it was spent *actually reading* the book? He was asked to note the time when he began reading and when he stopped. The answer was surprising: about 75% of the "studying" time was actually spent doing something other than reading the material. Probably it was spent staring at the material, worrying about what would happen if he failed college, being frightened, and looking around the library. This suggested an initial self-modification program: to increase the percentage of time actually spent reading the books.

The advisor was using chain-of-events reasoning. The desired goal for the student was to do well in college. This, of course, requires studying, so the advisor first checked to see whether that necessary behavior was occurring. The student assured him that it was, which implied that the student was not studying efficiently.

Whenever some desired outcome is not occurring, make the assumption that there is a chain of events involving your behavior that would normally lead to the outcome, and that somewhere along the chain you are not performing some behavior, causing the chain to break down. First, state what the chain of events has to be. Second, ask yourself "Am I performing the necessary behavior at each stage of the chain?"

In specifying the chain of behaviors leading to some desired goal, don't overlook the obvious. In both examples given above, the missing behavior—once it was pointed out—was quite clear. Almost always some obvious simple behavior not being performed is what causes the chain to break down.

"I don't know why, but John doesn't like me."

"Are you trying to be nice to him? Are you reinforcing for him?"

"No. If he is not going to like me, why should I reinforce him?"

"On the other hand, if you do not reward him, why should he like you?" The point is obvious, but even more obvious when chain-of-events analysis is employed.

It is sometimes helpful to ask yourself "Why do I want to modify that particular behavior?" The answer to this question should be a statement of some cause-and-effect relationship: by changing behavior X, goal Y will result. If you cannot tell yourself the reason *why,* in terms of cause and effect, it may be that you have not specified correctly the behavior that will lead to your goal.

The following example illustrates how this process works. An older male student reported that he wanted to eliminate scratching his head while he was studying.

"Why?" he was asked.

"When I am studying," he replied, "I don't concentrate very well. Maybe if I could stop scratching my head, I would concentrate better."

Of course, the next question was to ask him what he thought was the cause-and-effect relationship between not scratching his head and concentrating. He could not name one. His real goal was to increase concentration while studying, so it was suggested that he try to identify other target behaviors that would lead to success in achieving the goal.

Sometimes your answer to the question "Why do I want to modify that particular thing?" will be a value statement: "Because I would be a better person." "Because I would be happy." "Because I feel less guilty." Reaching one of those states is itself a goal and can be achieved through changes in your behavior. Asking yourself "Why?" should help identify the cause-effect relationship between some aspect of your own behavior and that goal.

Seeking advice

There will always be problems that will not yield to your efforts at observation and analysis. This is most often the case when you are trying to create hypothetical chains of events involving behaviors and goals entirely outside your previous experience. Sometimes the effective behaviors do not occur to you; at other times you really do not know how to perform the needed behaviors. In such cases, the advice of others may be helpful.

Even in this early stage of self-modification—specifying the problem—you may find yourself unable to manage alone. In cases like this, the advice of professionals may well be sought. Various kinds of counselors—psychologists, college counselors or teachers, psychiatrists, social workers, ministers—can be of great help in defining your problems. In fact, traditional psychotherapy's greatest effect is probably its ability to help an individual define his own problem so that he can set about solving it himself. Self-modification programs do not imply that others cannot help you. At any stage—even near the termination of your intervention programs—professional advice may be indicated. We do not emphasize professional help in this book because the vast majority of adjustment problems will probably yield to intelligent self-help. But for any stage in the behavior-modification process, professional help is available to untangle your analyses when you cannot manage them alone. Often all that is needed to identify a problem is the extra experience the professional brings to the situation.*

Professional advice is not the only advice that may be useful. The advice of friends, family, or others whom you respect may sometimes help you over difficult moments in your self-analysis. This is particularly true in the stage of problem definition. If you are unable to determine your own contribution to an unsatisfying chain of events, someone who knows you may be able to offer suggestions. If you are unable to imagine desirable alternatives to your self-defeating chains, someone who *does* handle these chains well may be able to offer advice. A general rule for seeking this kind of advice is to seek it from someone who either knows you well or knows the kind of problem well.

In seeking advice, *you should remember that it is advice you want, not punishment.* Suppose your advisor suggests that you are really behaving stupidly. "Don't tell me I am a stupid jerk," you may observe politely to him, "tell me what behavior I could change so I would not be a stupid jerk."

It will be just as useless to have an advice-giver assure you that nothing is the matter with you, that you are really wonderful. The point is that if you involve advisors, you often have to teach them the principles and language used in behavior modification.

---

*If you are having great difficulty in specifying your problem as behavior-in-a-situation, it may be appropriate to read Chapter Thirteen at this point.

Using models

When you are having difficulty defining the problem or its solution, another useful technique is to observe the behavior of others who successfully achieve the goal you have set for yourself. This is especially true when you cannot figure out the target unit in a chain of behavior. For example, the girl who wanted to increase her social activity might be able to analyze part of the problem accurately:

"I can see that I must go to the Student Union more. I guess that's obvious. If I'm not somewhere to meet boys, I won't meet them. But after I get there, then what? I've done this kind of thing in the past, but even at a party where you talk to lots of people, I never seem to get into a really good conversation with hardly anybody."

"Do you have any idea what you could do to improve that?"

"None. I really don't. I feel friendly; I want to meet boys; but it just doesn't happen."

"Do you know anyone who handles this situation very well? Someone who does achieve the goal you want?"

"Karen does. She lives down the hall and is in my German class. She talks to every boy at a party and gets asked on more dates than she has time for."

"Why don't you watch her. Just observe how she handles the party situation; observe her as closely as you can. Make notes later."

This student actually did make these observations and returned later, very excited.

"You know what she does? She starts smiling even before she's sure he's even talking to her. It makes her look so *interested!* And she says something back, very quickly. I suppose it makes guys think that she really likes talking to them."

By carefully choosing a model who *does* achieve the goals you want, you can observe full chains of events that will contain behaviors you may wish to adopt. Some of these behaviors, as in the example above, might never occur to you. If you can get ideas for behaviors from models, then you can complete the problem definition—that is, fill in any missing links in your chain of events.

But is it desirable to "imitate" others? For some reason many people feel that this is distasteful. Imitative behavior is seen as the opposite of your *own* behavior and believed to be somehow not genuine. It is certainly possible to imitate artificially, in a way that makes you and those around you uncomfortable.

The use of models does not imply that kind of imitation. Actually, the most economical kind of human learning is imitative learning: by observing good models, you can often unreel very complicated behavior sequences accurately on the first performance. In childhood, imitation is the way that complicated social behaviors are typically learned. This kind of imitation occurs constantly throughout our lives and is a very natural process. Furthermore, observing models will give you *ideas* for behaviors, not necessarily the exact behavior that you will ultimately perform.

Our example continues:

"But if I use 'smiling-and-answering-boys-quickly' as my solution, and try to behave that way, won't I turn out looking like an imitation Karen? That will turn everybody off, especially me."

"No, it's unlikely to turn out like that. If you decide to smile and answer quickly, you will be smiling your own smile, not Karen's; you will be answering with your own comments, not hers; and everything you do will be in your own style. Your new behaviors will become integrated with your old ones, and you will be only yourself, but yourself smiling and answering."

When the goal does not seem to be a behavioral one

There are instances when your desired goal is something that does not seem behavioral. It may be some kind of favorable outcome, such as loss of weight.

If the desired outcome is to lose pounds, the question, of course, is how to produce a situation that will lead to achieving the goal. Ask yourself what chain of behaviors will lead to losing weight. You will have to eat less, push away from the table earlier, cut down the number of meals, eliminate in-between meals, eat different foods. These are all behaviors. To reach your goal, weight loss, you must engage in some or all of them.

If your goal were to get better grades in school, you would be in a similar situation. The desired outcome is not behavioral, but in order to reach it, you must engage in certain behaviors, studying being the most obvious. If your goal were to gain more attention from the opposite sex, it is also true that to attain this outcome you would have to perform certain behaviors, such as being socially attractive.

If your goal does not specify a behavior, it is still true that the way to gain that goal is to engage in certain behaviors.

Thus your task will be to increase those behaviors that will produce a desired goal and to decrease those behaviors that interfere with the desired event. Always think of the problem in terms of *your* behavior.

The reason for this is simple: your behavior can be brought under your control.

Has the problem been analyzed correctly?

How will you know whether you have analyzed the chain of events correctly? How will you know whether you have identified the antecedent situations accurately and have chosen the right behavior to change?

You must know the answers to these questions, because it would be absurd and wasteful to continue a program of self-change that was having no effect at all in helping you reach your goals. It would be even more unfortunate if you stopped an effective program because you erroneously thought it *wasn't* working.

In order to accurately assess your self-modification programs, it is necessary to compare the situation *before* and *after* your intervention. In this way, you will know when you must reanalyze the events surrounding your target behavior. This comparison will identify both mistakes and successes. To obtain the necessary data, self-modification again specifies a scientific procedure: you count and record the frequency of the target behavior *before* you intervene and also *during* your intervention. Differences in frequencies indicate that some change has indeed occurred.

The frequency counts taken before intervention are called *baseline* rates. The next chapter is devoted entirely to specifics about baseline-rate collection; here we will simply show you how such counts can help determine whether or not you have correctly specified the problem. For example, suppose a girl sets out to increase the number of dates she has and erroneously tries to reach this goal by increasing the amount of time she spends at social gathering places (when her problem really is that she rarely smiles at men). She will be able to see that she has picked the wrong behavior to modify when the number of dates does not increase. Whenever you modify some aspect of a behavior chain successfully and still fail to achieve the desired goal, you must consider modifying some *other* behavior in the chain.

The girl would say to herself "I have increased the amount of time I spend in social places by 50%, but my number of dates has not increased. This implies that I must be making a mistake. Maybe the problem is that I don't engage in some necessary behavior when I am at the gathering place."

This kind of program correction is possible only if you have accurate baseline data, because only accurate baseline data will show you

whether or not any change has occurred. Gathering baseline data, therefore, is of great importance in self-modification programs.

Deciding on categories

The purpose of specifying the problem is to know exactly what
behaviors to change in which situations. Once specified, such behaviors
can be counted. But before you can count, you must decide exactly *what*
to include. For that reason, you establish *categories* of behavior and
situations. The aim of this chapter is to give you the ability to *state your
behavior-in-a-situation observations so clearly that the words will cover all
instances of the problem.*

For example, the student who had difficulty in actually reading his
study material defined his problem very precisely:

Situation	Behavior
When-I-have-sat-down-to-study-and-gotten-everything-ready	really paying attention, in spite of distraction, and really working
R (Ready)	W (Working)

This table illustrates a good specification, because it is general
enough to cover all the problems: seeing a friend, falling asleep, listening
to the radio instead of studying, and all the other problems that interfere
with his goal of increased study behavior. It is also a good specification
because it is precise enough to exclude behaviors that really work differently. For example, his statement correctly excludes "not studying"
when it is due to extra time in the stacks searching for a misfiled volume,
or "not studying" because he is sick in bed. These are *not* instances of
the same inattention problem that concerned the student, so the *category*
describing his behavior-in-a-situation does not include them. It is also
a good specification because it is stated positively, in terms of *behavior*
to be increased, rather than negatively, in terms of behavior to be
avoided; notice that he specifies "working" rather than "nonworking."

Notice also that he developed a symbol to stand for the category.
A good category specification is often so long that it is awkward to use
when noting occurrences of the behavior. The use of symbols is convenient in keeping records; this student used R (for Ready) whenever that
situation occurred and W (for Working) whenever his attention was

truly on his work. The symbol allows the student to say "My goal is to increase W in situation R." You should be able, at this point, to make this kind of statement for your own problem.

Of course, if your goal is much simpler, the specification will also be simpler to state. For example, one student who wanted to stop cracking his knuckles established a simple category and a simple goal: "Stop CK's in *any* situation." This goal was so simple that he did not even want to specify an alternative or positively stated behavior.

Sometimes problems are more complex. Consider the girl discussed earlier in this chapter who was distressed by having few dates and chose a friend as a model for behavior change. How do you think she might have specified her problem? What categories of situation and behavior might she have used? Because this problem was a complicated one, several good strategies were possible and there was no single right answer. However, this case can be used as an exercise for you to check your grasp of the procedure involved in specifying categories: you should now be able to make a reasonable suggestion for this girl, in the following form:

The goal is to increase *(behavior)* in *(situation)*.

Try developing a good description of these categories and some symbols for them. If you can do this, you are probably ready to do the same for your own self-modification project. If you are not yet able to do so, try rereading this chapter before going on to the next.

Your own self-modification project: Step five

You should now specify your problem as some behavior-in-a-situation that you wish to decrease or as some behavior-in-a-situation that you wish to increase. Ideally, even if you want to decrease some undesirable behavior, you will be able to state, as your goal, an *increase* of some other behavior that is incompatible to the undesired one. You should specify a category that includes all instances of the target behavior so that you can identify an instance of the behavior when it occurs. If you cannot now state your problem as behavior-in-a-situation, you should go through each of the procedures in this chapter, step by step, for your own chosen problem.

Before going on to the next chapter, complete the description of your own problem behavior-in-a-situation.

Chapter Six
Gathering Baseline
Data

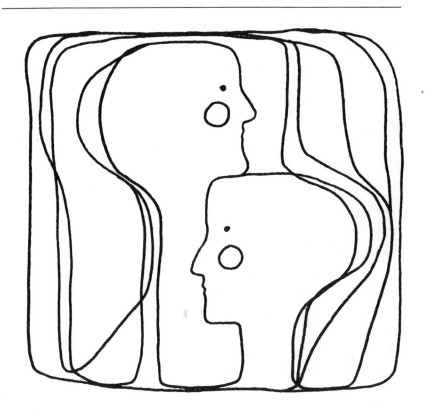

1. The data gathered before intervention begins are called baseline data.
2. Your goal is to count all occurrences of the target behavior.
3. The mechanics of recording your behavior:
   a. The recording system must be truly portable.
   b. It must be present when the target behavior occurs.
   c. Recording must be easy.
   d. You should keep written records.
4. You should almost always avoid immediate intervention.
   a. Sometimes it is allowable to skip the baseline period.
   b. Sometimes just gathering the baseline data will have an intervention effect.
5. You should build record keeping into your pattern of habitual behaviors.
6. What to do with behaviors you perform without thinking.
   a. Negative practice.
   b. Using others to remind you.
7. Reinforcing the act of recording the baseline data.
8. How long should you gather the baseline?
9. How can you know if your baseline data are accurate?

The data gathered *before intervention begins* are called the *baseline* data. The baseline becomes the standard of comparison for later effects. Because the baseline is so important, this chapter is devoted to a discussion of baseline-gathering issues: how, why, and for how long.

How are baseline data different from prebaseline observations?

You have been observing your behavior and environment for some time before the baseline period. In fact, you have observed accurately enough to establish categories and formulate goals. How are baseline data different? Basically, these data are quantitative: they result from *counting* something. As you move into the baseline phase, then, you begin to *count* things, and your records are kept in numbers.

What do you count?

The answer to this question is simple: *you count the occurrences of the behavior-in-a-situation categories you have just established.* Remember the nonstudier who, in the last chapter, formulated his goal in terms of symbols: "My goal is to increase W in situation R." This student, during baseline, would then *count* occurrences of W and R.

We can use this student's case as an example of the counting procedure. At this stage, his task was to invent some record-keeping system that would help him accurately record the occurrences of W and the occurrences of R. Immediately he was faced with a question: *What is an occurrence?* Are occurrences of R all the same, no matter how long they last? Or would he count the *duration* cf R and the *duration* of W? That is, should he record the number of *minutes* he was "ready" and the length of time he actually "worked"? Each case will be different, of course, but there are some elements common to all.

The student constructed this chart.

	Mon	Tues	Thurs	Fri	Sat	Sun
R	45					
W	15					

He decided to record the *number of minutes* actually spent studying and the *number of minutes* when he was in R condition. The actual count of the minutes is shown for his first day. Notice that the chart did not include Wednesday. This student worked at a part-time job on Wednesday, and there was never an opportunity for R to occur on that day. He believed it to be a more accurate description of his study-week if Wednesdays were not included in the records. Thus he restricted his chart to occasions when the categories *could* occur.

Should you always record in duration units—minutes or hours? No. If the target behavior is smoking, then you count the number of cigarettes smoked daily. If the target behavior is practicing dance, on the other hand, you will probably count the number of hours—or minutes —you practice each day. Smoking cigarettes is a behavior that will occur a number of times each day: ten, twenty, or forty. Studying, on the other hand, is not something that will occur so frequently. You won't study twenty *times* each day. Instead, you may study only twice but for twenty *minutes* each time. In that case, you would count not the number of occurrences, defined as separate acts, but the number of minutes. Another alternative would be to count the number of pages read or math problems solved.

The number of occurrences will always be either the number of separate times you perform some behavior or the amount of time you spend at some behavior. Use a simple rule of thumb: *if it is easy to count the number of separate times you perform the target behavior, count that. If it is not easy, or if the target behavior runs on for several minutes at a time, count the amount of time you do it.*

A young man said "I want to decrease my telephone talking. I seem to spend half the evening on the phone, and it wastes my time. But I tried counting the number of phone calls I make, and it doesn't make any sense. One evening I made only one call, but it lasted two hours. Another evening I made a bunch of calls, but they were all short." To solve this problem, he began to count the *total amount of time* spent on the phone each evening.

A male student, who was extremely afraid of women, mentioned that it would be silly for him to count the amount of time he spent with eligible young women because it probably came to about five minutes per week. He began counting the occasions on which he could (and/or did) say at least "Hello."

Remember, too, that your goal is to count *behaviors,* even though the goal may not be behavioral.

Dieting is a good example. In dieting, the goal is to reduce weight, so you need a daily record of weight. What produces this goal? Reducing food intake and/or increasing exercise. You may find it necessary to keep a record of not only how much you weigh but also what food you consume, the number of calories, and perhaps how much you exercise.

Whenever your goal is not behavior but some other event such as decreasing your weight, increasing the number of good grades you receive, or increasing the number of dates you have, the first task should be to work out the chain of behaviors you would have to engage in to bring about that desired goal. Since it is your behavior that will bring about the goal, it makes sense that you should keep a record of that behavior. A rule of thumb: always keep a record of the *behavior* that you have to produce in order to attain some goal.

Some examples of record-keeping systems

A young man had the habit of cracking his knuckles. He wanted to stop, and his fiancé also wanted him to stop. He carried a 3 x 5 card around with him and, every time he cracked his knuckles, he made a check on the card. Each day he started with a fresh card. He was counting the daily frequency of knuckle cracking.

A female student wanted to increase her vocabulary. Whenever she encountered a word she did not know, she wrote it down. Later she looked up its meaning in a dictionary. She was then able to count both the number of words written down and the number actually looked up.

An older woman wanted to stop smoking. She began by counting the number of cigarettes she smoked daily. She also noted the *situation* in which the smoking occurred. She had already established categories for these situations and codes for the four major categories:

Category	Code
After or during eating or drinking	E, for eating
While nervous in a social situation	S, for social
While driving the car	D, for driving
Other times	O, for other

Each letter is the code for one category. Using an abbreviation makes recording less tedious. Her daily 3 x 5 card looked like this for the first Monday:

Smoking Record		Monday the 7th
Morning	Afternoon	Evening
E E D O S S S E	O S S D S E E E	E O

She was surprised to see her pattern of smoking so clearly revealed. Actually, her records for several days were very consistent, and she was later able to plan an intelligent antismoking program.

Case #5. A very attractive young woman was bothered by what she considered her sexually promiscuous behavior. She wanted to have intercourse less often. More particularly, she wanted to know her boy friends better and longer before she went to bed with them. Following the idea of specifying the chain of events that produces some desired goal, she reasoned that if she reduced the number of times she got herself into physical or social circumstances that would permit intercourse, she would be able to refrain more. She began counting the number of occurrences each week of *situations* in which the circumstances would or would not permit intercourse—for example, how often she was at a large social gathering with a date versus how often she was alone with him.

The mechanics of recording

These plans for recording categories are good, but they will come to nothing unless the mechanical problems of actually *doing* the recording are solved. For example, if our smoker forgot her 3 x 5 card one day and later tried to remember her smoking behaviors, she would be unlikely to remember accurately. Inaccurate data are worse than no data at all because they will both deceive you and make you falsely secure. So you must develop a system for recording that will actually work. Several general suggestions can be made.

The recording apparatus must be truly portable. Many of our students use a 3 x 5 card or some other small piece of paper that will fit conveniently in pocket or purse or stash bag. This, along with a pen or pencil, is all the "equipment" one needs. But sometimes even such a simple arrangement won't work. The man who is recording his frequencies of knuckle cracking has no pocket for his card when he goes to the beach on Sunday. The promiscuous girl finds herself reluctant to pull out her 3 x 5 card just as she declines an offer or, worse, just after she accepts!

These examples may seem petty, but such issues arise in almost every self-modification project. The reader should expect them and should also work to solve them, because they can be solved. For example, the girl discussed in Chapter Five who wanted to increase her frequency of smiling and encouraging conversation, decided that a paper-and-pencil system would be ridiculous, since a series of smiles-then-write-it-down might appear more bizzare than attractive. She bought a small golf-stroke counter from the sporting-goods store. It was not much larger than a healthy peanut and could be easily hidden in her hand. When a social situation with an eligible boy arose, she slipped the counter out of her purse, and the recording—accomplished by pushing the thumb-lever—did not interfere with the smiling at all.

The knuckle cracker at the beach found a big leaf and tore little notches in the side for each crack. He later transferred this "record" to his regular chart.

The smoker, who often left her 3 x 5 card at home in the morning, decided to cut the card down so that it would slip inside the cellophane of the cigarette pack. Thus, it was always present when the problem behavior occurred.

Actually, that is the central issue: *the recording apparatus must be present when the behavior occurs.* By carefully analyzing the problem, as discussed in the last chapter, you can anticipate most of these situations. The recording technique should be selected to meet the requirements of these situations. There is room here for much inventiveness.

One of our students carried a few pennies in his left pocket and, every time he engaged in his undesirable target behavior, moved one of the pennies to the right pocket. Then, in the evening, he could count the number of pennies to see how often he had performed the target behavior that day.

A girl who wanted to increase the number of times she performed a particular desirable behavior carried toothpicks in her purse and moved one into a special pocket of the purse after each occurrence.

A cigarette smoker started out each day with a specific number of cigarettes, thirty, and when he got home in the evening, simply counted how many he had left.

Daily records and storage records

When using bits of paper, leaves, golf-counters, or other devices for record keeping, you need to transfer their information to a more permanent storage record. This storage record may not be exactly the same as the daily (or occasional) record. For example, on Tuesday morning our lady smoker transferred the daily record (illustrated on p. 84) to her storage record.

It looked like this:

		M	T	W	T	F	S	S	M	T	W	T	F	S	S
E	7														
S	6														
D	2														
O	3														
Total	18														

Our smiling girl with the golf counter transferred her daily records to a chart that was simpler than the one for the smoking record because she was recording only the one category of smiling-and-encouraging:

M	T	W	T	F	S	S	M	T	W	T	F	S	S
5	7	3	6										

Sometimes a double record is not necessary. For example, the non-studier (whose chart appears on p. 82 of this chapter) was able to clip the chart to the inside of his notebook. It was always with him, and it served as his daily record and storage record both.

Sometimes, too, a self-modifier will transfer his daily record directly to a *graph*. That issue will be discussed later, on p. 95.

The important point here is that record keeping and record storing must be adapted to each reader's own behaviors and own situations. Do not be afraid to improvise or adopt a system not mentioned here. The aim is to get the data and, if an accurate baseline results, that is the proof of the system.

Be strict in your counting

One major benefit derived from counting the occurrences of your target behavior is that it forces you to pay close attention to the target behavior. Because, as humans, we are not careful observers of our own behavior, what counting uncovers about our behavior is often very surprising.

Record all occurrences of the target behavior.

The goal of your intervention plan is to reduce or increase the frequency of the target behavior. Only if you have kept an accurate count of the frequency of the target behavior will you be able to work out an adequate intervention plan. In science, the accuracy of counting is called *reliability.* You must have a reliable, accurate count; otherwise it will be impossible to judge the effectiveness of your program.

You will also want to be strict in your definition of an occurrence. Your target behavior might be to increase the amount of time you spend studying. You would begin by counting the number of minutes each day actually spent studying. Suppose that you sit down, open the book, and immediately go into a daydream that lasts five minutes. Don't count that five minutes. Count only the amount of time actually spent doing the target behavior.

At the end of your daydream, when you snap back to reality, say to yourself "Well, I didn't really study for that five minutes, so I won't count it." If you had written on your daily record "Began studying at 7:45 P.M.," you would change it to read, "7:50 P.M."

Maintaining a strict count like this helps you understand the difference between engaging in the actual target behavior and engaging in other related behaviors. You might come to realize, as in this example, that you seem to spend a large amount of time daydreaming when you are supposed to be studying. By starting out to make a strict count of the amount of time you actually engage in the target behavior, you can sometimes learn what you are doing *instead* of the desired behavior or what you are doing that interferes with the target behavior.

Keep written records

It is sometimes tempting to say "I'll just remember how much time I spend doing the target behavior, so I won't write it down." Avoid this type of thinking. You will find that if you don't keep written records, you won't keep any records at all. You might forget; you might rationalize.

One of our students reported that, whenever he was working successfully on his diet, he faithfully kept a daily written record of how much he weighed. But then would come that fateful weekend: a dinner party on Saturday night followed by a spaghetti supper on Sunday. Monday morning would dawn, and he would know very well that he had gained weight over the weekend. His solution was simple: he would not weigh himself on Monday! Thus he wouldn't have to be confronted with the awful evidence. Not weighing when expecting bad news could easily become a habit, and soon weighing would stop altogether. Then —fat again!

Many smokers report that because it is so disturbing to realize exactly how many cigarettes they consume each day, they want to avoid keeping a record. In cases like this, it is obvious just how important record keeping is to achieving the desired goal.

One of our very bright students reported that he had the bad habit of being rude to his friends. He seemed to insult them and to do it often. He began record keeping by carrying in his pocket a 3 x 5 card with two columns on it, labeled, "Did insult" and "Did not insult." As soon as he had finished some conversation with a friend or acquaintance, he would take out the card and make a check in one of the two columns. For example, he might run into a buddy on campus and stop to talk for a few minutes, then the two would go their separate ways. Our student would immediately make an entry in one of his columns. The major advantage of this system was that it allowed him to make a decision immediately after a conversation rather than later, at the end of the day, when his memory was hazy. It also had the advantage of providing immediate reinforcement for not insulting a friend. *It is vital to obtain data as the problem occurs.*

Another effect of recording each occurrence of a particular event at the time it happens may be to make you aware of pleasant events. In some cases it is just as easy to forget these as it is to forget bad things you have done. A girl who was troubled with feelings of depression started out by saying "There is nothing good or happy in my life. The whole day is a bummer." She started off trying to count the number of times each day that she felt depressed but soon stopped; basically she felt that she was depressed all the time. Remembering that when in doubt, you should begin by counting the frequency of desirable behaviors, she started counting the number of times each day that she felt good or happy or at least content. In three days she said "Hey, there are actually periods of time every day when I feel good!" She had never remembered these, probably because she was so involved in trying to cope with the depression.

Always keep written records.

Avoid immediate intervention

Once you have decided to modify some aspect of your behavior, you will want to begin immediately. After all, you are not concerned with a scientific analysis of the cause-and-effect relations in your behavior, so why should you first gather baseline data? Why not begin at once?

The reasons are several. First, without adequate baseline data, you might not notice early subtle changes in your behavior. Thinking that nothing is happening, you might become discouraged and stop the plan when, actually, it was just beginning to have an effect. Second, one of the things you will do when you gather baseline data is search for antecedent conditions—situations that have stimulus control over your behavior. If you do not discover them, obviously you will not be able to eliminate their control over your behavior, and the intervention plan will fail. A third factor is that if you have not solved record-keeping problems during the baseline period, you will first encounter them when you are trying to intervene. Then you might not be able to tell if your intervention plan is having any effect because of faulty record keeping.

There are other reasons as well, but the main point is this: *one of the most common reasons for the failure of intervention plans is inadequate baseline data.*

Is there ever a time when no baseline period is needed? Only two actually, and they are rare. The first instance is when the behavior *never* occurs.

If your plan calls for some behavior that you *never* perform, then there is little point in gathering baseline data. If you can honestly say that you have not studied in several months, then the amount of time you spend over the next few weeks would obviously be zero. If you never do it, and are really sure you never do it, then you already have your baseline data: over a period of several months, your baseline is zero. In that case, since you already have your baseline data, you can begin to intervene. (On the other hand, it may still be of value to record the baseline frequencies of *opportunities* for the new behavior.)

If you are performing some behavior only a little, however, then you should gather baseline data. Suppose you do study a little bit each week, maybe about fifteen minutes. You should gather baseline data in this situation because it will suggest how you should start to increase the desired behavior. If you were studying about fifteen minutes, you might begin an intervention plan by reinforcing yourself for studying twenty minutes. You would know where to begin only if you had adequate baseline data. Another common reason for failure of intervention plans is starting with too high a criterion for reinforcement. This can be avoided by initially gathering adequate baseline information.

Your first step, then, would be to ask yourself "Am I performing the behavior at all?" If the answer is "No," then you can intervene immediately. If the answer is "Yes," or even "Maybe," then you should gather baseline data.

The other situation in which you should intervene immediately is the one in which your behavior is dangerous to yourself or to others. What is defined as dangerous, of course, differs with different people. If the danger is slight or in the distant future, then you have to weigh the advantages of immediate intervention versus the advantage of starting with good baseline information. Realize, of course, that without adequate baseline information, you increase the risk that the intervention plan will not be successful. Thus, if your target behavior is smoking, which is dangerous, you should gather the baseline; in the long run, the increased chance of success is a greater advantage than the short-run advantage of stopping today but resuming next week.

There are also some kinds of behavior that occur only at certain times but then occur with a high frequency. Studying during exam period is a good example. You may not want to study very much throughout the semester but wish that you did study more when exam time comes around. Or you might very rarely have a date, but when you do, seem to always act stupidly. What to do about the baseline?

In this kind of situation, you cannot gather the baseline until the occasion arises. If it arises quite irregularly, like exams coming only once each semester, you can do two things. First, be prepared to gather the information *when* the situation does occur. Second, practice ways of dealing with the situation. If a girl knew that she always acted much too aggressively toward her dates, she could begin to practice a counter-behavior of acting in a friendlier fashion. Or if a student knew that he didn't study enough during exam week, he could begin practicing studying *before* exam week.

Some situations are worth sacrificing the baseline period for, and others are not. Most are not, even though there is a frequent tendency to skip over this important phase. Alternatives can often be adopted before you decide to abandon the baseline. For example, it would be simple to *contrive* an exam-like period and let this serve as a baseline phase. A person could, for instance, mock-up a two- or three-day period during which he resolved to study at least five hours daily. Observations on daydreaming, desk avoiding, and actual studying could well serve at a later date as baseline data for the actual intervention.

Intervention effects of gathering the baseline information

When we teach our students how to modify their behavior, we necessarily put a great deal of stress on working out a good intervention plan. Occasionally, a worried-looking student will approach us after a lecture and say "I'm sorry, but I cannot work out an intervention plan."

"Why not?" he is asked.

"My problem is that my problem has gone away! I started to gather the baseline data and was doing it regularly, just as you said, but then I just quit the undesirable behavior I was counting. Will that lower my grade?"

It sometimes happens that simply counting how often you engage in some undesirable behavior will be enough to decrease it (Rutner and Bugle, 1969). Or counting how often you do not engage in some desirable behavior will be enough to somehow increase it. This has been called the intervention effect of the baseline period (Tharp and Wetzel, 1969.) In other words, just gathering the information sometimes has a beneficial effect (McFall, 1970). If that occurs, fine. The whole point, after all, is to modify behavior, and if all you have to do is to count it, then you can only wish all behaviors would be so easily modified. However, you will want to guard against temporary success; if the problem returns, you may then have to institute an intervention plan.

Building record keeping into the pattern of habitual behaviors

Keeping a record of how often you engage in some behavior is itself a behavior that, unfortunately, is not often practiced. For that reason, you may encounter some problems in keeping records. Think of ways to build record keeping itself into a habit. One way to increase a behavior is to build a *cue* that will trigger the behavior. In the early stages, you may need cues as support. For example, a weight-watcher developed the habit of weighing as soon as he got up in the morning. It became one of his first daily chores, like brushing his teeth.

If you always perform some behavior at the same place, it is easy to keep records by simply keeping your chart at that place. If you always study at the same desk, the chart can be kept right there. Or if you study at various places, but always have your notebook with you, you can tape your chart into the notebook.

Building record keeping into the pattern of the target behavior is another way to build cues. A dieting student taped her record of foods consumed onto the refrigerator door. She also kept a chart and pencil taped to the wall just above her scales so that, when she weighed each morning, she could note her weight immediately.

Another way to make keeping records an effective habit is to *increase the attention you pay to the target behavior.* If you do not attend to the behavior, simply do not notice it, you cannot very well record it. Often you must teach yourself to attend. There are several ways to increase attention. One way is through the technique known as *negative practice.*

Negative practice for "unconsciously performed" behaviors

Some behaviors, such as nail-biting, talking too loud, or overeating, have been so well practiced for so long that you do them without noticing. Under such circumstances, it is very hard to get accurate recordings and even more difficult to intervene. There is an available strategy, however, although it may seem peculiar at first. It is called negative practice.

When you are performing any undesirable behavior without paying attention, your first step is to deliberately practice doing the behavior while consciously paying attention.

Our reasoning is easy to follow: you want your attention to be readily switched on when you begin to perform the undesirable behavior. To achieve this, you take the same approach you would take for any other behavior that is not occurring; you practice it. In this case, you need to practice paying attention while you are performing the target behavior.

A young man who habitually cracked his knuckles—baseline, seventeen times daily—spent five minutes each morning and five minutes each evening deliberately cracking his knuckles while paying close attention to every aspect of the knuckle cracking. If he had allowed his attention to wander, the purpose of the practice, associating the target behavior with paying attention, would have been lost.

A sophomore girl had developed a habit of scratching her arms while she was sleeping. In the mornings she would sometimes awaken to find herself bleeding where she had been scraping away at herself all night. Being asleep, of course, makes it rather difficult to pay attention. We suggested that each night, when she first went to bed, she deliberately scratch her arms for several minutes while paying close attention to the scratching. Being awake, she was not in danger of scratching until she bled. We had suggested that she do it just before going to sleep, instead of at some other time during the day, because that situation was most similar to actually being asleep and thus would generalize most easily. It worked. After a few nights' practice, she was not scratching in her sleep anymore.

Once you have learned to pay attention to the habitual target behavior, you can then begin some intervention plan to eliminate it. The scratching girl worked out a plan so that she gradually replaced scratching with rubbing, then with patting, then with just touching.

Using others to remind you

A second way to deal with "unconsciously" performed behaviors is to ask others, usually friends, to point out instances of the target behavior.

One of the authors had developed the habit of always saying "Okay?" when mentioning a difficult point in a lecture. What was meant was something like "I know I just mentioned a difficult point. Do all of you understand it? If not, please let me know and I will explain." Somehow this had been shortened to "Okay?" The baseline (believe it or not) was nine times in every five minutes. (That's what one of our irritated students recorded, at any rate.) The solution was to ask one of the friendly students in the first row to waggle her finger every time the word "Okay" popped out. Using other people who have not developed the habit as you have will supply a cue for you to notice when you are performing the target behavior. In this case, fortunately, just gathering the baseline had an intervention effect. Another student, bright but excitable, had developed the habit of talking much too loudly—not all the time, but regularly when she was enthused. It was so habitual that she would start the behavior and perhaps continue it for several minutes before becoming aware of it. To get a count, she asked her friends to remind her when she was talking too loudly. In another case, an overweight student had his wife remind him whenever he appeared to be overeating.

One common problem in using other people to remind you that you are engaging in some undesirable target behavior is that you may find it punishing—socially embarrassing—to be reminded. Also, the person who is supposed to be reminding may misinterpret his job and think that he is supposed to be punishing the target behavior:

"John, you fool, you're biting your nails again!"

Whenever this occurs—when you feel punished—change the system that is being used to notify you. The student whose wife reminded him of his overeating reported that, initially, he became very irritated when she said "Ed, you're overeating"; That was too bald a statement. They changed her phrase to "Ed, dear, are you . . . ?" Then she dropped the subject. This indirect way of reminding him was not frustrating.

Never allow yourself to be punished for noticing or recording your behaviors. This, after all, would make recording a less frequent behavior, exactly the opposite of what you want.

But suppose the very act of gathering the baseline data is punishing to you, even if no one knows but you? Sometimes a person has a difficult time keeping the records because he does not like what the records are telling him. The scales may tell you, every day, that you are overweight. The record of number of cigarettes smoked may tell you, every day, that you are killing yourself. Because it is so painful you may be tempted to stop keeping records. If record keeping is punished, it—like any punished behavior—will be suppressed. This can be overcome *by introducing positive reinforcement for the behavior of recording* (Stuart, 1971).

Reinforcing the recording of behavior

The simplest reinforcement is the target behavior itself. If you are going to engage in it anyway, then it is easy to use that behavior to reinforce record keeping. For example, one of our smokers simply set a rule that she could smoke, but she always had to note down that she had smoked. Every time she wanted a cigarette, she simply made a mark on a piece of paper she carried in her purse and then allowed herself to light the cigarette. Another student who usually overate allowed himself to eat all he wanted, but he had to first note down what he was eating. A third student, an older man who had the unwanted habit of getting angry very easily allowed himself to do it but first had to move a penny from one pocket to another to record blowing his top once again.

If this kind of reinforcement will not work for you, then you can work out some other positive reinforcement for keeping the record. For example, one of our overweight students had initially had some success in weight loss by recording only his daily weight. But when he could lose no further pounds, he decided to keep a record of not only how much he weighed but of all foods that he consumed each day. However, his new plan was unsuccessful because it seemed like a lot of trouble to keep a record of every calorie consumed and it was embarrassing for him to see how much he sometimes ate. Result: no records. Thus, his first step was to reinforce record keeping. In this case, he worked out a plan that allowed him to spend one dollar on a pet hobby for each day he kept accurate records. The result was that he began to keep the records. He then discovered where his food intake problem was and worked out a plan to eliminate it.

Self-modification of behavior is itself a behavior and follows the same rules as all other behaviors. It can be influenced in its frequency by its consequences. You want to be positively reinforced for each attempt at self-modification, for that will increase the chances that you will attempt self-modification again when it would be desirable. The best way to ensure success is to have every aspect of the system working well. If you are failing to produce the necessary behavior at any stage —if you are not gathering the baseline, if you are not reinforcing your- self—*you should view your failure as a result of the nonperformance of a necessary behavior and work out a system to increase that particular behavior by positively reinforcing it.*

Analyzing the baseline data

For most forms of baseline data, you want to understand how the behaviors vary from one day to the next (or from one week to the next). In other words, you want to see the data *in relation to time.* Only in this way can you judge the reliability or the stability of your observations.

For this reason, the *graph* is often a useful device for inspecting your baseline data. Ordinarily, in behavior-modification work, the time units are entered on the horizontal axis and the behavior units are entered on the vertical axis.

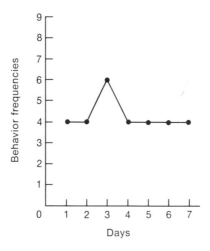

Figure 1. Recording baseline rates.

In the graph in Figure 1, for example, you can see very quickly that there were four instances of the behavior on each of the seven baseline days, except for day 3, when the behavior occurred six times. Making a graph is easy, and the visual aid is valuable in several ways. For one thing, it can tell you quickly *when your baseline rates have stabilized.* A stable baseline rate ordinarily means that intervention can begin.

The easiest way to know that you have a stable baseline is that the line on the graph levels off. Figure 2 gives an example of a rather stable baseline rate. In the figure you can see that, on the first few days, this cigarette smoker showed some degree of variation in the number of cigarettes smoked, but by the end of ten days the daily number seemed to average about twenty-five. After ten days of baseline, he was ready to begin his intervention plan.

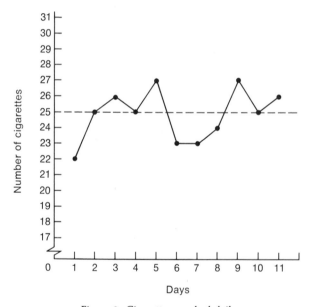

Figure 2. Cigarettes smoked daily.

The question we are dealing with is "How many days would this cigarette smoker have to gather baseline data before he could feel that he had an adequate estimate?" Our rule of thumb is: *if the behavior is daily, always gather the baseline for at least one week.* If, by that time, it seems to show only small swings up and down, you will have a usable estimate.

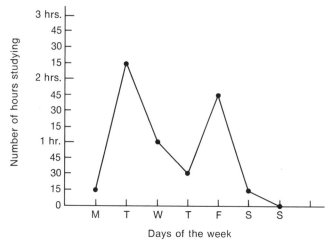

Figure 3. Number of hours studying daily.

Figure 3 shows the number of hours a college freshman studied each night. You can see that, at the end of the first week, he would have had only the roughest idea of his weekly study time because within the week he had shown such variation. This suggests a second rule: *when the behavior shows large swings from one day to the next, it is best to gather the baseline for at least two weeks.*

The general answer to the question, "How long should you gather baseline data?" is: *long enough to have a good estimate of how often the target behavior occurs.*

There is no absolute rule for judging how adequate a baseline record may be, and there is no absolute rule for how long you should collect data prior to intervention. After all, the purpose of the baseline is to establish how often the behavior is occurring. *You end the baseline period when you have some confidence that you understand the actual patterns of your behavior frequencies.*

There are some considerations that can offer help in deciding whether or not you have a stable baseline.

First, it is rare to get a stable estimate in less than a week. Each day's activities are somewhat different from all others and, even with frequently occurring behaviors, it will take seven days to notice any consistency.

Second, the greater the variation from day to day, the longer it will take to get a stable estimate. A good rule of thumb to follow is that if, after three weeks, you still have a lot of up-and-down swings on your graph, use a simple average. At the extreme are very irregular behaviors that occur with great frequency only at certain times—for example, cramming at exam time. In this case, you can use a practice period, as suggested earlier, and rehearse the conditions and behaviors that you expect to occur at the time in question.

Third, ask yourself if the period of days or weeks during which you have been gathering the baseline is representative of your usual life. If you were counting number of hours spent studying, for example, and last week was mid-term time, then that is not a typical week and should not be used to make an estimate. Or if you went to an unusual number of parties over the last five days, and if you smoke more at parties, then you could not use that period as a good basis for estimating how much you smoke. Every day has something unusual about it, which necessitates gathering the data for at least a week. But we are suggesting that you look for special occurrences that would artificially inflate or deflate your estimate of the frequency of a target behavior.

In general then, always run the baseline period for at least one "normal" week, and rarely go beyond three or four weeks.

Are the baseline data reliable?

Reliability, in science, refers to a particular kind of accuracy of recording. Data are *reliable* when two or more observations of the same event result in the same recording. In the self-modification of behavior, the question you must ask yourself is: "Am I really recording each occurrence, and am I recording the same events in the same way each time they occur?"

In psychological research, we usually try to use two or more separate observers, and these observers practice recording together until they reach an acceptable level of agreement (usually 85–95%). But in self-modification, you are your only observer which can lead to some difficulties.

A young man was determined to increase his housekeeping behavior. Two sets of roommates had already thrown him out because he sloppily threw things around, never washed dishes, never cleaned the bathroom, and so on. He established a category called "acts of good housekeeping." The baseline, after two weeks, was very irregular. He asked for advice; it turned out that his definition of "acts of good housekeeping" changed from day to day: sometimes putting his empty beer glass in the sink would earn a check mark for good behavior, while on another day—when he was in a more depressed mood—he would count only "acts" as major as making his bed or taking out the garbage. The category definition drifted from day to day and thus his records were hopelessly unreliable.

There are several common reasons why a person has a difficult time trying to make reliable observations. All of them have been discussed earlier and are summarized briefly below.

You may not have defined your target behavior in terms of behavior-in-a-situation. In short, you may not have not been specific enough.

The behavior may be an "unconscious" habit that you perform without paying attention to it.

Perhaps engaging in the behavior is so upsetting to you that you'd rather forget about it than record it.

You may not have developed a record-keeping system that is simple enough.

Each of these problems can be reduced by consulting the sections of this chapter that discuss them and following the recommended procedures. But you still may have doubts about the accuracy of your data.

In some cases, when you have such doubts, you may ask for help from another person. You may ask him to record along with you, each of you keeping separate records. This procedure may bring problems of its own, since observers also make errors (McFall, 1970). Nevertheless, the level of agreement can then be calculated, and 80% or more may be considered acceptable.

Enlisting the help of a second recorder may be useful when the behavior is public and especially when the frequencies are high, but it will not be helpful if the behaviors occur infrequently and unpredictably. Other observers cannot help much when the behaviors are private or when they involve such feelings as fear or unhappiness or joy (Kanfer, 1970b). Much of your concern with your own adjustment involves these private feelings, yet they *are* private and not available for observation by anyone else. Thus they are particularly vulnerable to unreliability, to drift, and to being unnoticed. The depressed girl who recorded her "good" and her "bad" feelings could never rely on anyone but herself to make these judgments and these recordings.

Because the achievement of reliability is one of the inherent difficulties in self-modification, you must be particularly careful to use techniques to maximize your reliability: Use (1) *specifically defined categories* of (2) *behaviors-and-situation* recorded on a (3) *device always present* at the occurrence with a (4) *simple system* that is (5) *not punishing* and that may even be (6) *positively reinforcing.*

Your own self-modification project: Step six

You should begin to gather the baseline data for the behavior-in-a situation chosen at the end of Chapter Five. You will need to count every instance of the target behavior and keep records of your count. In order to be successful, you must make record keeping easy and build it into your life pattern. Avoid immediate intervention. If you have difficulty in getting an accurate count, reread the sections of this chapter on tactics for dealing with that problem.

It may require two or three weeks to get a stable estimate of your baseline. While you are gathering the data, you should read the next four chapters, which deal with techniques of intervention; when you do get a stable baseline, you will want to have an intervention plan nearly ready to begin.

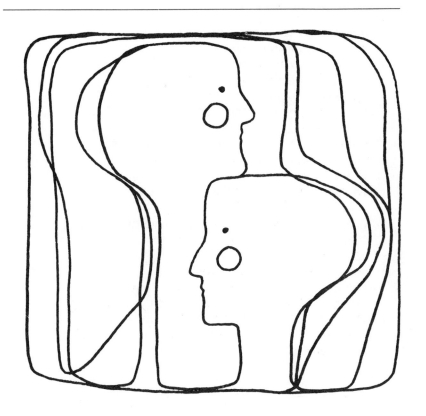

1. You will need to arrange things so that reinforcement follows desired behaviors.
2. If you observe that some reinforcer is currently maintaining an undesired behavior, then you can rearrange the contingency so that the same reinforcer is used to strengthen the desired target behavior in the same situation.
3. You can select any reinforcer from your life and make it contingent on the target behavior.
   a. There are a series of questions that you can answer in an effort to list your own personal reinforcers.
   b. The reinforcer you choose must have three characteristics: it must be a reinforcer for you, it must be manipulatable—so you can put it on contingency—and it must be potent.
4. The Premack principle: Any behavior that you perform frequently can be used to reinforce some target behavior that you do not perform frequently, by making the frequent behavior contingent on the infrequent behavior.

The simple formula for self-modification is to rearrange the contingencies so that *reinforcement* follows desirable behavior. Thus you need to know about the reinforcers that you have available for rearrangement.

During the baseline period, you should be searching for reinforcers. This chapter discusses ways of discovering and cataloging them.

Direct observation of reinforcing consequences

Sometimes it is possible to discover the consequence that is currently reinforcing your undesirable behavior. Behavior analysis generally asserts that most habitual behaviors—including undesirable ones—are maintained by some form of reinforcement. Occasionally you can readily discover these reinforcing consequences. For example:

Case #6. A male student kept careful baseline records of his studying behaviors. He recorded the situations and opportunities for studying (for example, "at library, 42 min."). He also recorded his actual attentive time ("4 min.," "15 min.," and so on). The baseline rate of actual study time was very low—less than 20% of the time he was in an appropriate study situation. What was the reinforcer for all this inattention-while-in-study-situation? He was able to report it instantly: instead of reading, he spent his time watching girls, especially girls climbing the stairs beside his usual study table.

This reinforcer, incidentally, was not only clear but very available for rearrangement. He designed an intervention plan that required him to spend at least sixty minutes studying in his room, a behavior he would then reinforce with a trip to the library where he could girl-watch with single-minded devotion. He reported that this plan increased both his study time and girl-admiring time.

A professor we know reported that he had developed the bad habit of bluntly telling others when he thought they were not acting very intelligently. "What do you think reinforces this behavior?" he was asked. "I guess it's the feeling that I have that *I* am smart. By showing others when they do something dumb, it shows them that I am smart. The trouble is, of course, that it makes them angry." We suggested that he could gain the same reinforcer (feeling intelligent) by intelligently choosing a positive statement instead of making some deprecating remark.

These two examples illustrate how an easily discovered maintaining reinforcer can be rearranged to support new, alternative behaviors. In both cases, the same reinforcer is gained but for a different behavior.

It is likely, in this kind of situation, that you will have discovered the reinforcer for your undesirable behavior while you are gathering baseline data. *The easiest kind of intervention plan is simply rearranging the reinforcers that you are already getting so that they are used to reinforce some desirable behavior rather than some undesirable behavior.*

Of course, life is not always so simple. There are situations in which the reinforcers, though evident, are not so easily detached from the problem behavior.

Consummatory responses

Difficulty in detaching reinforcers from a problem behavior is particularly evident for *behaviors that consume the reinforcer:* for example, overeating is reinforced by the food (in addition to other things); excessive beer drinking is reinforced by the beer itself; pot smoking, by the effect of the marijuana; cigarette smoking, by inhaling the smoke. It is certainly easy to identify these reinforcers but not so simple to detach them and rearrange them into an intervention plan. Problem sexual behaviors also resist change in the same way. Case #7 illustrates this point.

Case #7 was concerned with excessive masturbation, an activity in which he indulged two or three times daily. The reinforcer was fairly obvious here: the sexual pleasure itself. (Although he also gained some temporary relief from social anxieties this way, the sexual pleasure was apparently the most powerfully reinforcing consequence.) The reinforcer was thus easily identified but could not be detached from the activity. He found it necessary to control the *antecedents*—the situations in which he observed that masturbation usually occurred.

He was able to eliminate some of the antecedents but not all of them, probably because masturbation usually occurs when a person is alone, and it is neither possible nor desirable to eliminate all situations of aloneness. Thus, he was only partly successful in his effort to reduce the frequency of the undesired behavior.

Finding a reinforcer more powerful than sexual gratification might have been a better strategy. This case illustrates the need to catalog a wide variety of reinforcers, even when you know the one that maintains your problem behavior.

Problems can arise when the reinforcing consequences of behavior are not so obvious. Sometimes the most careful observer cannot discover what they are. Two conditions that commonly obscure reinforcers are *intermittent reinforcement schedules and avoidance behaviors,* both of which were first discussed in Chapter Three.

Intermittent reinforcement and avoidance behaviors

Some habitual behaviors are reinforced only *intermittently.* If each instance of your problem behavior were followed by reinforcement, then careful observation could reveal the reinforcer in question. But some of your more persistent actions are followed by reinforcement only some of the time. Remember that intermittent reinforcement leads to greater resistance to extinction. Thus, you might expect to find that an intermittent reinforcement schedule is responsible for maintaining especially persistent problem behaviors.

Suppose, for example, that some problem behavior receives reinforcement on an average of only once every twenty-five times. If this were a behavior that occurred five times per week, it would take five weeks of observation to detect the *first* instance of reinforcement. Before you could establish that a one–to–twenty-five ratio was the intermittent schedule, you would need hundreds of observations, and the baseline period would necessarily extend for a year or two. This kind of observation might be interesting scientifically, but it would not be at all appealing to the individual who wanted to change his behavior.

Avoidance behavior creates even worse problems for the person trying to discover his reinforcers, because the aversive consequence may not occur at all. When you have been punished for a behavior in the presence of a cue, that cue will come to control avoidance of the behavior. Thus, if you are successful, you will not be punished again, and you will not be able to observe the negative reinforcer. While avoidance learning probably accounts for many problems, you might observe forever and not detect the specific punishment you are avoiding.

Case #8 was a sophomore who wanted to go out for his dormitory's intramural basketball team. He had not played competitively in high school and had not even played many pick-up games since he was about fourteen, although he enjoyed shooting baskets alone. He told us that he really had a baseline: during three semesters of college in which he wanted to go out for a team, he just couldn't make himself do it. He wanted to know how to discover the reinforcer for non-going-out.

Of course, Case #8 couldn't discover such a reinforcer, and neither could a professional. It did not appear that any alternative behavior was particularly attractive to him. He did not, for instance, prefer studying to practicing with a team. In a case like this, we can suspect a pattern of avoidance learning. During high school, some unpleasant consequence probably followed his efforts to participate in organized basketball. That consequence might well be lost in his history of learning. Even if he were able to remember the punishment he once received, he would need new positive reinforcers to strengthen the behavior he now wants —joining the dormitory team.

To summarize: If you can discover the reinforcers that are supporting some undesirable behavior, you may be able to rearrange them so that they will reinforce some desirable behavior. But three conditions can interfere with this process: the behavior may lead to consuming the reinforcer or may be otherwise inalterably attached to it; the problem behavior may be on an impossible-to-detect intermittent reinforcement schedule; you may be engaging in avoidance behavior. For these three conditions, the reinforcers may not be discoverable or controllable. *Your strategy, then, must be to discover reinforcers that are controllable. The reinforcers do not need to be those that are currently maintaining your problems.* You can use *any* reinforcer, as long as it will increase the frequency of your desired behavior.

Cataloging reinforcers

If you cannot rearrange or even discover the reinforcers for a particular behavior, it is still possible to modify your behavior by selecting some reinforcer that is presently not supporting the desirable target behavior but that can be arranged to do so.

Positive reinforcers

A positive reinforcer is anything that will increase the occurrence of the behavior that it follows. Reinforcers can be things, people, or activities. A "thing" reinforcer might be a doughnut, a five-dollar bill, a new dress, a fancy shirt, a stereo record—anything you want or would like to have. A "people" reinforcer would be something like being able to go on a date with your girl friend, talk to your boy friend on the phone

—spend time with anyone you enjoy. An "activity" reinforcer is any event that you enjoy—playing a game, going to a movie, and so on. Sometimes you treat yourself to a movie. Or you buy a good meal at a restaurant. Maybe you "do nothing"—talk with friends, loaf. Usually these kinds of potential reinforcers are not limited to any one behavior or situation. You may just feel like going out for a few beers. Any kind of special occasion like this can be used as a reinforcer. *The task is simply to connect the occurrence, contingently, to the target behavior.*

The range of reinforcers is potentially as wide as the range of objects in the world, as wide as the range of human activities. How can an individual decide which of these will be among the catalog of potential reinforcers for him?

To demonstrate the variety that is possible, a partial list of the reinforcers used by our students follows:

taking bubble baths
making love
going to a movie or a play
going to the beach
mountain climbing
smoking pot
smoking cigarettes
spending time at a favorite hobby
spending money
playing records
listening to the radio
eating favorite foods
going out "on the town"
playing sports
getting to "be the boss" with a girl friend or boy friend
spending extra time with a friend
"spoiling" or "pampering" oneself
reading pornography
reading mystery stories
taking long breaks from work
putting on makeup
not going to work
"doing anything I want to do"
going to parties
being alone
"doing only the things I want to do, all day long"
"not doing my duty sometimes"
goofing off
watching TV

How to catalog your reinforcers

How can you decide which are the potentially effective reinforcers for yourself? Here are some questions to answer:

1. What kinds of things do you like to have?
2. What are your major interests?
3. What are your hobbies?
4. What people do you like to be with?
5. What do you like to do with those people?
6. What do you do for fun, for enjoyment?
7. What do you do to relax?
8. What do you do to get away from it all?
9. What makes you feel good?
10. What would be a nice present to receive?
11. What kinds of things are important to you?
12. What would you buy if you had an extra five dollars? Ten dollars? Fifty dollars?
13. What behaviors do you perform every day? (Don't overlook the obvious, the commonplace.)
14. Are there any behaviors that you usually perform instead of the target behavior?
15. What would you hate to lose?
16. Of the things you do every day, what would you hate to give up?

You can construct your own additional set of questions. Determining reinforcers is an individual matter. You should feel confident in the reinforcers that you feel are present, whether or not they are used as examples in this book.

Wherever you are in your own self-modification project, stop at this point and take a few minutes to think about the questions above. In our experience, there are two stages in self-modification that are most difficult. One is specifying the problem behaviorally, the topic covered in Chapter Five. The second is selecting reinforcers to use, the present topic. You should be able to specify several answers to each of the questions listed. If you can, you will have a good-sized catalog of possible reinforcers.

Three considerations in choosing a reinforcer

You have to consider three things when choosing a reinforcer. *First,* the consequence has to be a reinforcer *for you.* You will have to select consequences that are individually tailored to your needs and desires. *Second,* the consequences you select to use as reinforcers must be accessible to you. You must be able to manage them, to make them contingent. *Third,* they should be relatively strong reinforcers: the more potent the reinforcer, the more likely it is to be effective in helping you to change your behavior.

Reinforcers must be accessible. For example, there is no point in cataloging "$1,000" as an effective reinforcer if you cannot arrange to collect and give yourself $1,000. Perhaps you cannot afford to use even one dollar as a reinforcer. In such a case, you must look further. You will be able to tell if a particular reinforcer is accessible simply by asking yourself "How will I be able to deliver that reinforcer to myself when I have performed the target behavior?"

The easiest way to evaluate the strength of a reinforcer, its potency, is to ask yourself *"Do I really think that I will stop performing the undesirable behavior—or start performing the desirable behavior—just because I will gain X (the reinforcer)?"*

Case #9. This student intended to reinforce her new behavior of getting-in-by-midnight. She considered using a reinforcer of a morning bubble bath. It could be put on contingency because there was no other demand on her to bubble her morning bath. But, she decided, it wasn't really potent. Staying out late, her problem, was more pleasurable to her than the bubbles. She decided to use listening-to-the-radio-while-she-dressed-in-the-morning as the reinforcer because it was manipulatable —could be put on contingency—and, in addition, was more potent: the music was an important part of her morning ritual.

What if no reinforcers seem to be available?

Often it will appear that there are no reinforcers available for manipulating. Sometimes it seems this way when you are locked into a rigid and demanding schedule.

Case #10. This coed, nineteen years old, struggled to stay in school. She registered for morning classes only, starting at 7:30, and at 2:00 each weekday her job at the bakery began. When she finished at 10:00 P.M., she frequently had papers to write, exams to study for, and other numerous demands on her time. She lived with her mother, who was partly disabled, so housework, laundry, and shopping occupied most of the weekend. She dated only occasionally. Sundays she slept. She wanted to increase the amount of time spent in pleasant activities.

For this girl, each reinforcer that she cataloged seemed to require time for its enjoyment, and there seemed to be no time. For example, she wanted new clothes, but there was no time to really enjoy wearing them. She wanted a new FM stereo receiver, but what she really wanted was time to listen to music. Case #10 had a rich catalog of things she wanted but she could not manipulate them.

Another situation where selecting a reinforcer is a problem is one in which nothing seems to be a reinforcer, nothing seems to be any good. Observe yourself the next time you feel depressed: one of the components of your depression is the feeling that nothing is desirable or worth doing, or, in the language of behavior modification, stimuli lose their reinforcing function. Things no longer matter. Depressed students often report that their reinforcer catalogs are blank.

Another problem, that of not being able to specify an available reinforcer, occurs when everything in your reinforcer catalog costs more than you can afford.

Case #11 turned in a reinforcer catalog that looked like this:

1. Guitar
2. New amplifier
3. New boots
4. Trip to Alaska next summer
5. Quitting school for a year and doing *nothing.*

This student was entirely self-supporting, currently living on his previous summer's earnings, but budgeted so close to bankruptcy that the first four items were out of the question. He was having so much academic trouble that a part-time job seemed unwise. The fifth alternative was unrealistic, both for financial reasons and because of the military draft.

These are unhappy cases. However, a student sometimes reports that he has just the opposite problem: he is already receiving all the major positive reinforcements he wants and cannot rearrange them without losing something. His situation may not be so unhappy, but it has exactly the same effect. Specifying a reinforcer that will be effective in helping him change his behavior is very difficult. What can you do when, for any of these reasons, no practical reinforcer reveals itself? For an answer, we turn to the Premack principle.

The Premack principle

Named after the psychologist who has studied the phenomenon most systematically, the Premack principle states, in effect, that if behavior B is more likely to occur than behavior A, then behavior A can be increased in its likelihood by making behavior B contingent on it. An example from an experiment by Homme, de Baca, Devine, Steinhorst, and Rickert (1963) follows: Nursery school children are very likely to run around and make noise. They are much less likely to sit quietly in their seats. If you wanted to increase the probability of their sitting quietly in their seats, you could do so by arranging events so that *if* they sat quietly, then they could run about freely. Sitting quietly is behavior A; running around is behavior B. Initially, B is frequent but A is not.

The Premack effect works like this: First the children sit quietly for a few minutes. This is followed by the opportunity to run around and make noise. Sitting quietly will then increase in its frequency, as long as it is a necessary step to the behavior that was already very frequent —running around.

Notice that in the definition of this kind of a reinforcer, there is no mention of fun or pleasure or feeling good. The point of the Premack effect is that an activity does not have to "feel good" in order to be useful as a reinforcer. *Any behavior that you frequently perform can be used to reinforce any less frequently occurring behavior.* (It should not be actively unpleasant, however.) This kind of reinforcer has all the functional characteristics of other types of reinforcers.

Can you see the usefulness of this principle? Suppose that you have defined your problem in terms of behavior-in-a-situation and realize that there is a particular target behavior that you would like to increase. You try to think of some pleasurable, positive reinforcer to connect to the target behavior, but nothing seems available. There are, of course, certain behaviors that you engage in every day, such as taking a bath, going to work or school, eating, watching TV, or talking to friends on the phone. Any one of these may be used to reinforce the target behavior by connecting its occurrence to the target. *The design of the plan is to require yourself to first perform the target behavior before you perform the behavior that occurs frequently.*

Case #12 was a young woman who wanted to increase her exercise time, up to fifteen minutes each day. A very frequent behavior for her was taking a shower. Following the Premack principle, she simply arranged this contingency: she could not take a shower until she had done her exercises.

Case #13 was a studious young man who wanted to spend a few minutes, just before he went to sleep, reviewing the material he had learned that day. The trouble was, he reported, that when he lay down to sleep, he started having random fantasies and, before he knew it, he was asleep. "It's like my brain started showing me movies of the day's events. Should I get rid of these fantasies?" he asked. "Don't get rid of them," he was advised. "Take advantage of the fact that they always occur." So he put them on contingency; just before he lay down to watch the movies his brain had in store for him, he would go over the lessons he wanted to review. Then he could have his fantasies. Having the fantasies reinforced his reviewing.

Another example was a married couple who wanted to increase the frequency of their lovemaking. They used their highly regular and frequent visits to the barber and beauty shop as reinforcers for their less probable sexual activities! (Goldiamond, 1965)

A good strategy is to employ the behavior that you usually perform *instead* of the target behavior as the *reinforcer* for that target behavior. For example, a man who wanted to spend some of the time in the evening reading "cultural" materials, such as current events and "good" books, instead spent all of his time reading escapist materials, such as whodunits. This was a very frequent behavior, and it obviously interfered with reading the cultural material. So he used the whodunit reading as a Premack-type reinforcer: if he spent a certain amount of time reading "cultural" material, then he would reinforce that by allowing himself the more frequent activity—reading mystery stories.

The possibility of using this strategy is why, in listing questions to be answered when cataloging reinforcers, we ask "Are there any behaviors you perform instead of the target behavior?"

Since everyone has certain activities that they often engage in—we are all creatures of habit—the Premack principle can be used as a resource even when reinforcers seem discouragingly scarce.

Even relatively automatic behaviors can be used as reinforcers. Brushing the teeth in the morning, using a pillow to sleep on, taking a coffee break, eating lunch, taking a nap after lunch, calling a friend, going to the Union to play bridge—all of these behaviors can be used to reinforce less frequent behaviors. You can see, now, why one of the questions we suggested for cataloging reinforcers is "What behaviors do you perform every day? (Don't overlook the obvious or the commonplace.)"

Now we can return to the cases discussed before. Case #10 was the girl who had no time for reinforcers. Yet there were many things she did every day—perhaps too many. She decided that her target would be to increase one of three things she wanted to do but never had time for: going to visit a favorite aunt, practicing yoga, or attending a sensitivity group. She was a fastidious housekeeper, so she selected one of the duties that she regularly performed (cleaning the bathroom) and allowed herself to do it only *after* doing any one of the three target activities. Thus she used the Premack principle to increase the amount of time she spent doing things that she desired. Case #11, the draft-eligible student, presented a list of reinforcers that were, in reality, impossible to manipulate because they were financially unrealistic. He eventually used talking with his friends, a frequent activity, as the reinforcer for his target behavior.

Limitations of the Premack principle

There are some behaviors that you engage in frequently but that you would stop immediately if you only could. It is best not to choose such behaviors as Premack-type reinforcers, for they are usually aversive and will transfer their aversive characteristics to the target behavior by emotional conditioning. For example, a young man had unfortunately developed a strong fear of riding in automobiles and consequently walked everywhere. He asked if he should use this distasteful walking as a reinforcer. We advised against it; to do so would be punishing himself for the target behavior, which is not the point at all.

Select, for a Premack reinforcer, some behavior that is not aversive. It can be simply neutral; for example, few people find brushing their teeth actively pleasurable, but it is not often really unpleasant.

Putting a plan together

Once you have cataloged your reinforcers, you are ready to construct an intervention plan. The real art of self-modification is to achieve a simultaneous increase in both the reinforcement and the desired behavior. Whether or not you succeed will depend on the skill with which you construct your intervention plan. We turn to that topic in the next chapter.

Your own self-modification project: Step seven

You should have a written list of your answers to the sixteen questions we listed in this chapter under "Cataloging your reinforcers." Each answer will suggest possible reinforcers to use. For each possible reinforcer, ask yourself the three questions: Is it a reinforcer for me? Is it a strong reinforcer? Is it manipulatable?

Introduction to chapters eight, nine, and ten

Our discussion of techniques for self-analysis and self-observation is now complete. If you have followed the recommended procedures presented in the first seven chapters, you should now have enough data about yourself—your problem behaviors and your own reinforcers—to construct an actual intervention program for your self-modification project. To help you do this, we now turn to the actual process of changing behavior.

This topic is discussed in three chapters, each of which focuses on a particular set of problems and techniques. Chapter Eight discusses the management of contingencies—the techniques for arranging reinforcers so that they will strengthen desirable behavior. Chapter Nine treats the other end of things—ways of rearranging antecedents or cues to behavior. Chapter Ten discusses emotional reactions, both as problems in themselves and as ways of fostering thorough and desirable self-modification.

The separation of these three topics is, in a way, unfortunate. We have separated them only because it is not possible to present them simultaneously on the same printed page. The problem is that *until you have read the material in these three chapters, you will not be sure which set of techniques is appropriate for your self-modification;* the antecedent, consequent, and emotional aspects of a behavior-in-a-situation truly are not separate. By the end of these chapters, you will see that the same stimulus may have all three functions simultaneously—that is, the same event is often a cue *and* a reinforcer *and* also elicits an emotional response. When you rearrange any situation, you simultaneously adjust all three. Therefore, self-modification must attend to all three elements.

You should continue to create your intervention plan as you read these chapters. The material is organized so that a minimum of redoing is likely to be necessary. However, remember that many plans will require some consideration of all three chapters. Therefore, we suggest that you first read quickly through to the end of Chapter Ten and then review Eight, Nine, and Ten more carefully as you apply the procedures discussed to your self-modification project.

Chapter Eight
The Basic Form of
Intervention

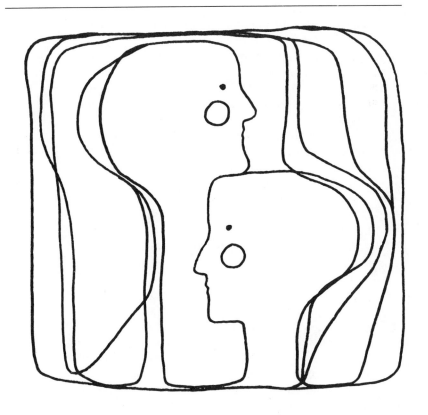

1. Self-modification begins with a contract—an agreement with yourself to gain some reinforcer only if you perform some target behavior.
2. In specifying the reinforcer, you should be sure it is potent and accessible.
   a. The sooner the reinforcer occurs after the target behavior, the more it will reinforce the target behavior.
   b. Tokens—symbolic reinforcers that can be converted to real ones—may be used to bridge a time period between performing the behavior and getting the reinforcer.
   c. There are problems to avoid in using reinforcers.
   d. Other people can be used to dispense the reinforcers.
3. The major technique for developing new behaviors is shaping—the method of successive approximations to the final goal.
   a. Two rules for shaping: you can never begin too low; the steps can never be too small.
   b. *Plateaus, cheating* by taking the reinforcer without performing the target behavior, and *lack of willpower* are presented as problems in shaping.
   c. You can observe models to learn how to begin to develop new behaviors.
4. Even when your goal is to eliminate an undesired behavior, the best technique is to find an alternative, incompatible behavior that you can increase.
5. Self-punishment is covered in detail. Rules are presented for those rare situations when self-punishment is advisable.

A very common form of self-modification is one in which consequences are arranged to support new behaviors. You will have to choose the consequences to employ, and you will arrange the relationship between your behavior and its consequences so that reinforcement follows desirable behavior. The details of exact planning can now be considered.

Contracts

In Chapter Four, on p. 53, an example was given of an informal "contract" for a self-modification program. Self-modification profits from such a "contract," even though the agreement is only with one's own self (see Chapter Fourteen on "Rule setting"). Ideally, a contract should be written and signed, and it should specify each detail of the intervention procedure. Just making each element of the plan specific is a great benefit, and having the plan in written form helps in those inevitable moments of weakness.

How does a self-contract differ from a New Year's resolution? New Year's resolutions have several flaws: they usually specify the ultimate goal—"This year I will lose ten pounds!" or "This year I am going to always be nice to my friends!"—and they usually rely on the "intrinsic" value of the goal—"How good I will look when I've lost ten pounds!" Self-contracts, on the other hand, specify how to reach the ultimate goal, and they specify the values to be gained along the way—the reinforcement at each stage.

You should write a self-contract as soon as you are ready to start the intervention plan. In it, you should specify the stages of the procedure, the kinds of reinforcers that will be gained at each step, and—most important—the *self-agreement* to make gaining those reinforcers *contingent* upon performing the target behavior. You may, of course, change the contract as you go along but, even so, initially each stage should be firmly stated. Written this way, the self-contract is an important aid to clarity.

Contracts in action

The example that follows illustrates an intervention plan that required several changes in the contract. Like all good intervention plans, this one used several principles of self-modification. Although we will discuss each of these principles in detail later in this chapter, it will be helpful to first see an overall plan in action. This case will also illustrate how contracts fit into the intervention process.

Case #14. Female, college sophomore. "I almost never talk with my professors. They scare me. Sometimes I have questions or would just like to talk with them, but I have spoken only to one, Professor A, all year, and that's only for a few sentences at a time. Target behavior: to increase talking with my professors.

"*Baseline:* it is very nearly zero. I rarely say anything to my professors."

Our analysis: She has chosen one basic tactic: to increase talking with professors instead of attacking her fear. She is using the principle of increasing a desirable, incompatible response and has a reasonably adequate baseline already.

"*Intervention plan* #1. Since I rarely talk with a professor, I should develop my behavior gradually. I worked out the following schedule:

Step 1. Say "Hello" to a professor.
Step 2. Talk with a professor for fifteen seconds.
Step 3. Talk with a professor for thirty seconds.
Step 4. Talk for one minute.
Step 5. Talk for two minutes.

I decided to use a combination Premack and food reinforcer. I eat lunch every day at school, so I set a rule that I could not eat lunch until I had performed whatever step was required by the schedule."

Our analysis: This is the original contract. It is generally satisfactory, except that she should have specified how many times she would require herself to perform each step. Her plan has several excellent features: First, she realized that she would have to develop her behavior gradually, so she began with a relatively easy requirement and used small steps. Selecting "lunch" as the reinforcer may seem a drastic step but, since her schedule is reasonable and develops slowly, she should never actually have to go without food. At the same time she gains the reinforcing effect that lunch would have on the target behavior. When her plan did fail, she analyzed the reason for the failure and went on to change the plan.

"*Results:* this plan did not work. I could work at Steps 1 and 2 okay, but at Step 3, I got into trouble because the professor wouldn't quit talking to me, and suddenly I was involved in a complex conversation and became quite nervous. So I worked out a second plan.

"*Intervention plan* #2. The reason the first plan failed was that the professor carried me too far up the schedule. Looking back, it seems inevitable that this would have happened. I might have gotten up to three minutes, or something like that, but at some point some professor would have just continued talking to me, and I'd be in trouble. I decided to enlist the aid of one particular teacher.

"I stopped Professor A in the hall and quickly explained the situation to him. I selected Professor A because I liked him, and he was practically the only one I talked to during my baseline' period. I know he is interested in students. I explained that I wanted to use him to practice on. He thought this was kind of funny, but I got my nerve up and explained why the first plan had failed. This conversation was very difficult for me, and I could see that I needed a new schedule:

Step 1. Talk with Prof. A in the hall for fifteen seconds.
Step 2. Talk with him for thirty seconds.
Step 3. Talk for one minute.
Step 4. Talk for ninety seconds.
Step 5. Increase thirty seconds at a time, up to five minutes.

I was going to do each step three times before going on to the next step. There were two parts to this plan. First, I was going to do the talking in the hall. After I got pretty far up the schedule, I was going to repeat the entire sequence in his office, because it was more scary to talk with him in his office than in the hall. After I got to Step 4 for talking in the hall, I started Step 1 for talking in the office. Even that was too hard, so I put in a new Step 1a: just sticking my head in and saying hello. Step 1b was talking for five seconds in the office; Step 1c was ten seconds; then I went into the old schedule. Professor A agreed not to force me to talk longer than I was supposed to. Same reinforcer as before."

Our analysis: Here is a new contract, written when the first plan developed difficulties. She is using another person, Professor A, to help herself perform the desired behavior. By agreeing to cooperate, he ensures that she can proceed at a slow pace, gaining the reinforcer each time. Notice how she analyzed two separate antecedents (the hall and the office) and realized that these would require separate procedures. Note also that she changed her schedule for the second antecedent condition, which required a slower start. She continues:

"*Intervention plan* #3. Plan #2 works pretty well. Professor A and I are now talking for as much as three minutes in the hall and two minutes in his office. The trouble is that there are lots of other professors. I decided that I need to be able to generalize from Prof. A to others. I decided to use Prof. A again. Here is a new schedule:

Step 1. Go up to Prof. A while he is talking with another professor and say hello to both of them.

Step 2. Go up and talk to Prof. A while he is talking with another professor and talk with the other one for at least one sentence.

Step 3. Talk with the other one for five seconds.

Step 4. Ten seconds talking with the other one.

Step 5. Fifteen seconds.

Step 6. Thirty seconds, then on up from there by fifteen-second jumps.

Professor A has agreed to cooperate. He will know where I am in the schedule and will bail me out whenever I complete my time for that particular step. Also, some professors seem unfriendly to me, while others are pretty good, so I will only go up to Prof. A when he is talking with one of the friendly ones."

Our analysis: This is a critical step, for she is building the new behavior so that she can use it in a variety of situations. Also, she realized that an unfriendly professor is a different antecedent stimulus than is a friendly one, and she decided to deal with the easier antecedent, the friendly man. Plan #3 was successful. She is now able to talk with professors who seem friendly, which she considers a significant improvement. This plan illustrates the way that contracts specify the relationships among reinforcement, new behaviors, and antecedent situations. Now we will discuss the details of these three elements.

Reinforcement during intervention

Choosing the reinforcer

Go down the list of reinforcers in your catalog, and examine each one to see if it meets two criteria: is it accessible—that is, can it be put on contingency—and will it be powerful enough to cause the change you want?

Accessibility is usually obvious: either you can get the reinforcer or you can't. A trip to Afghanistan or $100,000 might be high on your list but of little use to consider.

What about the reinforcer's *potency* or power? It is not necessarily correct to choose the very most powerful of your accessible reinforcers. Choosing an unduly large reward can have two unfortunate results. It may make the plan seem inappropriate or absurd to you and thereby weaken the likelihood of success. Second, remember that the reinforcer may not be earned. Therefore, it should be something that you can tolerate losing. For example, making three meals a day contingent on not cracking knuckles could seem to be a case of overkill, and you would not take the plan seriously. Furthermore, if the daily criterion was not m,et, and the reinforcer not earned, the loss of three meals would seriously disrupt daily life. An intervention plan is not likely to survive such punishment. Nevertheless, a reinforcer must have sufficient power.

How potent a reinforcer should you choose? There are two basic guidelines. First, your own "intuition" or estimate of that potency will be a very reliable guide. You can ordinarily tell in advance if some incentive will motivate you to do a particular thing. In fact, your own prediction is the single best guide we know, prior to actual use. The second indication of sufficient potency is the result of the frequency counts, which should be continued throughout intervention. Your own data will tell you whether or not you have chosen a sufficiently powerful reinforcer. If your behavior does *not* increase, you can select another reinforcer from your list.

Rapid reinforcement

How often should you get the reinforcer? *The ideal situation is one in which the reinforcement occurs immediately after you perform the desired behavior. The longer a reinforcement is delayed, the less effective it is.* It may still feel good when it occurs, but its reinforcing effect on the more distant behavior will not be so strong. If it has to compete with some other strong reinforcer that is occurring immediately after the target behavior, it will not be effective. In order to decrease this risk, *you should always try to reinforce quickly after performing the target behavior.* Just as you must structure your life so that you have opportunities to perform the new target behavior, you should arrange things so that you will have opportunities to be reinforced for it.

One of our students decided to increase her study time. The reinforcement for studying was to have a carbonated drink. Before intervention, she had observed that she drank about five or six sodas each day. All she had to do was make them contingent upon studying the required amount. If she studied, she got the drink; if not, no drink. She would go to her study place, put in whatever amount of time was required by her schedule, and immediately go for a drink. Thus, she was providing reinforcement very quickly after performing the desired behavior.

Many times the Premack effect can be used to supply a quick reinforcement following performance of the target behavior. A young man who took a shower every night required himself to exercise fifteen minutes before he took the shower. If there is a behavior that you engage in daily (a Premack reinforcer), you can make it immediately contingent upon the performance of the target behavior by scheduling the target just before the Premack activity usually occurs.

A married student developed the habit of swearing excessively. His baseline average was more than 150 swear words per eight hours! He had worked out a plan in which he got strong reinforcers from his wife if he reduced his daily average by 10% for one week. Unfortunately, he never made it to the end of the week. After one or two days of good language, he would revert to his old habits. We advised him to reduce the delay of reinforcement. His new contract, agreed to by his wife, called for *daily* reinforcement if he reduced his undesired language by 10%.

While the general principle is that the reinforcer should be delivered as quickly as is reasonable after the desired behavior is performed, in some cases *it is vital that the delay be extremely short.* This is especially true when the undesired behavior results in consummatory responses or in fear responses. For example, a cigarette in the mouth *right now* is more reinforcing than imagining clean lungs six months from now. A piece of pie in the mouth *right now* feels a lot better than that distant day when your weight has dropped several pounds. Biting your nails *right now* feels better, too, than the movie you will get as a reinforcer Saturday night.

The same kind of problem exists for people who are afraid of some situation, such as talking in front of an audience or going in the water to swim. It feels much better to avoid the feared situation *right now* than it does to think about how nice it will be when you get a reinforcer at the end of a week.

Whenever the target behavior has to do with very strong habits, or when it has to do with feared objects, you should try to provide yourself with positive reinforcement immediately after performing the desired behavior.

There are two basic strategies for increasing the rapidity of reinforcement. The first is to break the behavioral improvement into small units. This technique is called *shaping* and was illustrated in the case of the girl who was afraid of professors. Shaping—gradual development of a behavior—will be discussed in detail later and should be kept in mind as a strategy for providing immediate reinforcement. Second, the reinforcer itself may be broken into smaller units. This adjustment is made through the use of reinforcement *tokens.*

Tokens

If your reinforcer is something that you can carry around with you, such as candy, or if it is something that you commonly do, such as talk with a friend, you can use these easy reinforcers to supply quick effects on the target behavior.

But suppose your reinforcement is not portable or is not some easily adjusted activity? Sometimes you *cannot* deliver the reinforcement immediately after performing the desired target behavior. When, for any reason, you cannot have the reinforcer quickly after the behavior, then *token reinforcers* may be appropriate.

A token is a symbolic reinforcer because it can be converted into real reinforcement. Money, for example, is a token reinforcer, for it is the things that money can buy—the reinforcements—that make money attractive. Such devices as poker chips, gold stars, check marks, ticket punches, and dollar bills have all been used as tokens.

Many people, in modifying their own behaviors, choose a *point system* of token reinforcement, rather than using actual objects. In a *point system,* the performance of the desired behavior results in gaining a specified number of "points." These points can then be "spent" for reinforcement. The cost—so many points per reinforcer—is also specified in the contract.

The main function of tokens, whether they are objects or points, is to bridge the delay between the time when you perform the desired behavior and the time when you can partake of the reinforcer. For many people, the chosen reinforcer is something they can do at the day's end. They may use a particularly nice supper, or the opportunity to watch TV, or a talk with friends in the evening, as their reinforcer, contingent upon their having performed the target behavior earlier in the day. For all of these reinforcers, tokens can be used during the day to provide the necessary immediacy.

A man who wanted to substitute being-nice-to-friends for being-rude-to-friends selected as his reinforcer *watching TV in the evening.* He couldn't be sure when the opportunity would arise during the day to be nice to his friends, and he couldn't rush off to watch TV as soon as he had performed his target behavior, so he used a token system. He carried a 3 x 5 card in his pocket and made a check on it when he performed the target behavior. Then, later in the evening, he would allow himself to watch TV if he had earned the number of points his shaping schedule required for that day. He used his tokens cumulatively: the more points he earned during the day, the more he could watch TV at night. His "menu" looked like this:

one token ———————————————— 30 minutes' TV watching
two tokens ——————————————— 60 minutes
three tokens —————————————— 90 minutes
four tokens ——————————————— as much as I want

Using a token menu like this has an advantage in that it makes it possible to employ a great variety of reinforcers instead of just one or two. Very few activities, such as watching TV, will be equally appealing (reinforcing) every day. One night you might want to watch TV, but on another you might want to go to a movie, and on a third you might want to go to a party. A young woman used a menu like this to deal with that situation:

one point————————————— can watch TV up to one hour
two points———————————— can watch TV as much as I want to
three points——————————— can watch TV as much as I want to or
                                                          can go to a movie
four points————————————— can do any of those things, plus can
                                                          read any kind of book or story I want
five points————————————— can do any of those things, plus can go
                                                          out with friends if they ask
six points—————————————— can do all that, plus can ask friends to
                                                          go out with me

An even broader net was cast by a student whose last menu item was this: "Every Saturday morning: *anything* I want to do requires four points." This kind of system will work if it is possible to create opportunities for the desired behavior but not if you have to wait for opportunities to come to you. For example, if you earn points for studying, you can always finish the required amount of studying on Saturday morning, but if you earn points by being nice to friends, you may not have the opportunity to perform the target behavior because they may not be around to practice on.

A token system makes it easy to increase a behavior slowly. For example, over time, you can gradually require more and more performances of the target behavior to earn a token. You might start a study program, for instance, by getting one point for every fifteen minutes spent studying but, after a few days, increase the amount of time you must study in order to earn a point.

The arithmetic of reinforcement

An ideal intervention plan should *increase the total amount of reinforcement that you receive.* That is, the gross amount of reinforcement should be higher during intervention than before intervention. For example, one of our colleagues is an avid stamp collector. His goal in self-modification was to increase the amount of time he spent writing professional material. During baseline, he recorded not only his writing time but also the amount of money he spent on his stamp collection. It averaged about two dollars per week. His intervention plan called for reinforcing writing with money-for-buying-stamps. If he reached his weekly goal for writing time, he rewarded himself on Saturday with five dollars in stamp money. Thus, increasing the total amount of reinforcement gave him an additional incentive for continuing self-modification.

Avoiding problems in reinforcement

Do not overuse reinforcers. If your intervention plan is going to require that you reinforce yourself very frequently for some behavior—particularly if the reinforcement is daily—you should select several different reinforcers to use. Otherwise, you will satiate on a particular reinforcer. To say that you are satiated means that the reinforcer has lost its reinforcing quality through repeated presentation. For example, think what would happen if you used chocolate candy as a reinforcer. On the first day and the second day, eating chocolate might be enjoyable. But anyone, even with the sweetest tooth, will eventually get enough candy. A stimulus for which the person is satiated is no longer an effective reinforcer.

If you are going to need daily reinforcement (and many plans call for just that) use a variety of reinforcers. Of course, a solution to this problem is the token system, *which can easily allow for a menu of reinforcement.* For example, your reinforcement menu might look like this:

One point is worth: one chocolate candy bar or
one carbonated drink or
one beer or
one pack of chewing gum

Do not use reinforcers that punish others. A second problem to avoid is selecting a reinforcer that will punish someone else. For example, if you want to pay yourself five dollars per week as a reinforcer, and you are married, you should get your spouse to agree to the payment. Otherwise the money in your pocket might be money out of your spouse's; this situation could cause arguments that would be punishing, not reinforcing. Thus, if your reinforcer will involve any inconvenience to other people, be sure that they agree with your plan.

Use a separate reinforcer for each plan. Use independent reinforcers for each intervention plan. Suppose that you decide to start two interventions simultaneously. In one, you are going to lose weight by eating less. In the other, you are going to increase your study time. Suppose that you pick one powerful reinforcer to apply to each: if you perform the desired behavior during the week, then you can do anything you want to do on Saturday and Sunday.

Suppose that you do very well on the study plan and succeed in putting in the required number of hours. But not so on the weight-loss plan: you give in to temptation and eat too much. What should you do on Saturday—get the reinforcements or not? If you do take the reinforcement, arguing that you did, after all, perform the required study behavior, then you will also be reinforcing *not* sticking to your diet, which is clearly a mistake. On the other hand, not giving yourself the activity would be failure to reinforce studying. The answer is clear: *if there is more than one intervention plan, use different reinforcers* so that if you fail on one plan, you still get reinforcement for the successful one.

This principle applies doubly when two people have interacting intervention plans. For example, a married student was reinforcing his studying behaviors, and his wife, who was interested in the scheme, had worked out a similar plan for herself. For each, the reinforcer was supposed to be spending happy hours together during the weekend. But suppose only one had done the required hours of studying for the week? The solution is to use separate plans with separate reinforcers.

Using others to dispense the reinforcer

Sometimes the reinforcers that you select are shared with other people or affect them as much as you; nevertheless, it is *your* behavior that establishes the contingency. For example, a young woman used going to the movies with her boy friend as her reinforcer. She needed his cooperation in her intervention plan because if she failed to perform the target behavior, she was going to have to miss seeing the movie with him. But not only would she miss the movie, *so would he.* The pleasurable experiences we have with other people—being together, doing favorite things, loving—are often very powerful reinforcers and thus are ideal for an intervention plan. But if you want to use them, you must have the cooperation of the other person.

Often it is helpful to reinforce a friend for his cooperation by telling him how much you appreciate his help, or by using some other reinforcer. Many times one person will select some aspect of his or her behavior to modify because a friend or lover is somewhat concerned about it. A man might smoke, for example, and his girl friend might disapprove. Often it is possible to use the other person, who is not changing his or her behavior, as a partner in the process of change. This is particularly true if you are trying to get rid of some behavior that the other person doesn't approve of anyway, or if you are trying to increase some behavior that the other person wants you to increase. The change in your behavior becomes the reinforcer for the partner's behavior of cooperation.

Using activities with others is not only a powerful reinforcer, but it brings another force to bear in your intervention plan. The other person, who may stand to lose if you fail to perform the target behavior, will put pressure on you to do it. If your determination begins to lag your friend may say to you "You better do it! I want to see that movie!" However, before choosing this strategy, be sure that the relationship will bear up under such pressure. The negative emotional conditioning may be a greater loss than the behavioral gain is worth.

If you have complete control over a reinforcer, it may be possible for you to give this control to another person. People who dispense reinforcement to someone else are called "mediators" (Tharp and Wetzel, 1969). If your reinforcer is something tangible like money, you may give it to another person and explain what you must do in order to get it back. Or if the reinforcer is some activity you commonly engage in with the other person present, you can structure the situation so that you must have his permission to engage in the reinforcing activity, and you gain his permission by performing the target behavior.

Whenever you use another as your mediator, it is important that the person understand exactly what he is supposed to do; that is, he is supposed to reinforce contingently, and he is not supposed to punish you. If you fail to perform the target behavior, and he withholds the reinforcer, that is unpleasant enough. You don't need further punishment, such as scolding. Such punishment may cause you to discontinue intervention altogether.

Summary

Your intervention plan will call for a written *contract* that you make with yourself. In the contract, you will specify exactly what you must do in order to get the reinforcement you have selected. The contract may be changed as necessary. In selecting the reinforcers to use, try very hard to minimize the *delay of reinforcement*—the time between actual performance of the target behavior and reinforcement for the performance. The more rapid the reinforcer, the more effective it is. One good method to bridge any unavoidable time delay between performance and reinforcement is the use of a *token system* in which you gain points, or tokens, as soon as you have performed the target behaviors, and these can later be turned in for real reinforcers. In the ideal reinforcement system, by performing the target behavior you actually *increase* the positive reinforcers you have been getting.

There are problems to avoid: Overuse may lead to becoming *satiated* on the reinforcer. You should not use a reinforcer that will punish someone else. You should use a separate reinforcer for each intervention plan.

Some of the most effective reinforcers are activities you engage in with other people. If they will cooperate—and you can reinforce them for cooperating—then you can use those activities as reinforcers. Or you can give over control of certain reinforcers to others so that they give you the reinforcer if you perform the target behavior.

Developing new behaviors

As you examine your own self-adjustment, you are often not content to merely remove some problem behavior. You may want to substitute a more adjustive behavior or develop some new competence. The development of these new behaviors is the heart of behavior modification. Three principal techniques of development have been studied and will be discussed in this section. They are (1) shaping, (2) modeling, and (3) the use of incompatible behaviors.

All three are concerned with a common problem. Behavior modification depends heavily on reinforcement, which comes *after* the behavior, to strengthen that behavior. But how do you produce the behavior in the first place? Reinforcement procedures cannot help you there. All the reinforcement in the world would not enable a typical college freshman to successfully pilot a commercial airliner on his first try. Sometimes all the reinforcement in the world would not enable us to suddenly produce desired social skills.

The problem is this: you must *first* produce the behavior, so that your intervention plan can then reinforce it. In ordinary life, many of your new behaviors may seem to be produced almost by accident. You first "happen" to perform some behavior and events then "happen" to strengthen it into a habit. In the laboratories of behavior analysis, however, certain processes have been discovered that lead us to believe that the accidental factor may not be so important as we think.

These processes—shaping, incompatible responses, and modeling—have been studied by behavior modifiers and developed into specific techniques for self-help. These techniques are merely the self-conscious application of principles that occur in learning in natural settings.

Shaping: The reinforcement of successive approximations

You cannot expect yourself to produce a behavior that you do not know how to produce. A behavior that you do not now possess, that you cannot perform, must be learned. New, complex behaviors rarely emerge spontaneously. Therefore, instead of waiting for some new, desired behavior to emerge, magically full-blown, the self-modifier should begin teaching himself the new behavior from the point in his store of behaviors that is the closest approximation of his ultimate goal.

Recall the woman who wanted to increase speaking to her professors: she began by requiring herself to speak to one of them for only fifteen seconds and then gradually increased upward toward her final goal. If approximations are reinforced, they will become the basis from which each next, improved step can be taken. This process—the reinforcement of successive approximations—is known as *shaping.*

One of the most common reasons for failure in self-modification projects is the lack of shaping. Everyone has a goal for himself, and it is agreeable to think of reinforcing yourself when you have reached that goal. But if you decide to reward only perfected behavior, you greatly decrease the chances that you will ever get to your goal. You must reward, step by step, approximations that may be *much* lower than your eventual goal.

Some students resist using shaping because they believe that they "should" perform at certain levels and do not "deserve" to be reinforced for performance that is below that level. This is an unfortunate attitude because it removes the possibility of both reinforcement and learning. Shaping increases your *ability* to do what you believe you should do.

Sometimes shaping at a very low step is embarrassing. If so, then keep it a secret and reinforce yourself heavily for starting.

By the use of shaping techniques, you begin at whatever level you presently find yourself and slowly but surely move toward the ultimate goal, reinforcing as you progress.

How the shaping process works in self-modification

You can now see an additional reason for having good baseline data. The baseline tells the *current* level of performance. And that—or just beyond it—is where the shaping process should begin.

Thus, you begin by reinforcing yourself for performing at the baseline level, or a level slightly above it. Call this Level 1. When you can consistently produce Level 1, you move upward one small step, to Level 2. Now performing at Level 1 is not enough to gain the reinforcement. You must perform at Level 2 to gain the reinforcer that you were previously getting for Level 1. You persist in this fashion until you arrive at your goal.

There are two simple rules for shaping: (1) *you can never begin too low,* and (2) *the steps upward can never be too small.* Whenever you are in doubt, begin at a lower level or reduce the size of the steps. This has the effect of making it easy to perform the desired behavior. Thus, shaping makes it possible for you to feel that your movement upward is *easy*. This is important, for it increases your chances of success.

Almost any self-modification plan that calls for increasing some desired behavior should have a shaping schedule built into the plan. You may have to change it, of course, if some of the projected steps turn out to be too large.

Here is an example of the shaping schedule of a student who wanted to attain the goal of eight hours of studying per week.

Baseline: I am now actually studying about 30 or 45 minutes per week.

Level 1. I will begin by reinforcement for studying 45 minutes per week. This should be easy to do, as I have done it several times in the past.

Level 2. The second week, I will require myself to study 50 minutes in order to get the weekly reinforcer.

Level 3. The third week, my goal is to study 60 minutes. I get the reinforcer only if I have done that much.

Level 4. One hour, 15 minutes.

Level 5. One hour, 30 minutes.

Level 6. One hour, 45 minutes.

Level 7. Two hours.

Higher levels. After two hours, I hope to be able to increase by 30 minutes each week until I reach the eight-hour goal.

Notice how carefully he followed the two rules for shaping: start low and keep the steps small. This allowed him, slowly but inevitably, to move toward his goal.

Notice also that the first steps were smaller than later steps; this is often a good idea, for in the beginning very small steps will ensure that some progress is made, while later it may be possible to make progress more quickly.

In following schedules like this, you must stay flexible. *Be ready to change your schedule.* What you plan on paper may not work out in practice: you may have to reduce the size of the steps; you may have to stay at the same level for several time periods; you may have to return to an earlier level if some setback occurs.

There is a rule for solving these problems: *do not move up a step until the previous criterion is met.* The study-shaping schedule just discussed has a potential flaw. This student may be tempted to move to Level 3 just because it is week 3. He should not do so, unless Level 2 has been performed.

While it is often useful to create a tentative time schedule as an additional motivator, these arbitrary calendar plans can retard your progress. We have seen many students, for example, who can advance more rapidly than they originally estimate. And we have seen many who, in order to meet their prearranged time plan, move to higher criteria before the lower are mastered. These potential problems can be overcome simply by remembering that you advance a step when the previous step is secure—then and only then.

The continuum along which you shape

We have been speaking of situations in which you shape your behavior by increasing the *amount of time* that you perform some desired behavior. Actually, shaping can be used in any situation in which you can gradually increase the criterion for the behavior required.

The young woman whose goal was to have more dates had followed chain-of-events reasoning and decided that the chain she needed to follow was: (1) go where men are; (2) smile at them; (3) talk with them; and so on. Actually, Step 3 could be broken down into talking with them about "safe" subjects like school or the weather, and then progressing to more adventurous conversational topics. After achieving the first steps in the chain, she decided to shape her behavior according to the degree of controversy she would bring into her conversation. She chose this dimension because she was made very uncomfortable by conversational disagreements.

Her baseline showed that she did very little talking with men on any subject at all. She reasoned that it would be a mistake to move immediately into conversations on controversial issues. Therefore, for the first step she chose to increase only talking about school. After she could comfortably perform at Level 1, she would raise her sights and try a foray into more exciting, but (for her) dangerous, topics, such as whether a movie was funny or not. That was Level 2. Level 3 was at an even higher level of controversy—university politics. Level 4 was interpersonal relations and sex, and Level 5 was the most difficult of all for her—national politics, student protest, the military, and other like topics.

Shaping in this fashion has two advantages. First, as with all shaping procedures, you can perform at a level that allows you to gain the reinforcement. Second, *it encourages analysis of the component parts of a situation*—to see, for example, that there are levels of difficulty in handling a conversation or that several different behaviors are part of studying. You can work on one part at a time instead of trying to deal with all levels of difficulty at once.

Problems in shaping

You should expect that the course of learning will not be smooth all the time; this seems to be everyone's experience. The important thing is to keep trying—to stay within a shaping program—even if it is the thirty-ninth revision of the original schedule.

Plateaus

A common experience in following shaping schedules is the *plateau.* Week after week, for example, you may make excellent progress and then suddenly stop. Moving up all those previous steps may have seemed so easy, but now a new step, which is the same size as all the rest, seems very difficult. *The easiest way to continue upward when you reach a plateau is to reduce the size of the steps.* If that is not possible, continue the plan for a week or so. The plateau experience is so common that it should be expected and "ridden out." You may try increasing the reinforcement. If movement still does not occur, it may be that you are at a comfortable upper limit and should think about terminating.

Cheating

It may surprise some readers to see *cheating* considered as a problem of shaping. After all, why should you cheat yourself? Nevertheless, many students have reported that cheating by delivering the reinforcer without meeting the criterion is a serious difficulty. One solution to this problem is to use someone else to deliver the reinforcer. An even easier solution is to require less of yourself by attempting to reach the final goal even more slowly.

A young man whose final goal was to save seven dollars each week began by requiring himself to save fifty cents each day (he put it in a bank), even though he had almost never saved any money before. He used the reinforcer of eating supper only after he had put the money in his piggy bank. After three days, he skipped his saving for one day but went ahead and ate supper anyway. This began a two-week period during which he more often skipped than saved, but ate his supper anyway. He realized that this cheating was a problem in shaping. So he wrote a new contract in which he required himself to save only twenty-five cents each day—a more realistic place to begin, in his case—in order to gain the reinforcer.

Cheating by taking the reinforcer even though you have not performed the target behavior is fairly common in self-modification. Almost everyone does it sometimes. You should watch yourself very carefully, however, for if you are cheating more than occasionally—say, more than 10% of the time—it indicates a shaping problem. You should redesign your shaping schedule so that you will be reinforced for performing at some level that you find possible. As long as you are able to provide a contingent reinforcement, you are building toward the final goal, no matter how small the steps are or how low you begin. If you cheat, don't abandon the project—redesign it.

Losing willpower

Chapter Fourteen presents a theoretical analysis of willpower. In practical terms, "willpower" may be seen as a shaping issue. Ordinarily, we think of willpower as an entirely internal thing. The reader now knows enough about the principles of behavior-environment relationships to know this: there are many reasons why you do not perform a given behavior. In our experience, the loss of willpower in the middle of intervention is most often due to a failure of adequate shaping.

For example, a student will say "To hell with it. I can't do it. I want to get in that library and stay there thirty minutes, but I just can't make myself do it. I haven't got enough willpower. And besides that, this whole idea of self-modification is ridiculous, because the whole problem is really whether or not you yourself have got the willpower to really improve yourself. I quit."

In our terms, this may be merely a problem of shaping steps. Thirty minutes in the library may be much too severe an increase over current performance, and this student should have set his first approximation at only five minutes. For some students with a near-zero baseline, we have suggested, as a first approximation, merely walking to the library and up the steps, then returning home to consume the reinforcer. Most self-modifiers are simply too embarrassed to reward themselves for such elementary steps. They then increase the step to a "respectable" level, which is often outside their performance capacity, and finally quit altogether in a huff of "willpower" failure.

This failure of willpower may be experienced in two ways. First, you simply may not get started on a self-modification project. You would like the final goal but somehow cannot get around to starting toward that goal. This is a shaping problem—you simply need to start with a very low step. Second, you may have started, but find that you are not making progress. This is also a shaping problem—you need to use much smaller steps.

The whole point of shaping is to make starting and continuing easy by requiring yourself to do so little more than you can presently do that it is easy to perform the target behavior. Then, after practicing a bit, it becomes easy to move up one more short step.

Summary of shaping

Most self-modification plans, particularly those that call for developing some desired behavior, will require shaping. Shaping means that instead of requiring yourself to perform the complete new behavior before gaining the reinforcement, you require yourself to perform only a part of it and gain the reinforcement for that. Then, in a series of successive approximations to the final goal, you gradually increase what is required in order to gain the reinforcer. The two main rules for shaping are: (1) you can never begin too low, and (2) the steps can never be too small. You can shape your behavior along any desired continuum.

Common problems in shaping are: plateaus, in which you level off, finding it hard to progress; cheating, in which you take the reinforcer even though you did not perform the required step in behavior; and lack of willpower, in which you are either requiring yourself to start too high or using steps that are too large.

Modeling

In virtually every development of new behaviors, the shaping of small steps is advisable. However, you are still faced with the problem of choosing the initial step—choosing the behavior that you *can* indeed perform. By referring to the baseline, as discussed earlier, you can determine your capability for some tasks. For some other problems, however, you may not know how to begin. You may not know exactly which acts do come first in a chain-of-events *sequence.* In this case, you may want to use someone else as a model to get an idea of a starting point. We have discussed this tactic earlier, in Chapter Five, in the discussion of the young woman who observed, as a model, another girl who was effective in getting acquainted with new people. The first behavior of the model was merely to smile responsively. This student then used "smiling responsively" as the first step in her shaping plan. Observing models, then, is especially appropriate when you are uncertain about the exact behaviors you should choose to develop.

Incompatible behaviors

Even when your problem seems to be ridding yourself of an old, undesired habit, you are actually concerned with the choice of new behavior. In these cases, the use of punishment might occur to you. But this might be an incorrect procedure. Even if you feel that your problem is that you too often engage in some undesired behavior, *it is usually true that the best way to eliminate that undesired behavior is to find some alternative, incompatible, desired behavior that you can seek to increase via positive reinforcement and, in this way, automatically decrease the undesired behavior.*

A young woman who was bothered by too-frequent arguments with her father began to observe her own behavior. She discovered a chain of events that usually went like this: her father would make some comment about some aspect of her behavior that seemed to bother him (for example, he thought she came in too late from her dates) and she would usually respond with a frown and comment that he should mind his own business. This would enrage him, and they would be off to another bitter argument. She knew that her father basically loved her and that he was simply having a difficult time adjusting to her new maturity, and its prerogatives. She reasoned that if she substituted kind remarks and a smile when he opened up some topic about her behavior, they would then be able to discuss it in a more friendly fashion. Instead of setting out to *decrease* frowning and unkind comments to her father, she set out to *increase* smiling and kind comments to him.

Thereafter, when he made some remark about her behavior, she would smile at him and strive to pleasantly disagree with his comment. (Of course, she reinforced her new behavior.) Increasing the desirable behavior had, in fact, the effect of calming her father, and they progressed through a series of amicable conversations to a new understanding.*

This approach of increasing some incompatible behavior is better than attacking an undesired behavior by trying to extinguish or punish it. (The problems associated with self-punishment will be discussed later.)

Consider the girl who always gets nervous when she has to talk with young men. She feels shy and tends to withdraw from conversations. She could set out to decrease "withdrawing from conversations"

---

*Notice, incidentally, that this is a case in which one goal is ultimately to change not one's own behavior but the behavior of another person. The young woman reasoned that (1) she wanted her father to stop treating her as if she were still a child, and (2) she wanted to stop arguing with him. But she took the important step of realizing that the way to effect these changes was to change her own behavior first.

—considering this to be an undesirable behavior—and she might conclude that she will have to punish herself for withdrawing. Doing so
would be a serious mistake. Even if it were possible to punish herself
for withdrawing, this would have an unfortunate effect on her emotional problem: she still would feel nervous, shy, tongue-tied when men
were around, and she would not have learned any of the new social
skills required to reach her goal. This would increase the likelihood that
she would be punished by rejection and disappointment in her interactions with men. This punishment, coupled with her own self-inflicted
punishment, would increase her problem by strengthening the negative
emotional conditioning to such situations.

The use of incompatible responses here would involve *rewarding*
herself for staying and talking. The staying and talking itself should be
shaped, of course, in small steps that could provide success experiences.
Thus, as this example shows, changing the way you define your problems can help you find a way to use positive reinforcements rather than
punishment.

Selecting an incompatible behavior

What exactly is an *"incompatible response"? It is a behavior that prevents*
the occurrence of some other behavior. Smiling is incompatible with frowning, simply because you have only one face and it can do only one thing
at a time. Sitting is incompatible with running. Going swimming is
incompatible with staying in your room. Being courteous is incompatible with being rude. It is easy to see that for many undesired behaviors
there may be several incompatible ones available. Then you have the
opportunity to choose the new acts that you would most like to develop.

A male student was active in campus politics and had been elected
to the Council of the Associated Students. In the meetings, he found
that he was talking too much and losing his effectiveness because he
was irritating the other members. He said he felt the impulse to talk
with "the force of a compulsion." He first tried simply not talking so
much. He did have some success, but after considering the use of incompatible responses, he reasoned that he could do better by choosing a
more active, positive, alternative behavior. He then began reinforcing
"listening." This was a genuine new act, not merely the suppression of
an old one. It resulted in greater silence, which he wanted, and also
greater listening, which he came to value more and more.

Sometimes, there is no positively desired incompatible response.
Then it may be useful to choose an incompatible behavior, even though
it is of no particular value in itself. A man who was bothered by knuckle

cracking decided that whenever he felt like cracking his knuckles, he would *instead* make a fist. His target behavior was *making a fist instead of cracking his knuckles.* Each time he performed this, he would gain a reinforcer. A man who habitually bit his nails first set out to reinforce the behavior of touching his finger to his mouth but not biting his nails. The young woman who sometimes scratched her skin until it bled substituted patting instead of scratching and reinforced herself for that.

In such a case, will the person simply develop the new behavior into a "nervous" habit? Usually not, because the undesirable "nervous" habit is something that has been practiced for years and was probably learned under unusual conditions (perhaps aversive). You will need to practice the new, alternative behavior only long enough to get rid of the problem.

Some smokers have tried the technique of substituting some behavior for smoking. Instead of lighting a cigarette, they might take a piece of chewing gum. This technique is rarely effective if they rely solely on the reinforcing quality of the gum, because, compared to a cigarette, the gum's value is rather weak for the person who is addicted to tobacco. It would be better to employ the alternative, certainly, but to also heavily and quickly reinforce the performance of chewing gum instead of smoking.

Do not make the mistake of relying solely on the mere performance of the incompatible response. *It must be reinforced,* or it will not be continued. If it does not continue, the old undesired behavior may be expected to return.

To summarize this section: *whenever possible, even when you want to eliminate an undesired behavior, try to select an opposite, incompatible behavior that you can increase via positive reinforcement at the expense of the undesirable behavior.*

To select the incompatible behavior, ask yourself these questions:

1. Is there some directly opposite behavior that I would actually like to increase, while decreasing the undesired behavior?
2. What behaviors would make it impossible to perform the undesired behavior?
3. Is there any basically meaningless act that I could nevertheless substitute for the undesired behavior? Would it fit into the formula: I will do *(the substitute behavior)* instead of *(the undesired behavior)?*

Counting the frequency of the incompatible behavior

If you are able to select an incompatible, desired behavior to increase at the expense of your undesired target behavior, you should

have a baseline count of how often you perform the incompatible behavior, as well as a count of how often you perform the undesired target
behavior. If your plan calls for simply substituting some act—such as
slapping your hand instead of cracking your knuckles—then it is likely
that your baseline for that behavior will be zero. But if your behavior
has been performed in the past—sometimes, for example, the woman
who quarreled with her father did smile at him—then the baseline will
be somewhere above zero. If you begin to increase an incompatible
behavior without any idea of how often it has been occurring in the
past, you are essentially working without a baseline and can make
errors. For this reason, *it is a good idea to select incompatible behaviors as soon
as possible and begin to get a baseline count on them* while continuing a
baseline count on the undesired target behavior.

The issue of self-punishment

So far we have concentrated almost entirely on positive reinforcement. It may have occurred to you that it would be possible to use
punishment in a self-modification project. The theoretical explanation of
punishment was given in Chapter Three. If the following discussion is
not clear, you may refresh your memory by reading the appropriate
parts of that chapter.

Why punishment alone is insufficient

Many intervention plans that rely solely on punishment do not work.
There are several reasons why this is so. The first reason is that the
undesired behavior may be *resistant to mild punishment.* Suppose you
have chosen some undesired behavior to eliminate. You may feel guilty,
depressed, sad, embarrassed, or nervous because you do it. In short, you
are already somewhat punished for it. *Yet you continue.* The implication
is clear: the performance of the behavior is already somewhat resistant
to punishment. To use punishment as an intervention technique would
require heaping on a large amount of additional punishment, and you
are unlikely to do that.

In fact, you could make things worse; one way behaviors become
resistant to punishment is by first being mildly punished and then
positively reinforced. If you are somehow being reinforced for the behavior but are unaware of the reinforcer, you might actually increase the
behavior's resistance to punishment by supplying a small punishment
followed by an (unnoticed) positive reinforcement.

The second reason for avoiding punishment is that punishment
alone does not teach new behaviors. Punishment merely suppresses the
behavior it follows, but what happens *instead* is determined by the

reinforcement that follows the various things you might attempt. Your self-modification plan should provide a plan for designating and reinforcing desired alternatives to your problem behaviors. Otherwise, the plan is incomplete.

The third reason for avoiding punishment is that punishment is likely to produce negative emotional reactions, such as feelings of dislike, anxiety, anger, or depression. These emotions will become associated with the stimuli present when they are elicited. Thus, punishment will increase the number of situations that elicit negative emotions in you—an undesirable side effect. If you use positive reinforcements, on the other hand, they will likely have the effect of adding positive emotional feelings to a larger segment of your environment.

You can see, then, that punishment alone is an undesirable strategy to follow. This is true for either kind of punishment: adding an aversive stimulus to a situation or removing a positive reinforcer. An example of a situation in which punishment would be most undesirable follows:

One of our students had three jobs plus a full load at college. Her first suggestion was that she punish herself for *not* performing a desired behavior by depriving herself of one of the few things in her life that she enjoyed. She had somehow managed to preserve two free hours every Friday afternoon, which she always used to go to the beach with a close friend. Her plan proposed to punish excessive eating by giving up this weekly pleasure. We strongly disagreed with this idea. Her life needed enrichment, not a further impoverishment of positive reinforcers. It was suggested that she reward dieting by adding another social activity (even, if necessary, at the expense of her quite adequate study time). To have lost her one weekly contact with a friend would have made her even more dependent on her only other real pleasure—food. Besides, her general happiness required a broader base of pleasant events. Punishment would have restricted her life and would have made dieting less likely as well.

Should you ever use self-punishment?

In some situations self-punishment seems the only answer. We are reluctant to discuss these, not because we feel that self-punishment is intrinsically wrong, but because self-punishment can so easily lead to failure. Most people do not enjoy punishing themselves and are likely to abandon any plan that calls for self-punishment. People who choose self-punishment report less often that their intervention plan had beneficial effects than those who used a positive reinforcement technique (Mahoe, 1970).

Even in situations in which punishment *seems* to be the only alternative, other strategies of positive reinforcement should be explored, especially *shaping* and *the reinforcement of incompatible responses.* When you are performing some undesired behavior, it may be possible to reinforce positively an incompatible behavior instead of punishing the undesired behavior itself. It may be possible to use stronger or more immediate reinforcements as incentives. *Before you definitely decide to use punishment, always search for an incompatible behavior that you can positively reinforce instead. Search for stronger or more immediate reinforcements, and consider shaping in smaller steps.*

Nevertheless, there are a few situations in which punishment may be necessary. If you are presently getting all the positive reinforcers that you can conveniently gain from your environment, you may have to deny yourself some of them in order to control your behavior. For example, a young woman whose life seemed very much in balance and very much under her control said there was nothing she wanted that she didn't get, so there was nothing she could use to reward herself. Therefore, she chose to punish herself by not taking baths when she failed to perform her target behavior.

It may be that engaging in the undesired target behavior is so reinforcing that there are no positive reinforcers you can bring to bear that will be as strong as performing the target behavior. Take smoking, for example. Once you are a steady smoker, almost nothing would feel as good as a cigarette after twenty-four hours without one. You may feel that it is necessary to build in some punishments to induce yourself to stay away from lighting a cigarette. In cases like this, a technique such as that used by Nurnberger and Zimmerman (1970) might work.

In their research project on smoking, these researchers had each participant make out a bank check to his most hated organization. For someone whose political leanings were to the right, this might be a Communist organization. For someone who was a firm atheist, it might be some organized church. Anyone can make a list of organizations he really disapproves of, perhaps hates. The agreement was that if the person performed his undesirable behavior, the check would be mailed.

Hall and associates (1971) used similar procedures, which involved tearing up dollar bills or contributing twenty-five cents to a charity for each cigarette smoked.

Rules to follow in self-punishment

I. *The only kind of punishment to use is one in which you deny yourself some positive reinforcer that you usually receive.*

If you must punish, use denial of a positive reinforcer rather than addition of something negative. A woman might not allow herself to take a bath because she has not studied enough. A young man might not allow himself to eat foods he likes because he has performed some undesired behavior. In self-modification, the sort of punishment in which you would actually apply some aversive stimulus to yourself should be avoided. Don't whip yourself; don't pinch yourself. If you are accustomed to going to a movie on Saturday night, you could require yourself to perform some target behavior before gaining the right to go. One of our students followed the plan of dividing the foods he usually ate into really nice ones versus so-so ones. If he did not perform his target behavior, he did not allow himself to eat the nice ones. Many people will use the general category of "things I do for fun," requiring themselves to perform some target behavior before they allow them-selves to engage in the "fun" activities. Another student, who was in love with a man in another state, used the daily letters she received from him as a reinforcer. Each day she handed the unopened letter to a friend. If she performed her target behavior, then she got the letter back, unopened. If she did not perform the target behavior, her friend was instructed to open and read the love letter.

Any positive reinforcer that you are accustomed to receiving can be used as a potential punisher by denying yourself access to the reinforcer until you have performed the target behavior. The crucial point is that *you must actually deny yourself if you do not perform the target behavior.*

In Chapter Seven, on page 108, we list two questions, numbers 15 and 16, that are applicable to this strategy. If you decide to use punish-ment as a technique, your answers to these questions will provide you with a list of positive reinforcers that may be withdrawn. However, *if you are planning to use self-punishment, be sure to use very small shaping steps so that it will be unlikely that you will have to punish yourself.*

It may still be possible to avoid using punishment. *Whenever you think of using this kind of punishment—denying yourself some positive rein-forcer that you usually receive—ask yourself if it is possible to increase the positive reinforcers instead of decreasing them.*

A housewife came to us with an intervention plan that called for the denial of certain pleasurable activities if she did not perform her target behavior. "Why don't you increase the amount of time you spend doing the nice things," she was asked, "instead of cutting down on them?"

"Well, I can't," she said. "You know how it is being a housewife. There are a lot of things I have to do every weekend—duties."

"What would happen if you didn't do some of those duties? Sup-pose the kitchen floor was not quite as clean, because you only washed it every other week. Suppose the kids wore their slightly dirty clothes a day longer, which would cut down on the washing. What duties do you perform that are really not absolutely essential to the health and happiness of your family?"

Like most housewives, this woman was actually doing many things that no one really cared about. It was suggested to her that she could avoid the use of punishment altogether. Instead of denying herself some positive reinforcers, she could reward her good behavior by getting to avoid doing some of her duties.

II. *Use self-punishment only if it will lead to more positive reinforcers.*

Often the positive reinforcer will be that you feel better because you have carried out some intervention plan. Maybe you have stopped smoking or biting your nails, or perhaps you have increased how often you perform some desired behavior. In those cases the positive reinforcer will be your good feeling. At other times the positive reinforcer will be some pleasurable response from your environment: someone is happy because you have stopped the undesirable behavior, or new positive reinforcers are available because you have some new competence.

If there is some reason to expect that these new reinforcers will develop quickly, then a short term of self-punishment may be acceptable. The punishment can tide you over until the new positive reinforcement takes effect. But if these new reinforcers cannot be expected to develop "naturally," then you had best program some positive reinforcement along with the punishment.

III. *If you must use punishment, try to devise an intervention plan that combines punishment and positive reinforcement.*

Suppose you decide to punish some undesired behavior by taking away money. You should arrange the intervention plan so that if you do *not* perform the undesired behavior, you get *extra* money. If you are bad, you lose, but if you are good, you gain. This double strategy is the best choice when punishment is employed.

Earlier we mentioned the necessity for immediate reinforcement for refraining from smoking, overeating, and undesired sexual behaviors. Some of our students have found that the only kind of consequence strong enough to counteract the reinforcing effect of the undesired behavior is some form of punishment. A commonly used punishment has been loss of money. A student might sign a contract to the effect that if he smokes any cigarettes, he will have to give away some money. One older student, who worked with a man he hated, signed a contract that if he smoked a cigarette, he would have to give his enemy ten dollars. That was such a horrible thought that he gained a rapid suppression of smoking. A young man who desperately wanted to stop cracking his knuckles signed a contract that he could not engage in any sexual behavior with his fiancée on the day he cracked his knuckles.

A token system can easily be used for a combination program of positive reinforcement and punishment. Suppose that each time you perform some undesired behavior, you lose one point. The gains and losses do not have to be balanced, of course. One man we know gained one point for each hour he did not smoke but lost ten points for each cigarette used.

Summary

Self-punishment is not often a desirable form of intervention. Although punishment has the effect of suppressing the behavior that preceded it, it does not necessarily teach any new behaviors. Punishment also produces unpleasant emotional effects, which may become conditioned to various stimuli present at the time of punishment.

Many intervention plans that rely *solely* on self-punishment do not succeed. There are some situations in which self-punishment may be necessary: if there are no positive reinforcers you can gain or if the undesired behavior is so strongly reinforcing that it requires a direct, counterstrength reinforcement for not performing it. Consummatory behaviors are typical examples of this situation.

If you do decide to use punishment, you should follow these rules:
  I. Remove something positive instead of adding something negative. (Always try to figure out a way to increase some behavior by *adding* something positive.) Use small shaping steps.
 II. Use punishment only if it will lead to more positive reinforcement.
III. Devise a plan that combines punishment with positive reinforcement.

Your own self-modification project: Step eight

You should now draw up a *contract*—a written agreement with yourself that states what the target behavior is and what reinforcement you will gain for performing it. Your reinforcer should quickly follow the target behavior. If it does not, then you should use a *token system* to bridge the gap. You should be careful that you will not become satiated on the reinforcer, that it will not punish someone else, and that you are using a separate reinforcer for each plan. Ideally, your plan should allow you to increase the total amount of positive reinforcement you usually get. If you cannot easily reinforce yourself, you can use someone else to do it if you gain his cooperation.

Your contract should specify a shaping schedule. Be flexible, and change it as necessary. Be prepared for problems in shaping, such as plateaus, cheating, and losing willpower.

If you are considering using *self-punishment,* you should be sure that your case meets the rules: (1) that it uses the form of punishment in which you lose a positive reinforcer that you normally get; (2) that you will ultimately gain more positive reinforcement; (3) that it combines punishment with positive reinforcement. Before finally deciding to use punishment, try to define your problem as increasing an incompatible, desired behavior that you can do *via* positive reinforcement.

Draw up this contract in written form, *but do not actually implement it until you read Chapters Nine and Ten.* You may expect to modify your contract somewhat after this additional reading.

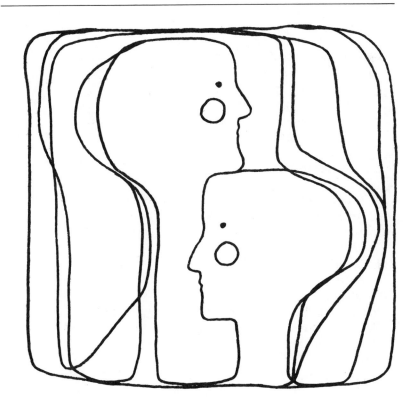

1. Some self-modification plans involve rearranging the *antecedents* to behavior.
   a. Discovering antecedents through self-observation.
   b. Aversive stimuli as antecedents.
   c. Discovering the antecedents after starting a self-modification project.
2. Techniques for controlling antecedents.
   a. Avoiding antecedents.
   b. The two-stage process: first, avoiding antecedents; second, learning desirable alternative behaviors.
   c. A two-stage process for consummatory behaviors.
   d. A two-stage process for interpersonal behaviors.
   e. Analyzing the chain of behaviors between impulses and undesired behaviors and building pauses into the chain.
   f. Breaking up, scrambling, or changing the chain of behaviors that leads to some final undesired behavior.
3. Increasing the control an antecedent has over a desired behavior.
4. Building stimulus generalization.

Behavior is embedded in a sequence: antecedent—behavior—consequence. We have been emphasizing the behavior and its consequences, but it is time now to turn our attention to the *antecedents.* Sometimes the most effective intervention plan is one in which you control the antecedents to your target behavior.

Case #15. A young married woman reported at first that her problem was to eliminate "giving excuses, rationalizations" to her husband when he questioned her behavior. He would notice something she was doing, or not doing, and ask her why. Sometimes her answer would be evasive or just an excuse. She began a self-modification plan designed to eliminate this behavior, replacing it with answers she considered more honest. But the plan did not go well, and she asked for advice. "Why do you think you make excuses to him?" she was asked. "Because sometimes I can tell, by the way he asks the question, that if I told him the truth, he would give me hell." It was clear why her plan of replacing excuses with the truth was not working: she was being punished for telling the truth!

We suggested that her husband, by his behavior—his tone of voice, his facial expression—was supplying the antecedent for making excuses. She agreed. She then worked out a new intervention plan that was designed to get her husband to do two things: (1) not punish her for telling the truth and (2) not supply the antecedent that produced her undesired excuses. She explained the situation to him and offered the following bargain: each time he wanted to question her, if he would refrain from frowning and using a certain tone of voice and would then refrain from punishing her if she did tell the truth, that evening she would cook one of his favorite meals. This bargain represented a new intervention plan in which she attempted to modify her husband's behavior in an effort to modify her own.

The control of antecedents does not really represent a different strategy from the ones discussed earlier. It only involves intervention earlier in the chain of events. One interesting point brought up in this chapter is that the behavior of other people is sometimes involved in your chain of events, and you can often alter their behavior by carefully controlling your own.

Discovering antecedents

Many forms of psychotherapy are designed to help people discover the antecedents to their behavior. This is perhaps one major strength of these approaches. Many people attempt to discover very obscure antecedents. In a psychoanalytic procedure, for example, you might attempt to discover the antecedents of behavior about which you were not consciously aware. This kind of self-understanding can often be helpful in producing self-change. In Chapter Thirteen we will recommend some kinds of professional help for instances when you are unable to discover important antecedents for yourself. More often, however, the key antecedents are not so mysterious and can be identified by your own careful observation.

By this time in your study, you should be somewhat skilled in the techniques and attitudes of self-observation. These skills are useful in locating antecedents to your behaviors. There are four kinds of antecedents for which you will be searching: physical circumstances, social settings, the behavior of other people, and your own thoughts.

If your target behavior is something undesired, you will have begun to count its occurrences in the baseline period. Once you are making these kinds of observations, you can also begin to search for the antecedents of the target behavior. The point of this search is to find out *when* you perform the target behavior—that is, the antecedent conditions.

One technique is to start at the performance of the target behavior, and think through the antecedents backward in time. You might say to yourself "I performed the behavior. Just before that I was in situation _____ or I felt the emotion of _____ or I thought _____ _____. Just before *that*, I was in situation _____ or emotional state _____, and so on."

You should be looking for and writing down events that occurred in a relatively short period of time, perhaps a few minutes. *Ask yourself:* (1) *What were the physical circumstances of the last few minutes?* (2) *What was the social setting?* (3) *What behavior of other people occurred?* (4) *What did I think or say to myself?* For each target behavior, fill out a list of the antecedents, under these four categories. After you have made the lists for a week or more, carefully examine them, searching for events that could be grouped together to form a category of antecedents.

For example, to discover the physical antecedents, you would describe to yourself the physical situation that immediately preceded the target behavior: the room, the time of day, the weather. This is often the easiest antecedent to discover. Be sure that you don't overlook the obvious: you might realize that you never study when the TV is on in the room, or you might find that most unpleasant social interactions occur in the first two hours of the morning, when you are still "waking up."

Social settings that serve as antecedents can also be discovered. A young man whose problem was an inability to act in an attractive manner with women discovered that this problem only occurred when he was in a large group or a party. When he was alone with the other person or in some small social setting, he felt that he was able to act in a personable manner.

The case of the married woman whose husband supplied the antecedents for making excuses is an example of the behavior of others serving as the stimulus for the target behavior. One of our students reported that every time he talked with a particular person (with whom he came in frequent contact), he felt "put down," and this produced undesirable "defensive" behavior. The other person's "put downs" were the antecedents. He first noticed this by examining his thoughts when he had to deal with that person. He reported that during each interaction, he would have thoughts such as "That arrogant so-and-so" or "He's so superior!" or "I better be careful; I'm not looking good in this exchange." Once his record of his thoughts alerted him to a possible antecedent, he was able to see in the other person's behavior those events that stimulated the put-down feeling and were the antecedent for his "defensive" behavior.

Many students report that they become nervous when they have to take tests. Some people become nervous in any kind of social situation in which they are likely to be evaluated by others, such as a blind date, a first date, a job interview, a talk with someone of higher status or prestige.

Direct observation

For all of these situations, the antecedent is discovered by observing the events that occur *before* you begin performing the target behavior. You might keep a chart like the one in the following case.

Case #16. Target behavior: "telling other people what I think of them, which is often unflattering."

Occurrence of target	Antecedents
Tues. A.M. told John he was "being dumb." It hurt his feelings.	He said he was pretty happy with the way the school elections had come out.
Wed. eve. told Ellen she was "full of bullshit."	She said that she thought the people who were making the most difference in the world were the scientists.
Fri. A.M. told Prof. X he was an "authoritarian old man."	He told me I should do the assignments.
Sat. night told my date she was "hopelessly middle class and dumb."	She said she was looking forward to getting married and having a family.
Sat. night told John he was "silly."	Don't know.

After two weeks of making observations of this kind, this young man was able to establish a category of the antecedents that seemed to produce his undesired behavior: "When people disagree with my personal philosophy, I tend to tell them off." This does not imply that his philosophy was either good or bad. It does imply that disagreement with it seemed to stimulate the response of "telling people what I think of them." He felt that this response was undesirable because it often angered the other people, and they were no longer interested in listening to his personal philosophy.

Whenever possible, write down the antecedents as soon as you observe that the target behavior has occurred. If this is not possible, write them down as soon as you can get a moment. The longer you wait, the more likely you are to forget them and thus be unable to establish accurate categories.

Sometimes stopping long enough to write down the antecedents is mildly aversive. It seems easier to forget about it or to wait until a quiet moment to write them down. In such circumstances, *your first self-modification plan might very well involve reinforcing yourself for just noting the antecedents to your behavior.*

It can be helpful to use other people in searching for the antecedents to your target behavior. The same rules that were discussed on p. 125 about using others' help apply here: do not allow yourself to be punished for seeking their aid, and reinforce their cooperation, if necessary. Many couples use this technique in ironing out their difficulties. After a series of arguments, they will sit down and discuss "just what is wrong." The woman may offer suggestions about behaviors the man engages in that evoke her undesired reaction, and he may counter with ideas about things she does that serve as an antecedent to his undesired behavior. Even if your target problem is not an interpersonal problem, it may be possible to seek the advice of another who has the opportunity to observe your behavior and its possible antecedents.

When you are searching for antecedents, you may engage in some armchair speculation—some introspection—as a way of getting ideas about possible antecedents. That is fine, but do not limit yourself to speculations. The armchair might be the place where you first form your self-hypotheses, but your real-life observations should be the place where you check them out. Your process may be a series of introspections and observations in which you first have an idea, then begin observing yourself to see if it holds up, and then find that it does not; you then revise your idea and make a new set of observations.

Discovering aversive antecedents

Many times the stimulus to some undesired behavior is aversive. Because of a past history of punishment, which you may no longer remember, some antecedents have come to have aversive stimulus control over your behavior. How can you tell when you are in such a situation?

There are certain signs indicating that some antecedent is producing an aversive reaction that you may be able to notice. First, you may feel nervous, anxious, tense. There may be physical signs, such as a queasy stomach, sweaty palms, a headache, muscular tension. You may feel "insecure." You may observe that your usually well-performed behaviors become less smooth or impaired; for example, you might stutter a bit, not think clearly, be awkward in behaviors you usually perform well. You may want to get away, to avoid the situation, and realize that if you stayed in it, you would be unhappy. You may find yourself thinking about some aspect of the situation over and over again, worrying about it but not solving the problem. Little things may be overly upsetting.

Situations are not simply either positive or negative. You may find that a certain situation has both aspects: you enjoy parts of it, but it also seems to produce some of the signs of aversiveness listed above. People are complicated, and some antecedents may stimulate both desirable and undesirable reactions.

If you find yourself showing any of these signs, it is worthwhile to search for their antecedents. Keep a chart, and record those things that occur *before* the noted indicators of an aversive condition. Some of our students have been successful in discovering the antecedents to their aversive reactions, but others have not. You may *not* be able to discover the antecedents if there is an intermittent reinforcement schedule or if you perform the avoidance behavior so well that you never come into contact with the aversive stimulus. In such cases, there are two strategies to employ.

The first has already been mentioned—seeking professional assistance. In conversations with professional counselors or therapists, you can often be assisted in identifying the chains of events. In therapy or sensitivity groups, *examples* of your behavior often occur that other group members can help identify.

Tinkering

Before resorting to these steps, however, you may choose a *second strategy—beginning an intervention plan along the usual lines of simple self-reinforcement for desired changes.* If consideration of the antecedents is indeed important, that fact will quickly become obvious by the difficulties you encounter. Most important, these difficulties will often *reveal* the obscure antecedent. If you begin a simple plan, you may soon discover which particular event is interfering with the plan.

The first example in this chapter illustrates this process. Case #15 was unaware of her husband's aversive cues *until she attempted to change.* It quickly became obvious that his behavior was in fact interfering with her change, through the cues he was providing. Before she started the simple project, she had not realized how important his behavioral cues were in affecting *her* behavior.

Thus, if you have begun a plan that is not working, and if you have fulfilled all the basic requirements of a good plan, ask yourself "What is interfering with my plan? What makes it difficult (or impossible) for me to perform the target behavior?" The *what* can be some antecedent: some part of the physical or social environment, the behavior of others, or even your own thoughts or feelings.

This kind of "tinkering" with your chain of events is often necessary to uncover the antecedents that have an "automatic" influence. You become aware of these mechanisms when the automatic sequences are changed. When using a "tinkering" strategy, apply the same observation-and-recording techniques during the period of trial intervention that were used during baseline.

Summary. You discover the antecedents to your behavior through self-observation. The antecedents will be some aspect of the physical or social situation, the behavior of others, or your own thoughts and feelings. As soon as the target behavior occurs, write down its antecedents. After you have gathered these data for a while, establish categories for the antecedents. If you have some of the reactions we listed on page 151, your antecedents may be aversive. Sometimes the best strategy is to "tinker," starting with simple reinforcement for desired changes and observing what interferes with your plan.

Controlling antecedents

Let's assume that you have been successful in discovering some of the antecedents to your behavior. What then?

Avoiding antecedents

One of the reasons why very strict diets work—ones in which every particle of food that you eat is determined beforehand—is that the dieter avoids the antecedents to overeating. If all you have in front of you are two pieces of celery and a bowl of soup, then you have avoided antecedents for overeating, such as a plate of spaghetti or a slice of cake. Chronic alcoholics who successfully stay away from drinking may accomplish this by never confronting one antecedent for overdrinking: the first drink.

The problem of the *consummatory response,* such as overeating or alcoholism, is that the behavior produces, automatically, its own reinforcement. Thus, it is impossible to separate the behavior from its reinforcer (Harris, 1969). Also, it is very difficult to find a stronger reinforcer that you can use to reward an incompatible behavior: if you are a habitual overeater or smoker or drug user, almost nothing is as reinforcing as your "habit." For such consummatory behaviors, perhaps the most promising type of self-modification plan is one in which you avoid the antecedents that set the time and place for your consummatory behavior. The smoker avoids cigarettes, the drinker avoids drinks, and the overeater avoids fattening foods; each knows that if he exposes himself to those stimuli, he will very likely perform the undesired behavior again. People with this kind of problem can work out self-modification plans in which they reinforce themselves for avoiding the antecedent.

Case #17 was a middle-aged, overweight man. He wanted to diet but reported that progress was always followed by disaster. He began to record the antecedents that produced his eating binges and realized that, while he normally stayed on his diet quite regularly, there was one situation in which he always ate too much. This was when he and his wife were invited to someone else's house for dinner, something that occurred at least every other week. His friends usually produced a delicious meal, and he always overate. He solved the problem by setting a simple rule to which his wife agreed: until he had lost twenty pounds, they would not accept any dinner invitations. When someone called to invite them for dinner, he would explain that he had to lose weight and that, because his would-be host or hostess was such an excellent cook and he could not possibly resist the food, he must regretfully decline.

The problem with this kind of avoidance of a controlling antecedent is that, when you do reexpose yourself to the antecedent, you find yourself performing the same old behavior. Research has shown that dieters usually are doomed to a lifetime of dieting, and alcoholics do best to stay on the wagon forever.

About fourteen months after Case #17 had lost his twenty pounds, he was back at our door, having regained ten of the twenty. He then went on a more permanent diet in which he gained reinforcements for exercising and for permanently avoiding the most fattening foods.

If you can reasonably expect to avoid the antecedent permanently, then reinforcing yourself for avoiding it will modify your behavior. If you cannot avoid it permanently, you may have to remodify your behavior from time to time, as reexposure to the antecedent brings the old, undesired habits back.

Reinforcement for avoiding these situations is often difficult. Indeed, the use of important interpersonal reinforcement is often the only sufficiently powerful plan. Case #17 used his wife's support and encouragement to avoid overeating. Alcoholics Anonymous and Synanon (for drug addicts) use the same principle: powerful reinforcement from other people for avoiding the problem antecedents. These techniques cannot alter the physiological addictions and cravings for alcohol, drugs, tobacco, or food, but they can reinforce the behaviors of avoiding them.

A two-stage process for consummatory behaviors

If your problem concerns consummatory responses, such as smoking or overeating, you may want to use a two-stage process. In stage one, you deliberately avoid the antecedent. For example, don't go to parties where you will be strongly tempted to smoke, or don't confront yourself with high-calorie food. Then, in stage two, you build in new behaviors so that you can go to parties or eat a small amount of high-calorie food.

In stage one, you gain the reinforcer for simply avoiding the tempting antecedent situation. In stage two, you gain the reinforcer for being able to withstand exposure to the antecedent without performing your old, undesired habit.

A man who had unsuccessfully tried to quit smoking several times did an analysis of the situations in which he had returned to smoking after having "quit" for a few days. He found that he was likely to go back to smoking at work if he took a coffee break or ate lunch with his friends, several of whom smoked. Their cigarettes looked so inviting that he would bum one and then be "hooked" again. In stage one of his plan, he avoided these antecedents for two weeks, carefully explaining to his friends what he was doing, and reinforcing himself for successful avoidance. He was not tempted so much on the weekends because he spent them with his wife, who did not smoke. After he had been off cigarettes for two weeks, he entered stage two, in which he gained the reinforcer (a big one) not simply for not smoking but specifically for not smoking with his friends at lunch. After this had worked for a week, he added taking coffee breaks to his daily schedule and reinforced himself specifically for not smoking at coffee breaks. Now his task was to remain vigilant for tempting antecedents and to reinforce himself for not smoking when the antecedent occurred. He was able to tell when such an antecedent was occurring, because he would suddenly remember how much he wanted a cigarette. The morning cup of coffee, a meal, a relaxed period, another smoker, a party—these were often the kinds of tempting antecedents that he had to learn to deal with.

In some ways, giving up smoking is easier than giving up overeating, because you can eliminate smoking entirely, but you cannot eliminate eating entirely (Harris, 1969). An overeater can also follow a two-stage self-modification process, however. In the first stage you may concentrate on bringing your eating habits under immediate control; for example, you might avoid all high-calorie foods or eating at restaurants or at the houses of friends. At the same time, you try to lose weight by increased exercise and/or decreased caloric intake. This is a difficult process, and you should use as many different reinforcement-delivery techniques as you can: immediate reinforcement, potent reinforcement, the use of other people, shaping, narrowing stimulus control (see p. 163).

In the second stage, your task is to build in new eating behaviors (Ferster, Nurnburger, and Levitt, 1962) so that you will be able to maintain your weight loss. Most people who lose on a crash diet regain the lost weight because their overeating behaviors have not been changed. Your goal should be to learn to eat properly, and you do not have to wait until you have lost the weight in order to begin the second

stage. A good plan would involve *increasing* your desirable eating behaviors at the same time that you are *decreasing* your actual weight.

You want to eventually learn to eat the right things in the right
amounts at the right times. Much overeating is associated with other
behaviors, such as watching TV, reading, or going to parties, so that
those antecedents become discriminative stimuli—that is, cues for overeating. Therefore, to break up this pattern, you should restrict your
eating time to eating only: don't do anything else during the meal
(Harris, 1969). Concentrate on eating, savor the food, eat slowly; don't
start moving food from your plate to your mouth until the previous
mouthful is swallowed. Put your fork or spoon down between each bite;
don't take a drink until your mouth is empty (Stuart, 1967, 1971).

You can even use food reinforcers to maintain these new, desirable
behaviors. For example, pick a favorite food, and use it to reinforce
staying on your diet or eating properly, but be sure you limit how much
of that reinforcer you consume. At the end of the day, if you have
stayed within your diet, allow yourself a small portion of the favorite
food as a reinforcer.

The general idea is to increase new, desirable eating *behaviors* that
will allow you to eat without growing fat. You accomplish this by (1)
learning to avoid overeating when the old, discriminative stimuli—the
antecedents—occur and (2) learning a new set of proper eating behaviors. Like any new behaviors, these will have to be shaped and reinforced.

The technique we have been suggesting, the two-stage process, is
one in which you follow avoidance of antecedents with developing a
new behavior. This principle can be applied to other kinds of problems
as well as to problems of consummatory behaviors.

Interpersonal problems

Case #18 involved two women who worked together. Over a year's
period their relationship had deteriorated to the point that just seeing
each other made each of them angry. When they did talk together, the
inevitable result was anger and hurt feelings. They had to work near
each other, however, so one of them decided to try a two-stage intervention program. The first stage was an effort to control the antecedents
for them both.

Stage one: she instituted a "cooling-off period," in which she simply
did not talk with the other except when it was absolutely necessary.
When she did talk, she would confine her remarks to their joint work
and try to be either neutral or mildly pleasant. This was reasonably

effective; after a couple of weeks, they settled down for two months of occasional, brief, relatively calm interactions. The evocation of anger seemed to have ended.

This is an example of initially avoiding an antecedent—in this case, talking with the other person—long enough to begin to develop other, more desirable reactions. However, unless some new behaviors were created, there was a real danger for these women. Eventually their work would require that they have more substantial conversations, and they might gradually return to their old behavior: stimulating each other to anger.

Stage two: the woman who had begun the cooling-off process now went into a second stage in which she would (1) not respond to any "anger-producing" remarks from the other person; (2) positively reinforce the other for more pleasant remarks (if the other woman said "I'm not sure you're doing a good job," she would be ignored, but if she said "That seemed to work out very well," the first woman would say "Why, thanks very much. It is kind of you to say that."); and (3) praise the other woman for her good work and refrain from criticizing her less-than-good work.

When the antecedent for your undesired behavior is the behavior of another person, it is sometimes possible to change his behavior by reinforcing him for another action. The woman in the example above was doing this. The young married woman whose husband produced the antecedent for her making excuses was doing the same thing.

Very often interpersonal problems develop because one person begins to punish the other. Receiving punishment often incites people to revenge, so that a vicious circle becomes established in which one punishment leads to the next, inciting the first person to another punishment, and so on until the relationship is destroyed. One way of breaking out of such vicious circles is to realize that the other person's reinforcing acts are also behavior: *you can reinforce the other person for reinforcing you!*

Also, you can reinforce yourself for reinforcing someone else. You might reinforce the other person by paying attention to him or making some statement that is rewarding to him. When you are involved in a problematic interpersonal relationship, you can ask yourself "What kinds of antecedents am I providing for the other person? Could I reinforce his desired behavior?" Your intervention plan might involve paying attention to the "good" things the other person does and reinforcing him for them. You then reinforce yourself for this behavior.

Two girls had been rooming together for more than six months and, while they liked each other very much, they had also developed a pattern of arguing that seemed likely in the long run to make their friendship much less rewarding for both. The vicious circle went like this: Anne would do something that Betty thought was very arrogant. Betty would then put down Anne. This would anger Anne, who would attack Betty. From Anne's point of view, Betty was a "put-down artist." From Betty's point of view, Anne was arrogant. Each seemed to us to be partially right; Anne was arrogant, and Betty seemed to enjoy putting her down. Deciding who was "right," however, was not the task and *would not have helped very much* in any case. The two worked out a mutual agreement in which Betty would ignore Anne's outbursts of arrogance, and Anne would ignore Betty's "put downs." Each also agreed to tell the other when an act particularly pleased her. Thus, they agreed to provide new antecedents and new reinforcers for each other.

Building in pauses

Usually the behaviors of others that serve as antecedents for your behavior will have been well established in their stimulus control *before* you realize that a problem exists. For any well-established antecedent, you may find yourself responding without thinking, whether the antecedent is a rude statement or a plateful of food. One technique that is helpful in dealing with this automatic quality of antecedents is to pause before responding. A man who had developed the undesired habit of becoming aggressive when others said something he thought was foolish worked out a scheme to reinforce himself for pausing a few seconds before responding aggressively. Often, in those few seconds, he would think of something less rude to say. Dieters have sometimes been successful by requiring themselves to pause between every bite, lay the spoon or fork down, and just sit for a second before resuming eating. Also, having no prepared foods in the house builds in a pause between the impulse to eat and the consummatory behavior (Stuart, 1967). Of course, you can reinforce yourself for pausing.

This technique for controlling antecedents gains support from (1) making careful observations, (2) establishing categories of antecedents, and (3) giving the categories *labels.* Consider the young man who always told off people who made statements that did not agree with his personal philosophy. Just being able to notice occurrences of an antecedent sometimes makes it possible to control your responses to the antecedent. *Labeling* the antecedent also provides a pause and an alternate behavior. For example, when someone contradicted this young man's philosophy, he could say to himself "Now that is an example of the disagreement-with-my-personal-philosophy antecedent that usually leads to my telling the other person off . . . I had better pause a moment." The pause itself is a new behavior that can become the antecedent for a more desirable link in the chain of events.

Earlier we discussed the student politician who increased listening instead of talking at campus meetings. In the early stages of his program, he used the technique of reinforcing himself for pausing and listening to one more sentence before he said anything.

This kind of technique essentially involves *lengthening the chain of events* between the first antecedent and your behavior (Ferster et al., 1962). For the student politician, the original chain had been: occurrence of a thought followed immediately by the behavior of talking. His new technique involved lengthening the chain by inserting a pause. This pause allowed the development of a new behavior: listening.

Another strategy that can be used in controlling antecedents is to *change the chain of events that produces the undesired behavior.*

Breaking up chains

Many behaviors are the result of a fairly long chain of events. An antecedent produces some behavior, which leads to a particular consequence, which is itself the antecedent for yet another behavior, and so on. The end behavior, which may be an undesired act, is the result of a long series of antecedent-behavior/new antecedent-new behavior. By the time you reach the end of the chain of events, the impulse to perform the final but undesirable behavior is so strong that it is very difficult to restrain. This may be particularly true for consummatory behaviors, in which the end of the chain is the behavior that consumes the reinforcer and is thus very strongly established. In such cases, a good strategy may be to interrupt the chain of events early. Bergin (1969) has described the clinical use of such techniques. Ferster et al. (1962) have applied this self-control method.

In this kind of situation, the final behavior in the chain is usually the one that you recognize as the problem behavior. For example, you may say to yourself "The problem is that I drink too much." But the act of drinking is embedded in a sequence of behaviors, which involves getting the alcohol, making some kind of drink, perhaps sitting down, and then drinking. Sometimes, by analyzing the chain of events that culminates in the final behavior, it is possible to identify an early, weak link in the chain. An interruption there can prevent the occurrence of the final behavior.

Annon (1971) reports the case of a person who used a complex "scrambling" of previous chain links. A problem drinker had consumed up to a pint of vodka before bedtime each night for several years and could no longer sleep without it. He analyzed the components of the usual chain of events that led to drinking: coming home, turning on TV, going to refrigerator, putting ice in the glass, pouring drink, going to bathroom, undressing, showering, going to bed, pouring more drinks, and so on. The man reorganized this chain into a different order: for example, he moved showering to just after coming home, delayed going to refrigerator until after undressing, and substituted cola for vodka in the glass. This scrambling had the effect of decreasing the vodka-drinking probabilities, since it broke up much of the antecedent control.

Changing the chain of events

Case #19 was a young woman whose target problem was excessively frequent urination. She reported that she went to the bathroom an average of thirteen times per day. She was upset at this, as it was personally and sometimes socially embarrassing. She had seen a physician, who reported that there was no medical problem.

In gathering the baseline data, she realized that two separate antecedents led to urination. First, she almost never went into a bathroom (even to wash her face) without using the toilet. Second, she would go to the toilet at the first hint of bladder pressure. To break up the control that entering a bathroom had over urination, she used a simple plan: she would reinforce herself for going into a bathroom, performing some behavior that did not involve using the toilet, and then walking out. For example, she would enter, wash her hands, and leave. Or she might comb her hair or put on lipstick and then leave. In this way, she broke up the inevitable relationship between going into the bathroom (the antecedent) and using the toilet (the behavior).

In order to change the antecedent control of urination by the stimulus of the first hint of bladder pressure, she used the *pause* technique. Upon feeling the first hint of pressure, she required herself to pause for five minutes before urinating. This simple pause technique was sufficient, because the passage of five minutes usually found her engaged in some other behavior. This no doubt stretched the actual delay time to far more than five minutes, making a formal shaping schedule unnecessary in her case.

This girl, then, determined two separate antecedent controls over her problem behavior and instituted separate interventions for each. In this kind of intervention strategy, the crucial step is being able to analyze the chain of events leading to the final, undesired behavior.

Suppose your problem is that you eat too many between-meal snacks. The statement "between-meal snacks" defines the target behavior and situation: consuming the food between meals. What is the chain that leads to this final step? First, you might feel slightly bored or have nothing to do for a minute. Second, you start moving toward the kitchen. Third, you open the refrigerator or pantry and search for food. Last, you eat it. If this were your chain, you might start to interrupt it by having an intervention plan that called for performance of some other behavior at step two instead of moving toward the kitchen. It might be *any* other behavior; for example, you might make a phone call, for which you gain a reinforcer. Each time you interrupt the chain, you gain the reinforcer.

You can't always avoid being bored or having nothing to do, so you cannot reasonably expect to eliminate step one. You should interrupt at step two. If you smoke when you feel tense, for example, you would probably not be able to eliminate all sources of tension in your life, but you can change what you begin to do as soon as you feel the state of tension building up.

Summary

There are several techniques for controlling antecedents. You can simply avoid them. If that is not practical, you can use a two-stage process, in which you first avoid and then build in desired alternative behaviors to perform when the antecedent occurs. This is particularly important for consummatory behaviors. A similar strategy can be used to improve interpersonal relations. You can reinforce others for reinforcing you—and then reinforce yourself for having done it! You can control antecedents by building in pauses between the first step and the final behavior and by breaking up, scrambling, or changing the chain of events that leads to the final, undesired behavior.

Increasing antecedent stimulus control

Because ridding yourself of undesired behaviors has been the focus of the discussion, we have dealt with methods for breaking up or eliminating the control that certain antecedents have over your behavior. Sometimes your strategy would be just the opposite. If you want to increase some desirable behavior, one way to start—besides the obvious techniques of shaping, positive reinforcement and so on—is to deliberately build in stimulus control. This will make it likely that you will perform the desired behavior in the presence of a particular antecedent.

Often you will want to be sure that you are able to perform the behavior, at least under *some* conditions. By deliberately attempting to create an antecedent control over the desired behavior, you can be more sure that you will perform the behavior somewhere. This technique is particularly appropriate when you want to establish long-term changes. For example, you might want to build in studying over a period of several years or learning to eat properly for your entire life.

An antecedent comes to have stimulus control over some behavior when the stimulus is present for the behavior's performance and reinforcement and not present when the behavior is performed but not reinforced. We first discussed this process in Chapter Three, page 43. Goldiamond (1965) has presented excellent illustrative cases.

Suppose you want to increase your *concentration while studying.* If you are to increase the control of some antecedent over the behavior of concentrating, you must arrange a situation so that first, *whenever you are in that situation, you are concentrating and gaining reinforcement for it.* It also means that second, *you must not perform any other behavior that may be reinforced, in that situation.*

This second feature is very important. Otherwise, the same stimulus could become a cue for more than one behavior, and the competing behaviors could interfere with the target.

Thus, you should begin learning to concentrate while studying by studying at a place in which you never do anything else and leaving that situation whenever you are not concentrating. When you are studying at a particular desk and realize that you are not concentrating, you should leave the desk until you can come back to it and concentrate once more. Reinforce yourself for this, of course, and shape the behavior in small steps.

If you don't have a place that you can reserve for one behavior, you can still make one particular *arrangement* of stimuli the cue. One man had only one desk for writing letters, watching TV, eating, and performing many other behaviors, but he always pulled his desk out from the wall and sat at the other side of it when he wanted to concentrate. That way, sitting at the other side—an antecedent—was associated only with studying.

A dieter used a similar procedure. She found that it was impossible at first to go through all the steps we recommended for breaking up the chains of behavior that resulted in her overeating. So she began by requiring herself to sit at a particular place for one meal each day. During the meal, she concentrated on performing all the acts necessary for learning new eating behaviors. In this way, sitting at that particular place acquired antecedent stimulus control over her behaviors of learning new ways of eating. Ferster et al. (1962) present similar cases and theoretical analyses.

This same general technique can be used when the *elimination* of a behavior is the goal. The logic is this: if a behavior can be firmly linked to an antecedent, that antecedent can then be successively narrowed in scope, down to a point where the behavior is unlikely to occur at all.

Nolan (1968) reports on a smoker whose self-agreement allowed her to smoke only in her "smoking-chair" at home. The chair was placed so that no reinforcement other than the smoking itself was provided: it faced away from the TV set, was not comfortable, and so forth. Once she established smoking only in the chair, she moved it to the cellar! Under this plan her smoking decreased markedly. Similar strategies for achieving stimulus control over nail-biting and hair pulling are advocated by Kanfer and Phillips (1970, p. 434). Goldiamond (1965) reports narrowing sulking behavior in a client so that it occurred only on a special sulking stool.

In summary, increasing the control of a *specific* antecedent stimulus can be chosen when you want either to build a desired behavior or to eliminate an undesired one.

The opposite strategy can now be discussed: *broadening* the range of effective antecedent stimuli.

Creating stimulus generalization

Of course, you don't want to spend the rest of your life being able to perform some desired behavior only when you are in the presence of some particular set of antecedents. You will want to be able to concentrate in several kinds of situations or to eat properly whenever you are eating or to use social skills with many people. In short, you want your newly learned behaviors to *generalize* from one situation to a variety of situations. *Stimulus generalization is the process by which a behavior that has been learned in the presence of one antecedent is performed in the presence of other, similar antecedents.*

Recall the young woman whose case was presented at the beginning of Chapter Eight who wanted to learn to speak with her professors. After she had developed the behavior of speaking to Professor A, she deliberately developed her ability to speak to other professors as well. She was facilitating stimulus generalization.

The more similar the new situation is to the original situation, the easier it will be to generalize your newly learned behavior. Therefore, you will want to think about the similarity of other situations to the one in which you can perform the desired behavior. You should begin generalization by performing the target behavior in the situation that is most similar.

A middle-aged woman had suffered from a very strong fear of

speaking in front of groups. Using some of the procedures we recommend in the following chapter, she developed the ability to speak to a
group of three or four friends. She then wanted to generalize this ability
to new groups. She decided that it would be easiest if the "new" group
contained at least two friends from the old one. That situation would
be most similar to the one in which she first practiced. She arranged
things so that such an opportunity would come up. When it did, she
performed the target behavior and then reinforced it.

Once you have developed a behavior that you can perform in certain situations, you should gradually take small steps into similar situations. You can see that this process is very similar to shaping. In shaping,
the *behaviors* are gradually extended; in generalization training, the *situations* in which the behavior occurs are gradually extended.

Your own self-modification project: Step nine

1. List the probable antecedents for each of your problem behaviors.
2. For each of these antecedents, perform self-observation to verify (or
   disconfirm) your hypotheses.
3. For antecedents that appear to have a firm relationship to the target
   behavior, establish categories and add them to your recording forms.
   Begin collecting frequency data on these antecedents.
4. Write an intervention plan using at least two of the principles discussed in this chapter. *Do not implement this plan yet.*
5. Attempt to coordinate these plans with the one that you wrote after
   reading Chapter Eight. Eliminate any contradictions in the contract.
   Do not implement this contract either, until you have read the next
   chapter.
6. Read Chapter Ten.

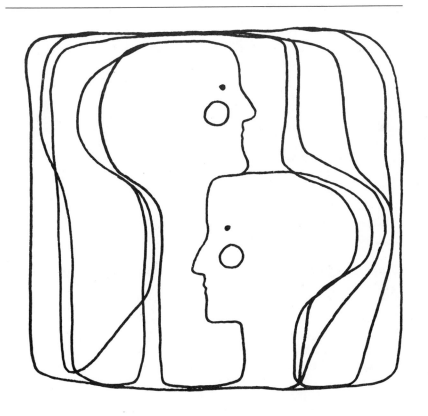

1. Emotions, our inner feelings, are learned reactions. They are learned *via* respondent conditioning.
2. Systematic desensitization is a technique for alleviating unpleasant emotional reactions by replacing them with incompatible feelings, through reconditioning.
3. Positive reinforcement has a conditioning effect. Whenever possible, in self-modification, it is best to use some positive-reinforcement technique to change both your behavior and your emotional reactions.
4. *In vivo* desensitization is a technique for gradually approaching some feared stimulus in a relaxed state.
   a. *In vivo* techniques can be combined with positive reinforcement.
   b. The process of *in vivo* desensitization involves: arranging a hierarchy of the feared stimulus; producing new behavior in its presence; maintaining relaxation while you do this.
5. Systematic self-desensitization is a process for gradually approaching feared stimuli *in your imagination* while you are in a relaxed state.
   a. The process involves: arranging an imaginary hierarchy of the feared events; learning how to achieve deep muscle relaxation; progressing through the hierarchy while maintaining the relaxation.
   b. Detailed instructions for building the hierarchy, attaining relaxation, and progressing through the hierarchy are given.
6. General rules for using *in vivo* and systematic desensitization are given.

Emotional reactions, as well as overt behaviors, can be a source of self-dissatisfaction. You may be fearful but wish you were not, or you may be inappropriately embarrassed or sad or too often angry. Thus, it is not an overt, observable behavior that displeases you but the way you feel inside. Indeed, people often think of their problems in terms of the way they feel—their emotional reactions—rather than in terms of the way they behave.

An emotional reaction is, in part, an inner feeling. This inner feeling will be observable only to yourself. You might tell others about your inner feelings, but only you can directly observe them.

For decades psychiatry concentrated on the understanding and treatment of emotional disturbances. Historically, psychotherapy assumed that an emotional disturbance lay at the heart of every maladjustment; thus, each problem behavior could be corrected only by relieving the associated emotional problem.

Today, psychologists see behavioral and emotional reactions as intertwined. Most chains of events contain both behavioral and emotional components. For example, picture two people who love each other, and who see each other from opposite ends of an open field. They might start running toward each other with their arms outstretched (their observable behavior) while experiencing inner feelings of joy and love at the same time. Many environmental circumstances will produce *both a behavioral reaction and an emotional one.*

Recall the married woman who found that she often gave excuses to her husband. His frowning produced in the wife both the *emotion* of anxiety and the *behavior* of self-justification. These appeared to result simultaneously. In other cases, the two reactions appear serially. Many nail-biters, for instance, report that the biting behavior occurs in reaction to a stimulus, such as reading, and is followed by the inner feeling of dismay when they realize they have bitten their nails.

Most of our personal dissatisfactions are rarely simply behavioral or emotional; they are usually both. Staats (1970) has detailed the processes that interrelate these reactions.

Most behavioral psychologists now believe that *emotional* reactions are learned—and unlearned—according to a set of principles that is somewhat different from the principles discussed for the learning of *operant* behaviors. Because these principles are different, a program for self-modification may require specific attention to the emotional reactions that are being learned. Before discussing ways of coordinating efforts, we must review the principles involved in learning new emotional responses.

Emotional responses

Emotional responses are usually learned according to the principles for *respondent* behaviors. These principles were mentioned in Chapter Three, but most of that chapter and the ensuing ones have dealt with the principles of *operant* behavior. To demonstrate *respondent* behaviors in Chapter Three, we suggested that you perform an experiment by having someone startle you. Your reaction to the stimulus that startles you would be to tense, jump, *and* have an inner, emotional reaction. You would feel emotionally full, uncomfortable, slightly fearful. This emotional reaction to a startling stimulus illustrates antecedent-stimulus control over emotional reactions.

The automatic, reflexive activities of our bodies are largely controlled by antecedents. The knee-jerk reflex is a simple example. Such reactions do not depend upon consequences for their maintenance, as operant behaviors do. Instead, they are classified as respondent behaviors because they occur in direct *response* to some stimulus. The reason this type of reaction is important is that it now appears that many, if not most, *emotional reactions are learned according to the principles that govern the entire class of respondent reactions.*

Respondent conditioning

Some behaviors are reflexive; they are not learned. For example, a baby does not have to learn to salivate when milk enters his mouth. He salivates automatically. Milk in the mouth is an antecedent condition that has control over salivation.

Does the baby also salivate automatically when he sees the bottle? No. Salivating to the bottle is not innate; it is learned. This process of learning is called *respondent conditioning.*

We begin with a stimulus-behavior connection that is built into the organism. The baby salivates to milk in the mouth. Suppose that always just preceding this, the baby sees the bottle, something that is quite likely if he is not being breast fed. Because he sees the bottle for a few seconds before milk in the mouth automatically leads to salivation, the simple association of the bottle with a stimulus that directly elicits salivation—if it occurs several times—will establish a conditioned response. Thereafter, the bottle will elicit salivation.

Respondent conditioning is the process in which previously neutral stimuli, through association with antecedents that have stimulus control over some reaction, themselves come to have that same stimulus control. First, you have an antecedent—call it A_1—that elicits a response. If A_1 is always preceded by another antecedent, A_2, then after a few such associations, A_2 will develop the same stimulus control over the response that A_1 has. If the response is some emotional reaction, then through this process of respondent conditioning, the new antecedent, A_2, will develop the capacity to elicit the emotional reaction, *even if A_1 does not occur.*

Emotional conditioning

Most emotional reactions are under antecedent stimulus control. Thus, they can be conditioned to other stimuli that were neutral before the process of association but that have acquired stimulus control over the emotional reaction since the conditioning or series of associations.

A number of years ago, John Watson and Rosalie Raynor (1920) demonstrated how an emotional reaction can be conditioned so that it comes to be elicited by an antecedent that was previously neutral. From the earliest days of our lives, a sudden loud noise is an adequate stimulus for a fear reaction. To associate that stimulus with one that was neutral, Watson and Raynor followed this procedure: a baby was presented with a soft, furry rabbit. A few seconds afterward, a very loud, unexpected noise was made behind him. He reacted automatically to the startling noise with fear. After several experiences in which the rabbit was presented just before the frightening noise—so that fear was experienced while seeing the rabbit—the rabbit became a conditioned stimulus. By itself, it became sufficient to elicit the fear, even if the noise did not occur. Thus, what had been a neutral stimulus became a frightening one.

In a similar way, emotional reactions can be transferred to many new stimuli in your life. As each person has new experiences, he may undergo new associations between conditioned emotional reactions and new stimuli, so that the new stimuli will come to elicit the original emotional reaction.

Once a conditioned reaction is established, a new stimulus may be associated with the conditioned stimulus, so that the new antecedent also acquires stimulus control over the emotional responses. This process is called higher-order conditioning.

Phobias, fear, and avoidance behavior

One of the best examples of conditioned emotional reactions is that of strong, socially inappropriate fears, called phobias. A woman may be so afraid of cats that she will not enter a house until she has been assured that there are no cats there. Some people fear heights to the extent that they are unwilling to go up elevators in tall buildings. Some fear sex to the extent that they do not respond with pleasure even when it would be reasonable for them to do so. A man may be so afraid of earthworms that he cannot go outside his house.

These are all examples of *phobias:* strong fears that most people consider irrational and that interfere with the life of the person who has them. These kinds of strong fears may be regarded as the result of conditioning processes. The man who fears earthworms, for example, has been the victim of a series of conditioning trials in which his fear, which was appropriate to some stimulus circumstances, has become conditioned through association to a stimulus, earthworms, for which fear is not appropriate. Even though the fear is irrational, it is nevertheless emotionally upsetting to the man who has it.

Sometimes a series of experiences will establish the conditioned fear; sometimes a single, very unpleasant experience will set up the conditioned emotional reactions. A common fear for college students is the test-taking situation. Some students become very nervous during a test, perhaps to the extent of actually forgetting material that they should easily remember. Another common fear concerns sex: despite all the talk about the liberation from Victorianism, there are still many people who become exceedingly upset when presented with sexual stimuli. A third common source of nervousness or anxiety are social situations such as interactions with people who evaluate us or introductions to strangers.

In all these situations, the stimulus acquires control over the emotional reaction. Whenever you have to take a test, for example, you may experience nervousness. Many people try to deal with these conditioned, unpleasant emotional reactions by avoiding the stimulus circumstances that elicit the reactions. They might try all sorts of ways to avoid taking tests—even going to the extent of dropping out of school. Or a woman for whom men produce fear reactions may simply choose to avoid men. But the person who has developed some kind of avoidance behavior may decide that this is not the most harmonious relationship with his environment. However, simply stopping the avoidance behavior would require experiencing the unpleasant emotion, which is controlled by some conditioned stimulus. Logically, you would correct this situation by attempting to *recondition* that stimulus, so that the situation would elicit some reaction other than fear. Such a technique has been developed by Joseph Wolpe and his associates (Wolpe, 1969). This technique, called *systematic desensitization,* has been carefully studied. It has been shown to have considerable effectiveness in the removal of unwanted emotional reactions.

Desensitization

Systematic desensitization is a clinical technique used by professional psychiatrists and psychologists (who are often called "behavior therapists") with their patients. Later we will discuss the implications of these clinical procedures for self-modification, but first, we will review the theory and procedures of systematic desensitization.

Desensitization is basically a process of *re*conditioning. Through prior conditioning, the patient has become unduly sensitive to some stimulus. For example, everyone gets a little tense when taking an important test, but a few panic. Most virgins are a little apprehensive on their wedding night, but some are terribly, unhappily nervous. Some people become so nervous when taking tests, or making love, that their anxiety seriously interferes with their performance. *The idea of desensitization is to recondition the person's reactions so that the stimuli that previously elicited an unpleasant emotion will, instead, come to elicit a different, tolerable emotional reaction.*

Desensitization usually follows a standard procedure. First, in a series of interviews, the behavior therapist tries to discover the stimulus situations that elicit fear or nervousness. After one or more categories of fear-producing stimuli have been discovered, the various elements of the category can be discussed. Suppose that a woman has an unreasonable fear of snakes. Not all snakes are equally fear producing: big, dangerous snakes probably elicit more fear than small, harmless ones. First, the varieties of such stimuli would be listed. Second, the stimuli are ranked according to how fear producing they are, from the least frightening to the most. Third, the patient is trained in a series of exercises that produce deep relaxation so that she can gain enough skill to readily put herself into a state of very comfortable relaxation.

Now the last, critical step can be taken: beginning at the least frightening stimulus situation, the person *replaces* her fear of that stimulus with *relaxation.* She does this by imagining the fear-producing stimulus while she is in the relaxed state. When she can relax while imagining the least fear-producing stimulus, she moves up one step to the next most frightening. She continues with this process, which is very much like shaping, until she has moved all the way up the ranked series of fear-producing stimuli, at each step replacing her anxiety with relaxation.

We have dealt with a very similar procedure already. Recall the case of the girl, discussed at the beginning of Chapter Eight, who was afraid to speak to her professors. She was basically using a desensitization procedure by gradually increasing the degree of exposure to professors in a carefully graded series of encounters. In that case, the young woman worked up her shaping ladder in real-life situations by gradually increasing how long she talked to her professors. The technique used in this case illustrates one of the major differences between her procedure and clinical, systematic desensitization. In the latter, the person goes up the shaping ladder *in his imagination.*

Positive reinforcement has a conditioning effect

Real-life techniques that apply positive reinforcement to behavior also involve an element of reconditioning. Return to the student who was afraid of her professors. If it had been possible to measure her fear of professors, we would have observed a decrease of anxiety as she gradually increased the length of her talks with them. Essentially, she was associating *feeling comfortable* with the stimulus of talking with her professors. *Any time you arrange your real-life situation so that you will gain positive reinforcement for attempting some task that was previously frightening, you are* (1) *reinforcing the new behavior and* (2) *reconditioning the emotional response to the present stimuli.*

As we observed earlier, a stimulus may produce an emotional response *and* have reinforcement value *and* be the cue for certain behaviors (Staats, 1970). The important point to remember is that if any *one* of these functions is changed, *all* may change. Thus, when you arrange intervention plans, you can anticipate that positive reinforcement will condition positive feelings to the antecedents of your behavior. These positive feelings explain why you so often come to like doing the things for which you are rewarded and why you even come to like the circumstances in which you do them.

Case #20. A young man and his wife had had a series of arguments over his lack of helpfulness around the house. She was carrying all the housework as well as a full-time job and felt that he should help more. He agreed but pointed out that his only other experiences with housework had been when his mother punished him by requiring him to work around the house, something he never had to do at any other time. You can see the effect this would have on him: since doing housework had always been a punishment, housework had acquired an unpleasant emotional tone for him. In short, he hated it. The couple worked out a contract in which he performed housework behaviors in return for which his wife reinforced him with extra affection and extra money to spend on his pet hobby. They followed a shaping procedure, so that his beginning attempts involved little work. We lost track of this couple for five months and then ran into them, holding hands, on campus one day. They were delighted with the results of their agreement, for now the young man was definitely doing his share around the house. "The really funny thing" he reported, "is not only that I'm now doing it, but I actually don't mind doing some of it. Sweeping, for example. It seems silly, but I almost like it. It's sort of a calm period during the day. It's not at all unpleasant any more."

This is an example of emotional reconditioning. By arranging contingencies so that the young man was positively reinforced for increased housekeeping behavior, not only did that behavior increase, but his emotional reaction to housekeeping was changed. He didn't love it, but it did change from a hated behavior to one that evoked a relaxed feeling.

You can often expect that your positive-reinforcement interventions will lead to more pleasant emotional reactions. Think back over the cases cited in this book; you can see that each person undoubtedly suffered some unpleasant emotional concomitant to his problem behavior. By changing the problem behavior directly, it is often possible to achieve a parallel alteration in the accompanying emotional feeling. This alteration comes about because of the emotional reconditioning that occurs through the association of pleasant (reinforcing) stimuli with the antecedent conditions and with the behavior itself.

Comparing real-life techniques and desensitization

We recommend that self-modification programs focus on reinforcement for behavior change, whenever this is adequate. However, some emotional problems will not yield to these procedures. We will discuss these limitations and explain the role of desensitization in self-modification later. But for the moment, consider the advantages of using a positive-reinforcement, real-life strategy.

First of all, because desensitization involves moving up a shaping ladder in your imagination, it is typically found that real-life behavior lags behind progress up the imaginary ladder (Bandura, 1969). Thus, it would be more efficient to choose some real-life technique, if possible, or to use systematic desensitization as a preliminary step.

Second, imagination is not so complete as perceptions of reality, and all the sights, smells, tastes, and background of real-life experiences are not totally duplicated in imagination or memories. People differ sharply in their abilities to produce and hold an imagined scene, and some virtually lack this ability. Even at best, the relearning in imagination will not be for as *complete* a set of stimuli as would be the case in real life. This is a disadvantage because the full array of stimuli that control the undesired emotions should be reconditioned.

There is a third reason why real-life techniques are preferable: they allow the learning of new behaviors to accompany reconditioning. Suppose a young woman has always been afraid of men. In school, while her girl friends were learning how to deal with boys, she was holding back because of her fear. If she were suddenly to get rid of her fear, she would still lack the years of practice in relationships that her agemates have had. She would find herself in novel situations in which she did not know how to act. She might not know how to graciously get a man to slow down a little in his advances, or she might not have learned how to be "cute" without acting foolish. There is more to being attractive than simply not being afraid. The effect of this might be that she would begin to relearn her fear, for she might well be rejected by men because of her relative lack of interpersonal skills. This possibility implies that she should not only get rid of her fear but also begin to practice the new behaviors that are required.

Summary.   There are three reasons why we recommend a real-life self-modification technique: (1) actual behavioral changes may lag behind changes achieved in desensitization; (2) your goal is to change some aspect of your real-life behavior, so it is most efficient to work there; (3) sometimes you will need to not only eliminate fear but also learn new behavior.

When to use desensitization

There are circumstances, however, in which some form of desensitization is the necessary technique. The first of these is when you know how to perform the desired behavior, but the appropriate situation elicits emotional reactions that prevent the performance. For example, a good student might spend several hours carefully preparing for a test, using good study habits, but become so nervous when he actually has to take the test that he "forgets" nearly everything he has learned. In this case, he might reason that he just needs to get rid of his test anxiety and all will be well. Desensitization, either systematic or some real-life parallel, would be appropriate whenever the *sole* problem is to eliminate some anxiety.

A young married woman complained "I don't see how behavior modification will work for me, because I don't need to learn anything new; I just need to get rid of my fears. When my husband wants to make love, I want to very much also; but when the crucial moment comes, I get so nervous that I can't carry on." This is another example in which the desired behavior is available but is inhibited by fear. In this case, also, desensitization of the fear seemed appropriate.

Another circumstance that calls for systematic desensitization is one in which it is not possible to use shaping techniques in a real-life situation. Suppose the student who wanted to increase how much she talked with professors had no friendly professor to practice on. She wouldn't have been able to use the technique of shaping and positive reinforcement. When you cannot engineer your daily life so that you can gradually move up some shaping ladder, then desensitization can be used to reduce your anxiety about levels higher than the one at which you are presently performing.

Summary. There are two situations in which the best choice for your self-modification will be to use some form of desensitization: *first,* if your only problem is to rid yourself of some undesired tension or anxiety, and there is no desirable behavior that needs increasing; and *second,* if your problem is that you cannot engineer your environment so that you can shape or practice some desired behavior without having to undergo too much anxiety.

When your anxiety does require desensitization, there are four basic strategies available. The first of these, positive reinforcement for gradually mastering the feared situation, has been discussed extensively in the course of this volume and needs no further treatment here. The remaining three are: (1) *in vivo* desensitization, (2) self-desensitization, and (3) clinical treatment. The rest of the chapter is devoted to a detailed explanation of these procedures.

In vivo desensitization

In vivo (from the Latin "in life") desensitization refers to a real-life process, of course, but the term is usually reserved for the *technique of gradually approaching an actual feared stimulus while being in a relaxed state.* Many individuals have been able to arrange for themselves to be relaxed, or be in some other emotional state that is incompatible with anxiety, and then move in gradual steps toward the most feared situation.

Case #21. college senior, female. She wrote "I am very afraid of birds, under almost any conditions. This sometimes makes me look like a fool—for example, I won't go to the zoo because there are so many birds around, loose as well as in cages—and often causes me unnecessary fear and trepidation. My life would be more pleasant with fewer fears!"

"Here is my hierarchy of *assertive* behaviors to be used for reconditioning."

    A. When *one or two* birds are fifteen yards distant:
        1. Turn and face a bird.
        2. Take one step toward a bird.
        3. Take two steps toward a bird.
        4. Continue until I have walked a total of five yards toward the bird.
        5. Then begin step B.
    B. When *more than two* birds are fifteen yards distant:
        1. Turn and face birds.
        2. Take two steps toward them.
        3. Take four steps toward them.
        4. Continue until I have walked a total of five yards toward the birds.

She then repeated the procedures, beginning at ten yards distance from a single bird, then from a group of birds. Next, she repeated the procedure from five yards. In the last stages of her complex hierarchy, she would begin three yards from the feared stimulus and move to within three feet of the birds, then gradually increase the amount of time, in seconds, that she spent close to them.

At first, she had difficulty in maintaining her assertive feelings but reported that, by getting her boy friend to hold her hand, her anxiety was considerably lessened. This worked well until, perhaps out of boredom, the boy friend gave her a "playful push," and she found herself frighteningly close to the birds, which set her back about three weeks. (It also set their romance back a bit.)

The student reported that she was not using systematic reinforcement for increasing her movements toward birds. She was relying on the "intrinsic" reward of being able to move around with birds nearby. When she got fairly close, she got stuck: she couldn't stay relaxed while moving any closer. At this point she introduced a token system: for each step up the hierarchy, she earned so many points which she could turn in that evening to "buy" certain privileges, such as allowing herself extra dates, doing "idiot" reading, and so on. In this case, she was careful to increase her total positive reinforcements so that she would gain something from coming nearer the birds. At last report, although she said that she still didn't like birds, they no longer made her feel nervous.

By positively reinforcing your movement up a real-life desensitization hierarchy, you provide incentives for getting into situations in which desensitization can occur.

Combining *in vivo* desensitization with reinforcement

Often some reinforcement is necessary to strengthen the approach behaviors that reconditioning requires. In the case of the bird phobia, two separate forms of reinforcement were employed. One was the formal token system, which she used to bolster the last, difficult stages of approach. But the earlier, less obvious one was the presence of her boy friend. The girl originally elected to include him because his presence made her feel more relaxed. But his walking beside her also had reinforcing value for the approach behaviors.

Often the stimulus you use to induce relaxation (or another incompatible reaction) will have reinforcement value as well. One of our students reported a fear of flying, which embarrassed and upset him repeatedly on plane trips. He achieved some relief by associating plane stimuli with mild sexual arousal. By choosing an aisle seat, he could concentrate on watching the airline stewardesses whenever he anticipated a fearful moment. By concentrating and using some fantasy, he could achieve some sexual titillation. This both prevented the anxiety arousal and provided some pleasant reconditioning to plane stimuli. The reinforcement, which consisted of the mild sexual pleasure provided by the activity, strengthened his desensitizing behaviors.

Other situations can provide both reinforcement and a new reaction incompatible with anxiety. The following is an example of the use of *intellectual curiosity* as the response that meets both criteria. A young law student suffered from an abnormally strong fear of "diseased organisms." An *in vivo* strategy was devised in which he enrolled in anatomical and obstetrical courses, thus replacing the response of anxiety with the competing one of intellectual curiosity. In his own words, he had, in this plan, the "double view of becoming acquainted with all conditions and of freeing myself from all apprehensions as to repulsive things . . . while I satisfied my thirst for knowledge" (Bringman, Krichev, and Balance, 1969, p. 3).

This student was the German author Johann Wolfgang von Goethe, and his "*in vivo* desensitization" occurred during his famous stay at the University of Strassburg during 1770–1771. Though Goethe did not use the language of behavior modification, of course, his sensible technique must have been remarkably successful. He later wrote extensively on his anatomical studies.

In summary, we have presented case examples of the use of three reactions—relaxation, sexual titillation, and intellectual curiosity—that may be incompatible with anxiety and have reinforcing properties.

However, you do not need to rely on the incompatible responses themselves to provide reinforcement. Just as the bird-phobic girl used tokens, various forms of reinforcement may be appropriate to motivate your taking the *in vivo* steps.

Rehm and Marston (1968) have reported an excellent research program of *in vivo* desensitization with college males, all of whom had social anxieties. Each student constructed his own hierarchy of feared situations and then sought to get himself into these situations in real life. Two forms of reinforcement were used for these behaviors: the experimenters' praise in a weekly meeting with the student and the student's own self-evaluation and self-praise during the actual situations. On a variety of measures, the *in vivo* desensitizing students improved much more than did a control group of students who received only weekly nondirective counseling or supportive sessions.

Summarizing the process of *in vivo* desensitization

In order to accomplish *in vivo* desensitization, there are some technical steps that you must take. *First, you should make a ranked list of the fear-producing situations, arranging stimulus items from least to most anxiety producing.* You should start the list very low and have small steps between the items. *Second, you must produce the new behavior and arrange positive reinforcement for it. Third, you must be sure that you are able to relax, or be in some state that is incompatible with being fearful, while you are progressing through the hierarchy.*

Arranging the *in vivo* desensitization in this manner is not always possible, because the world will not sit still for your plans. Just like the girl whose boy friend pushed her capriciously toward the birds (case #21), you are not always able to control events. Desensitization requires that the new, desired emotion always be strong enough to inhibit the appearance of the old fear. This means that you must control the stimuli that produce both the wanted and the unwanted feelings. Sometimes you cannot do this in real life. In those cases, systematic self-desensitization through imagination may be the answer.

Systematic self-desensitization

The advantage of desensitization through imagination is that you can regulate the appearance of the feared stimulus. If you are able to induce a state of relaxation, you can then produce the feared condition in a step-wise hierarchy in your imagination, and you will be less likely to be pushed too far by some event beyond your control. This control was a principal reason for the development of this clinical technique.

But desensitization *was* developed as a clinical technique, to be carefully administered by professional psychiatrists and psychologists. Can it be used effectively as a self-modification procedure? The answer is not yet clear. However, the preliminary results are encouraging (Migler and Wolpe, 1967; Migler, 1968; Melamed and Lang, 1967; Kahn and Baker, 1968; Rardin, 1969).

Because experience with self-desensitization is limited, we cannot yet describe its limitations or indeed the particular kinds of problems for which it is most appropriate. In our opinion, self-desensitization efforts are not likely to be harmful, even if they fail. Nevertheless, the reader should approach self-desensitization as an experimental procedure. It should be discontinued if the course of anxiety-reduction is not relatively smooth and *it should be immediately discontinued if any increase in anxiety is noted.*

Professional clinical desensitization is available, and such treatment should be sought for debilitating fears that do not yield smoothly to self-desensitization or to the techniques already outlined. Indeed, the one harm that might result from a failure of self-desensitization is that you might become discouraged and negative toward seeking professional desensitization. Although self-desensitization is in the infancy of its development, clinical desensitization is a well-developed, reliable technique, and fear that does not yield to self-desensitization may well be correctible by a competent behavior therapist.

Even though we present it as an experimental technique, self-desensitization is a most interesting and potentially promising procedure. Some students may wish to explore its use, and therefore we present an outline of the techniques, many of which follow suggestions in Kahn and Sandler (1966) and Paul (1966).

Steps in self-desensitization

There are four steps in self-desensitization. The first two are virtually identical to those used for *in vivo* desensitization: (1) listing feared situations and (2) arranging them into hierarchical categories. The third step is self-training in deep relaxation. The fourth step is the step-wise reconditioning.

Building the hierarchy. The hierarchy is a ranked list of situations that elicit the unpleasant emotion. Write each situation on a separate card, and arrange the cards in order so that the most disturbing situation is at the bottom of the stack and the least disturbing at the top. Some people begin to feel better just for having made the list; they experience some relief of anxiety. Others report the opposite effect. If building the hierarchy produces strong feelings of discomfort, this is an adequate signal that self-desensitization efforts should be discontinued and professional clinical treatment sought.

For example, suppose your problem is that you become nervous while taking tests. There are different kinds of tests, ranging from unimportant little quizzes to make-you-or-break-you final exams. Test taking is then the category of items. Within that category you might write down behaviors-and-situations like this in hierarchical order:

> taking a test that doesn't count for very much
> taking a test when I am not prepared
> taking a surprise test
> taking a test when the professor watches me all the time
> taking a mid-term exam
> taking a test that determines my whole grade in the course

Each hierarchy you create must represent a separate *category* of fear-producing situations. The category is established by arranging items together that seem related to one another.

Most writers suggest between ten and twenty items for the hierarchy. Follow the basic rules of shaping: begin with very easy items, and be sure that the steps between are small. Add or subtract steps as needed.

Sometimes your hierarchy will make sense if it is arranged in terms of *the distance in time* before some fear-producing event occurs. Here is a sample hierarchy recommended by Paul (1966) for anxiety connected with giving a speech in class.*

> Step 1. Reading about speeches alone in room, one or two weeks before you have to give the speech.
> Step 2. Discussing the coming speech a week before, in class or after.
> Step 3. In the audience when another person gives a speech (one week before your own speech).
> Step 4. Writing the speech in a study area.
> Step 5. Practicing the speech alone in your room.
> Step 6. Getting dressed the morning of the speech.
> Step 7. Activities just before leaving for the speech.
> Step 8. Walking to class on the day of the speech.
> Step 9. Entering the room.

---

*Adapted from Gordon L. Paul, *Insight vs desensitization in psychotherapy*. Stanford, Calif.: Stanford University Press, 1966, pp. 117–118. Reprinted by permission of the publisher and author.

Step 10. Waiting while another person gives a speech.
Step 11. Walking up before the audience.
Step 12. Presenting the speech (seeing the faces, and so on).

Other fears can be listed by *physical* distance. A fear of heights is an obvious example. A hierarchical list of such fears would include items steadily rising in number of floors or distance up the mountain.

Other cases may be more complicated and the category less clear-cut. For example, a woman with a phobic fear labeled her general category *accidents;* the hierarchy contained the following items (Evans, 1971):*

1. I am bending down inside a cupboard and then stand up too soon and bang my head against the cupboard door.
2. In my office building, I see a warning poster about avoiding industrial accidents.
3. The person walking in front of me stumbles and begins to fall; however, he regains his balance and continues without mishap.
4. I hear the squeal of tires as a car that I cannot see brakes violently on a nearby road.
5. I am watching television; the heroine of the story leaves a fire unguarded and causes a bad fire in her house.
6. I am looking through a magazine; I see a section titled "What to do in emergencies," and there are pictures of bandaging procedures and mouth-to-mouth resuscitation.
7. I am cutting vegetables, and the knife slips and cuts my finger slightly; I see blood beginning to trickle down my finger and on the blade of the knife.
8. I am standing in a line chatting idly to a woman I do not know, and she mentions that her husband recently fell off a ladder and broke his arm.
9. I pass the emergency entrance of City Hospital. I see ambulances parked outside, but there is nobody around. Inside the glass doors I can see stretchers, but they are empty.
10. In the morning newspaper I see a photograph of a very bad car accident on the freeway.
11. My neighbor's child is riding his tricycle in the front yard. I look out of the kitchen window and see him tumble off the trike and graze his knee.
12. I am listening to the radio and hear a news flash that there has been a train derailed in Scotland and that there have been many people hurt; no other details are available.
13. Out in the park I see a child slip and fall into the pond. A park attendant is nearby and soon fishes the child out of the water; he is wet and cold but otherwise unhurt.
14. I am about to step off the curb to cross the street; a bicycle comes past, very close, and knocks into me. My leg is slightly cut.

---

*Personal communication from Ian M. Evans. Reprinted by permission.

15. I am walking to the bus stop and see a crowd gathered on the street. Someone has been knocked down by a car. There is an ambulance with the doors open, and the victim is being placed onto a stretcher. There is blood on the side of the road, and people are crying.

In summary, you can construct hierarchies for very complicated emotions as well as very simple ones. Remember to begin with items that just barely elicit the undesired feeling and move in gradual steps to the more intensely unpleasant items.

You will then be ready to employ deep relaxation. If you wish, relaxation may be practiced while you are building the hierarchy.

Deep muscle relaxation. The next step in the desensitization process is to learn to relax. Your goal is to be able to produce deep muscle relaxation in your whole body and to be able to recognize when you have produced it. This state, like many complex goals, cannot be reached all at once, so you will follow a gradual procedure in learning it. First, you will learn to relax your arms; then your facial area, neck, shoulders, and upper back; then your chest, stomach, and lower back; then hips, thighs, and calves; then your whole body.

It may require twenty to thirty minutes at first, but as you learn, the amount of time needed will be shortened. The general idea is to first tense a set of muscles, then relax them, so that they will relax more deeply than before they were tensed. This is called the tension-release method.

You should focus your attention on each muscle system as you work through the various muscle groups, so that you can learn what each set feels like when it is well relaxed. With practice, you may not have to tense your muscles first in order to attain deep relaxation.

The process for achieving deep relaxation is as follows: Choose a private place, quiet, free of interruptions and distracting stimuli. Sit comfortably, well supported by the chair, so that you do not have to use your own muscles to support yourself. You may want to close your eyes. Then follow this procedure specified in a manual for desensitization (Paul, 1966):*

1. ... Make a fist with your dominant hand (usually right). Make a fist and tense the muscles of your (right) hand and forearm; tense it until it trembles. Feel the muscles pull across your fingers and the lower part of your forearm ... Hold this position for 5 to 7 seconds, then ... relax. ... Just let your hand go. Pay attention to the muscles of your (right)

---

*Adapted from Gordon L. Paul, *Insight vs desensitization in psychotherapy.* Stanford, Calif.: Stanford University Press, 1966, pp. 117–118. Reprinted by permission of the publisher and author.

hand and forearm as they relax. Note how those muscles feel as relaxation flows through them (20 to 30 seconds).

Again, tense the muscles of your (right) hand and forearm. Pay attention to the muscles involved (5 to 7 seconds). . . . Relax; attend only to those muscles, and note how they feel as relaxation takes place, becoming more and more relaxed, more relaxed than ever before. Each time (you) do this, you'll relax even more until your arm and hand are completely relaxed with no tension at all, warm and relaxed.

Continue this procedure until your "hand and forearm are completely relaxed with no tension (usually 2 to 4 times is sufficient)."

2. . . . Tense your (right) biceps, leaving (your) hand and forearm on the chair. Proceed in the same manner as above . . . using the right hand as a reference point, that is, move on when . . . (your) biceps feels as completely relaxed as (your) hand and forearm.

Now add the other muscle groups, one at a time.

Proceed to other gross-muscle groups (listed below) in the same manner. [Be sure to continue to note how each set of muscles feels as it relaxes.] Feel the relaxation and warmth flow through these muscles; pay attention to these muscles so that later you can relax them again. Always use the preceding group as a reference for moving on.

3. Nondominant (left) hand and forearm—feel muscles over knuckles and on lower part of arm.
4. Nondominant (left) biceps.
5. Frown hard, tensing muscles of forehead and top of head (these muscles often "tingle" as they relax).
6. Wrinkle nose, feeling muscles across top of cheeks and upper lip.
7. Draw corners of mouth back, feeling jaw muscles and cheeks.
8. Tighten chin and throat muscles, feeling two muscles in front of throat.
9. Tighten chest muscles and muscles across back—feel muscles pull between shoulder blades.
10. Tighten abdominal muscles—make abdomen hard.
11. Tighten muscles of right upper leg—feel one muscle on top and two on bottom of the upper leg.
12. Tighten right calf—feel muscles on bottom of right calf.
13. Push down with toes and arch right foot—feel pressure as if something were pushing up from under arch.
14. Left upper leg.
15. Left calf.
16. Left foot.

At this point, all the major muscle groups will be relaxed simultaneously.

For most groups of muscles, two trials will be enough. Check yourself to see if you feel tension anywhere in your body. If you do, go back and

repeat the tension-release cycle for that muscle group. It is often helpful
... to take a deep breath and hold it while tensing muscles, and to let it
go while relaxing. Should any muscle group not respond after four trials,
move on and return to it later.

If you develop muscle cramps or spasms from prolonged tension of
the muscles, shorten the tension interval a few seconds, and don't tense
your muscles so hard.

When you wish to terminate the relaxation period, count backward
from four to one. You should then feel relaxed, wide awake, and calm
(Paul, 1966).

You can practice muscle relaxation during the day between desensitization sessions. Some people find it pleasant to practice relaxation
before going to sleep.

The desensitization of an item.   Once you have constructed the hierarchy
and can deeply relax, you are ready to begin desensitization proper. Our
recommended procedures are adapted from Paul (1966), Kahn and Sandler (1966), and ultimately from Wolpe (1969).

You desensitize yourself by imagining a situation in vivid detail while
maintaining complete relaxation. Present the item to be desensitized by
looking at the card on which it has been written. The desensitization can
best be done at the place you have used for practicing deep relaxation.

Try to imagine the situation in complete, minute detail. For example, if your item called for imagining an introduction to a stranger, you
should think about the way the imaginary person looks, the expression
on his or her face, what he or she says, how you react, the details of the
physical situation. You may have to imagine the situation in its component parts while you concentrate separately on imagined sounds, tex-
tures, or elements.

It is very important that you attain a *vivid* picture of each item. It
doesn't have to be as clear as if you were watching a movie, but it should
be as clear as a very vivid memory. Sometimes your imaginary scenes
become more vivid with practice. A good way to check the vividness
of an item is to compare it with your imagination of some scene you
know and can visualize very well—for example, what it looks, feels,
smells, and sounds like to be lying on your bed in your room. First,
visualize the scene in your room. Then compare the visualized item on
your hierarchy; it should be nearly as vivid (Paul, 1966).

You should be able to start and stop an image on your own determination.

Inability to attain any one of the following is a clear sign that self-
desensitization should be discontinued and another intervention technique
chosen. You must be able to: (1) produce a vivid image, (2) start the

image on your own determination, (3) stop the image on your own determination.

During the relaxation training, you will have learned what it feels like to be very comfortably relaxed. When you can feel that same way while imagining any item, you are ready to go on to the next (Kahn and Sandler, 1966).

Be sure to understand that *this is not an exercise in courage.* You are not supposed to bravely experience anxiety while imagining an item. Rather, it is the opposite. Be sure not to leave an item until you are completely desensitized to it. You should feel totally relaxed, imagining it in all its detail while remaining completely at ease. *Once you have attained desensitization for a particular item, repeat that item once more before moving up to the next item.*

The number of sessions you will require depends on several factors. When working on relatively easy situations, you may be able to complete two or three in a single session. Harder items may require several sessions for each one (Kahn and Sandler, 1966).

The desensitization sessions.   Set aside fifteen to thirty minutes for each session. First, relax completely. When you are relaxed, begin with item 1 or, in a later session, with an item that you have already successfully completed. Allow about ten seconds per item. If you can repeat the first item three times while remaining relaxed, you are ready to start a new one. Between each ten seconds of imagining an item, spend thirty seconds or more working on just being relaxed. Then, begin a new item. Work on it for ten seconds, then relax for thirty or so, then repeat it, and so on. Repeat every item at least two times (Paul, 1966).

If problems develop

It is critically important to note that if the image fades or will not become clear or if your anxiety begins to increase or your relaxation to decrease, then you should immediately stop work on that item for that particular ten-second period and relax yourself comfortably.

When one of those things happens, you should concentrate on relaxing for one minute or longer, until you are as deeply relaxed as you were before. Then repeat the item, but for only three to five seconds. If you still become anxious or if your relaxation or the image fades, drop back to the previous item that you have already successfully completed.

If you can successfully manage that previous item, then move back to the item that gave you trouble. Use only a five-second exposure. If that works, try ten seconds; then try twenty seconds. If you can remain relaxed with that item at a twenty-second exposure, move to the next item on the hierarchy (Paul, 1966).

If these procedures for dealing with a difficult item will not work, you will want to create new items for your hierarchy. Kahn and Sandler (1966) suggest a way of inventing intermediate steps. First determine what aspect of the troublesome item makes it difficult; then think of ways to make that aspect less difficult. For example, suppose a person were desensitizing himself for test anxiety, and his item called for imagining a mid-term test for which he was not well prepared. He could imagine variations in how well prepared he was, going from very well prepared to moderately prepared to poorly prepared. If this difficulty arises with a very early item, you should invent easier situations to start with. Always begin no higher than the situation that causes the first bit of nervousness. When you have completed the entire sequence, repeat the hierarchy one last time to make sure that you have desensitized everything.

Summary

To accomplish systematic self-desensitization, you must (1) make out a hierarchy in which the items are arranged according to how frightening they are; (2) practice the tension-release method of deep muscle relaxation until you can attain deep relaxation; (3) proceed step-wise through the hierarchy, beginning with the least frightening items and systematically replacing tension with relaxation as your response to an imagined presentation of each situation.

General techniques for *in vivo* and systematic desensitization

Combining self-desensitization with *in vivo* procedures

Desensitization and *in vivo* techniques can be combined. A girl whose problem was acute test anxiety worked out an ingenious plan. She was worried that desensitizing the fear through imagination might produce too great a lag between her imagined sessions and the nerve-wracking realities of taking tests. Her solution was to work out a desensitization series but to combine this with real-life relaxation in testing situations. In addition to her self-desensitization sessions, she arranged to accompany friends to *their* examinations. She would sit quietly somewhere in the testing room, practicing her relaxation in the presence of all the actual testing-situation stimuli.

Systematic self-desensitization can be used to help yourself in situations in which you cannot easily arrange the environment so that you can use an *in vivo* desensitization procedure. For example, a person who has progressed several steps up an *in vivo* ladder in learning to converse with strangers cannot easily control exactly how many minutes he talks with some person. He might use systematic desensitization to cover certain situations in his imagination, so that when they occurred in real life, he would be better prepared for them. You should combine these techniques as it seems appropriate.

Adding reinforcement

Self-desensitization can also be combined with reinforcement procedures.

Case #22 was a young man suffering from a fear of crowds. He was rarely bothered by social situations unless they involved some crowding; then he began to feel "trapped." He was moving fairly well through his desensitization hierarchy but found it difficult to keep up the sessions once he had gained some relief from the problems he encountered in routine day-to-day life. He reasoned, though, that someday he would want to go to a movie or a ballgame, or he might accidentally find himself in a tight, crowded situation. He worked out a positive-reinforcement schedule, in which he earned the privilege of watching the 10:00 P.M. news on TV only if he had completed one further desensitization session that day.

Establishing equal intervals in your shaping ladder

A hierarchy is a kind of shaping ladder, whether you move up it *in vivo* or in your imagination. In order to be sure that your progress up the hierarchy will be relatively smooth, it is important to have the increases between steps approximately equal. How can you accomplish this?

Wolpe and Lazarus (1966) recommend using a numerical rating scale. This scale measures your "subjective units of discomfort"; abbreviated, it is called the *suds* scale. By devising a *suds* scale for your personal reaction to the items in your hierarchy, you can get an idea of the degree to which each item elicits your feelings of discomfort, and you can then use the scaled ratings to ensure fairly equal intervals between items.

Once you have made an initial hierarchy, you can rate each item separately with the *suds* technique. Here is the procedure. A score of zero means that the particular item would—if you were confronted with that stimulus in real life—produce no emotional reaction whatever. A score of one hundred, on the other hand, means that the item would produce total panic, falling apart, freezing. The partial *suds* rating for a hierarchy of a man with a severe fear of snakes follows:

Suds	Item	
2	1	the letter *S*
10	2	black-and-white photo of snake
19	3	seeing a live snake in a zoo cage
. . .	. . .	
65	18	seeing a loose snake at a distance
90	19	snake looking at me from 3 feet or less
95	20	snake touching my skin

Notice the advantages of making this rating. The man is able to see that going from item 18 to 19 in his hierarchy is likely to be exceedingly difficult. In fact, it represents more of a jump than the first three steps combined. He can now realize, before he gets to item 19 and runs into great difficulty, that he should introduce intermediate steps between 18 and 19. A rule of thumb might be that no item should advance more than five to ten *suds* points beyond the previous item.

Record keeping

The *suds* scale, besides helping you spot future points of likely trouble, has a second advantage: it can give you a good indication of just how much progress you are making. As in any other self-modification technique, it is important to keep records, to note your progress, and to look for the sources of your troubles. If you had a desensitization hierarchy composed of twenty items and had completed ten of them, you might think that you were 50% finished. But suppose that there were twenty-five *suds* points between items 10 and 11. In fact, you would not be halfway to completion. By doing a *suds*-scale analysis of your hierarchy before you started your desensitization, you would have arranged your items in approximately equal steps so that, as you progressed upward in the hierarchy, you could be sure that your progress was not deceptive.

The *suds* scale is helpful in another way. Often people find that establishing the ratings is very difficult; one item might be rated sixty *suds,* while another—which intuitively seems to belong lower—is rated at sixty-five *suds*. This is not unusual and ordinarily indicates that you are trying to force several fears into a single hierarchy. "Seeing a live snake in a zoo cage," for example, may be part of a snake phobia but also part of a "being trapped" fear, of which the individual is only dimly aware. Such cross issues may be revealed by seeming contradictions or confusions in the *suds* ratings.

If you are unable to establish smooth, steadily progressive, and noncontradictory *suds* ratings, you should discontinue your efforts at self-desensitization. This is probably a sign of multiple, interwoven categories, a condition that is best managed by desensitization by a professional.

One last topic remains in the discussion of record keeping for the modification of emotional disorders. Even *suds* represents only a subjective rating and is not a measure of real behavior. While a *suds* scale is extremely useful, it cannot entirely replace directly observing and recording your own behaviors. So when you are moving your improvement efforts into the real world, after or during desensitization, you should record appropriate behavior frequencies just as you would in any other program of self-modification.

Clinical desensitization

As we have pointed out earlier, the clinical practice of systematic desensitization by competent professionals can be a very helpful procedure, even when self-desensitization fails. Clinical desensitization is a pleasant and effective technique for specific emotional discomforts, and it can be of benefit even in rather mild cases. Many readers may attempt self-desensitization, and some may not succeed. Failure at self-desensitization should not deter one from seeking clinical treatment.

There are several signs that indicate that professional assistance should be sought. These are:

1. Uncomfortable anxiety during the creation of the hierarchies

2. Overlapping hierarchies, indicated by contradictory or paradoxical *suds* ratings of the items

3. Inability to produce vivid imagery

4. Inability to control the beginning or ending of an image

5. The inability to desensitize high enough up on the hierarchy to meet your goals.

This last inability could result, of course, from failure to master any of the steps: achieving relaxation, constructing hierarchies, and so on.

In Chapter Thirteen, we will return to the general issue of seeking professional help in self-modification. In the meantime, from your read-

ing of Chapters Eight, Nine, and Ten, you should be prepared to select
and implement your own self-modification program.

Your own self-modification project: Step ten

For Chapter Ten:

1. Select one of your problem behaviors for which there is an emotional component.

2. Devise an *in vivo* desensitization plan to recondition the eliciting stimuli. Include a detailed hierarchy of stages. Include a plan for reinforcement, if appropriate.

3. For the same emotional reaction, prepare a plan for systematic self-desensitization. Build the item hierarchy. Establish *suds* ratings.

4. Practice deep relaxation long enough to experience the entire procedure.

5. Write a paragraph, stating whether *in vivo* or systematic self-desensitization is the preferred procedure for your particular problem.

For Chapters Eight, Nine, and Ten:

1. You are now prepared to establish an actual, detailed intervention plan for self-modification. Reconsider the plans written separately for Chapters Eight, Nine, and Ten. You may wish to combine elements of each; you may wish to implement an entirely new plan. Choose the one best suited to your problem, whether it is a very simple plan or a more complicated one. Write one or more paragraphs justifying your contract.

2. *Begin this plan.*

Chapter Eleven
**Is It Working?
Analyzing the Data**

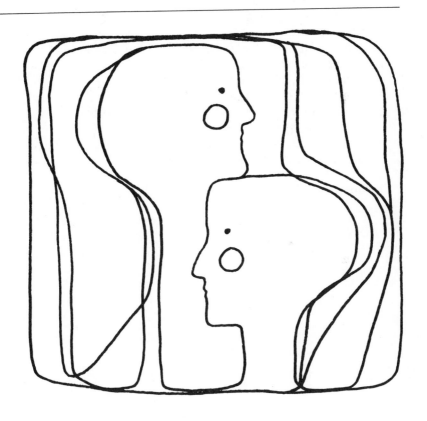

1. Counting the target behavior after intervention has begun. The best way to examine the data is to make a graph.
2. Examples of graphs that show that the plan is working and graphs that show that it is not working.
3. Changing definition of the target problem.
   a. Deciding whether to get new baseline data.
   b. Continuing with the old category while getting baseline data on the new behavior.
   c. Using an incompatible behavior while continuing to count the undesired target behavior.
4. Some of the most common reasons for difficulty in self-modification.

Are you achieving self-modification? This seems to be a simple question, to which a rapid "yes" or "no" could be given. Sometimes you can tell clearly and continuously. The student who never smokes again or the man who suddenly has a girl friend for the first time in his life or the overweight friend who quickly drops ten pounds—these self-modifiers know that they are succeeding, and they do not need elaborate techniques for assessing their progress. They know because there is a clear and rapid change in their situation from the baseline period to the intervention period. They measured the frequency of the target behavior *before* intervention and also *during* intervention. Differences in frequency indicated that some change had occurred.

More often, though, progress is gradual rather than dramatic. As you shape your responses, as you reach plateaus and go beyond them, and as you encounter unusual periods in your life, your behaviors gradually change. Often you do not clearly remember from one week to the next exactly how you felt or how often you actually did the things you wanted. In fact, most people seriously misjudge their progress, probably because they quickly adapt emotionally to current performance levels. We change our goals as we change our abilities.

A frequent misjudgment is that one is making *less* progress than is actually achieved. Readers who do not rely on their frequency recordings are often tempted to discontinue an intervention program even though it is succeeding. Of course, the reverse may happen, and an ineffective plan may be needlessly continued.

It is crucial that you continue to record behavior frequencies during intervention, because that provides the evidence you need in order to know if the plan is having the desired effect.

The best way to examine your data is to put them onto a graph. (Making a graph was explained in Chapter Six.) Each day or week you will have gathered the observations, perhaps on 3 x 5 cards or with some other easy system. At the end of a few weeks, you will have a stack of these pieces of information. By putting them all together on one graph, you can note progress or the lack of it.

Examining the graph

Case #23 was a young man who wanted to increase how much he talked in his classes. In his report, he wrote that he found it difficult to speak up in public. He was afraid that others would think his comments were silly or not worthwhile. This fear was particularly prevalent in very large classes where he felt that his speech had to be good to justify taking the time of so many people. His baseline was zero. He decided to begin by practicing in small classes and then, if that worked, to try it in large classes. He followed a four-step shaping schedule to change his behavior in class: first, just saying something to one class member; second, talking about something related to the group effort with one of the group members; third, addressing the whole group with a statement; fourth, "constant participation." He used a high-probability behavior as a reinforcer: "My reinforcer was playing in my band. This is a very powerful reinforcer for me in two ways: I really enjoy playing my guitar and, if I didn't show up for a gig, five other guys would wring my neck."

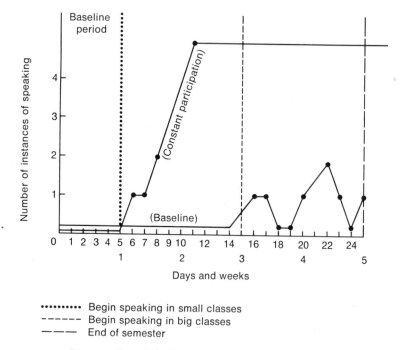

Figure 1. Case #23: Frequencies for speaking in class

Figure 1 is a graph of his data. Notice that in making his graph he counted only school days, so each week has five days in it. This is sensible, because he only had opportunities to practice his new behavior during the school week. Since he always had his notebook with him when he went to class, it was easy for him to make a simple check on a piece of paper each time he spoke up in a class.

Figure 1 shows a very rapid improvement in his speaking in small classes. Beginning on the first day of his intervention plan, he began to talk and within four days was engaging in what he considered to be constant participation. These are unusually good data. Most people progress at a slower rate, as this man did when he went into the second stage of his plan, speaking in large classes. You can see from the graph that he did make some progress but that his improvements were interspersed with days of no talking. This is the kind of situation in which a graph is helpful, for it will show that you are making *some* progress.

The following is an example of a case that did not make progress.

Case #24 was a young woman who was having an affair with a married man. He said he was happily married and was only interested in her as a source of sexual diversion—a break in his married routine. She was desperately in love with him. "I can live with that," she said.

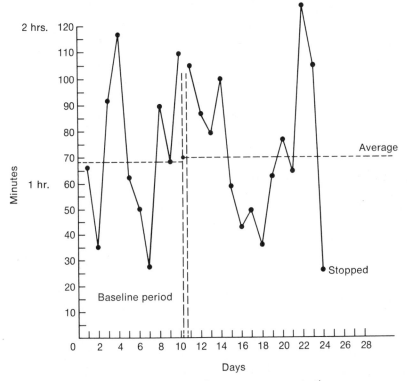

Figure 2. Case #24: Total daily time spent concentrating on activities, but *not* on lover.

"I know he will never leave his wife for me. But I don't see him very much, and I've gotten to the point where I spend all day thinking about him. My problem behavior is that I can't concentrate on anything else. It's becoming an obsession. I've got to stop it."

She decided to use her thoughts about him as a reinforcer. First, she would spend a few minutes concentrating on something she had to do or wanted to do, such as making a shopping list, reading a magazine article, or studying. She would then reinforce herself for this concentration by engaging in an orgy of thinking about her lover. She began keeping a record of the amount of time she concentrated on activities but *not* on him.

Figure 2 depicts the data that she brought to show us. The average daily increase of only three minutes is not a significant one. There are several problems with the data in Figure 2. The baseline data are very unstable, which makes comparison with the intervention period difficult. Furthermore, her record is probably very unreliable, because the category, "concentrating on activities," is too vague. She said that she had some difficulty in deciding whether to count a particular activity. Worse yet, "concentrating on activities" is an event that could occur in any number of different places—at the movies, at school, at the store, talking with friends, and so on—but she had not taken steps to be sure that she was always prepared to make a count when she needed to.

Her plan was really not effective. She had vaguely intended to use thinking about her lover as a reinforcer for concentrating on activities, but she did not ever make this contingency systematic. These problems make any judgment of progress difficult if not impossible.

Our advice to her was that further intervention could proceed only if she (1) refined the category so that it was not vague; (2) developed a new baseline; (3) constructed detailed reinforcement procedures, using a strong, manipulatable reinforcer. We also suggested that she was attacking the wrong problem and recommended that she consider not seeing the man while shaping other social activities which would enable her to meet men more likely to bring her happiness.

Public record keeping

Some people have used keeping graphs as an intervention technique. The idea is to keep your records in a relatively public place so that other people can see whether you are making progress or not. You may need some courage to use this technique. An older man, who had several employees, wanted to lose weight. He decided to keep a list of all the food he ate displayed in a prominent place in his store so that his employees would be able to see just exactly what he had eaten the day before. Others have simply required themselves to report to someone else, perhaps a small group, about their progress. It is a two-pronged approach, in which you gain positive social reinforcement if you are succeeding but social punishment if you begin to slip.

The problem of category shift

During the course of intervention, a *category* may shift, not in the behavior frequencies but in the definition of the category itself. Case #24 experienced a drift in her category, "concentrating on activities," almost every day. In her case, the drift resulted from a vague original definition.

Sometimes the category shift occurs in a valuable way. It represents a new level of progress, a new understanding. This kind of shift occurs when a new category is required to describe new goals.

Case #25 was a pretty but shy young woman. She felt that her problem was that she was too withdrawn, especially in groups. She reasoned that she would appear less withdrawn and would gain reinforcements from others if she could increase how much she smiled at them. Her original task, Plan 1, was to increase smiling, particularly at people she did not know well. She counted her smiling behavior by simply making a note on a card each time she smiled at someone she did not know well. After she had established a baseline, she worked out a plan in which she earned tokens, to be applied later to the purchase of elegant clothes, by smiling at people. She persuaded her roommates to help administer the token system.

Figure 3 presents part of her data. There are several interesting things to notice. First, she seemed to gain an intervention effect in the last part of the baseline period; at least, her graph shows an increased frequency that really didn't change much after she moved into the intervention period of Plan 1. Of course, she was quite pleased; for whatever the reason, she apparently increased her smiling at strangers. Her systematic reinforcement with the token system was maintaining her smiling at a new, higher rate.

Around day 11 or 12, she began to rethink the definition of her problem. "I started to realize," she later wrote in her report, "that although I was smiling more at people, I still seemed to be withdrawn because I was not looking at them. I was smiling but looking down at the ground. Most people feel that looking into someone's eyes is a good sign of interest, so I decided that just smiling at them wasn't enough: I had to smile, and *I had to make eye contact.*" What she has done is to

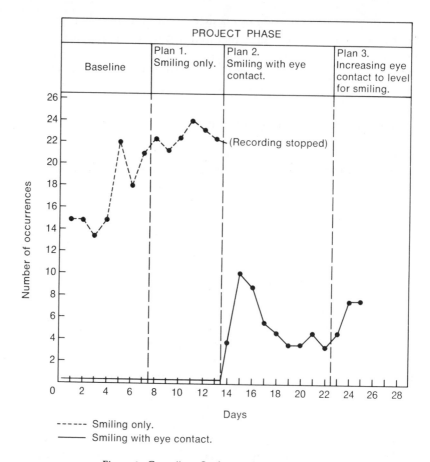

Figure 3. Case #25: Smiling and eye contact.

change her definition of the category, to broaden it. She counted eye contacts that lasted three seconds or more. Beginning on day 14, she started a second part of her plan, in which she gained her tokens for smiling plus three seconds of eye contact. This reflects her new understanding of the behaviors that are necessary for appearing interested rather than withdrawn when encountering people.

Her last step, Plan 3, was to begin shaping eye contact, so that it would occur as often as smiling alone had occurred.

She could have avoided this shift, of course, by starting out with a definition of her target problem that included both smiling and eye contact. This did not occur because, before she began the intervention plan, she had not realized how important eye contact is in appearing socially attractive. After she had increased her smiling, she knew that she needed to add eye contact.

As you continue with an intervention plan, your definition of some category of target behavior may change, as it did in Case #25. This is often desirable, for it indicates that you are learning more about your behavior and that you can make more subtle discriminations between various kinds of behavior. Don't stick blindly to your original category. But if you do change its definition, be sure that you are fully aware of the change, for you will want the increased sophistication to show in your data.

Category change and the new baseline

When changing categories in mid-plan, it is possible to establish the new baseline merely by withholding reinforcement for a time until you record the new category at a stable rate. For changes that are large and abrupt, establishing a new baseline is advisable; it is like beginning a new plan. For Case #25, self-improvement was so pleasing to her that she chose not to get a new baseline. Besides, she was fairly certain that her baseline for eye contact was zero.

Whenever you change the definition of a category, you must decide whether or not you need a new baseline period. Should you withhold reinforcement long enough to get a new baseline? Sometimes the necessary shift in the category will seem small, and you will feel that it is not worth giving up your intervention plan long enough to get the baseline.

If your category shift is so drastic that it really constitutes a new plan, you should definitely obtain new baseline data. For example, you might change your target behavior from "smiling at people" to "going to public places." For any large or abrupt change, you should have a new baseline.

Sometimes your change will be that you are *adding* something to an ongoing plan, as did the woman who added eye contact to her smiling. If she had not been sure that her baseline for eye contact was zero, she actually should have gathered some baseline data so that she could judge her progress during intervention. She could simply have continued reinforcing smiles for a few days while counting how often she also made eye contact. *You can get a baseline by simply continuing to reinforce the first target behavior for a few days while counting how often you perform the new target behavior, which will be added.* For example, you might have started out with "dieting" as your target and, after two weeks, decided to add "exercising" to your plan. In that case, you could continue to reinforce dieting for a few days while you get a baseline on exercising.

Lack of baseline for incompatible responses

If your initial problem was an undesired behavior, you probably began by getting baseline data on that behavior. Later, you might have selected an incompatible response to increase at the expense of the undesired behavior. You will find that while you may have a very good baseline for the undesired target behavior, you do not have a good baseline for the incompatible one. Furthermore, as a plan develops, the incompatible category may change as you develop new understanding and skill. Should new baseline data be recorded?

If the new, incompatible behavior is one that you intend to continue permanently, then you will want to get a separate baseline for it—for example, deciding to increase reading "good" books as a behavior incompatible with "wasting your time." You can use the same strategies that you would employ for any shift in categories.

If you do not intend to continue the incompatible behavior—for example, slapping your hand instead of cracking your knuckles—then it would not be necessary to get a separate count of the incompatible behavior as long as you are keeping a good record of the undesired target. Any number of shifts could be made in the incompatible behavior without affecting the category to be recorded. However, be sure to indicate on the graph each shift in the intervention strategy.

Common reasons for difficulties in self-modification plans

Throughout the book we have mentioned common problems that can occur, and we have suggested solutions. Here we want to remind you of potential sources of problems.

1. Faulty record keeping that results in unreliable data is a common source of trouble.
2. Inadequately defined behaviors-in-situations and overly vague categories of behaviors, emotions, or situations frequently give trouble.
3. Failure to make the reinforcer actually contingent upon the target behavior is a common cause of problems. Many failures are due to relying on the "instrinsic" reinforcing aspects of the target behavior. A related problem is to rely solely on the intervention effect of observing your own behavior.
4. Reinforcement delayed too long is a common problem.
5. Lack of proper shaping is another common source of difficulty.

There are, as well, many specific kinds of problems that you may encounter, which have been dealt with in the preceding chapters.

Summary

Inspection of the graphs will lead to decision about your plans. The change in frequency from baseline may be clear enough to warrant continuing the plan unchanged, as illustrated in Figure 1. Figure 2 illustrates the opposite extreme: data that suggest the necessity for carefully reworking a plan. This will involve rethinking each of its aspects: clarity of categories, accurate observation, adequacy of reinforcement. Figure 3 illustrates another outcome: changing the plan by shifting its goals. The fourth outcome, a decision to terminate the plan because it has been successful enough, is reserved for the next chapter.

Your own self-modification project: Step eleven

Make a graph of your data. Remember, the passing *time* is put on the bottom, horizontal axis, and the *number of occurrences* of the target behavior is put on the vertical axis. You should be able to look at your graph and tell clearly whether or not you are effecting changes in your target behavior.

Chapter Twelve
Termination

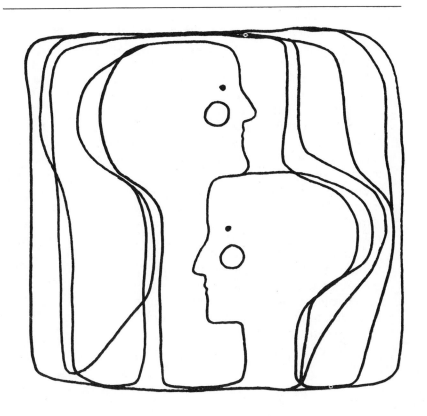

1. The decision to terminate an intervention plan is a value decision, which reflects satisfaction with the present level of performance.
   a. Many people evolve new values while they carry out an intervention plan.
   b. Formal termination is not the rule. More often, people just stop.
2. When considering termination, take steps to be sure that any newly learned behaviors will continue after ceasing self-reinforcement.
   a. Search for opportunities to practice and be reinforced for the new skills in the natural environment.
   b. Test and program for stimulus generalization.
   c. Build in resistance to extinction by shifting to an intermittent reinforcement schedule.
   d. Practice the new behavior sufficiently.
3. Some projects are almost never ending. Be prepared to reinstitute an intervention plan if some undesired behavior returns.

During the whole course of our lives, all of us constantly examine our goals and often revise them. It is a rare student who as a senior wants exactly the same things that he wanted at freshman registration. College itself is designed to foster such evaluation, since it constantly exposes one to new ideas and opportunities. At other times of life, when one is in a steadier groove, reevaluation is less likely simply because new situations, with changing feelings and changing behaviors, occur less often.

Evolving goals

The person who consciously engages in a program of self-change can expect that he is also in for a reexamination of his goals. This is because he will see new possibilities in his own behavior and situations. You do not simply bring your behavior up to some prespecified criterion and then continue contentedly into the sunset. Goals, too, are in a dynamic interplay with behaviors and environments.

Actually, ultimate goals (even in a precise self-modification contract) are not only unclear—they may even be unknown. All you can know for sure is that you want to take a step in some general direction. Of course, a particular goal is sometimes clear from the beginning—to stop smoking, to weigh less, to stop biting nails. More often, though, goals must be revised en route, because the information needed for the later decisions does not come until some change has already been achieved.

This issue arises most often when you have chosen a target behavior because it will lead to some greater goal. For example, studying is a behavior that most students value because it may lead to something else —mastery of the subject matter. In a sense, studying is not the goal at all; it is merely the route to the goal, one behavior selected for strengthening in the hope that it will thereby increase knowledge and understanding of the material.

But it may not. We have seen students greatly increase their study time, through self-reinforcement, but achieve only a minor increase in knowledge. Ordinarily, this problem is due to some failure in studying procedure—not making notes or writing summaries but only reading the material over and over. When the target behavior is redefined as "writing accurate chapter summaries," for example, such a student may find that he can use even fewer hours per week and nevertheless move closer to his real goal—subject mastery. Thus, your target behaviors may change as you observe their relationship to your ultimate goals. In that way, the achievement of some arbitrary criterion—for example, studying twelve hours a week—may have very little to do with the decision to terminate or not. That decision will be made according to whether or not the studying is having the desired effect.

Even when you have correctly chosen the target behavior, and it is leading to the ultimate goal, the quantity of performance that is desirable may not be clear until after you have experienced the new behavior.

Recall the young woman in the last chapter who wanted to respond more attractively when meeting people. At the beginning of her self-modification plan, she had little idea of what her upper goal should be: she didn't know what would later seem to her to be a reasonable amount of smiling and eye contact. Only after she had learned this new behavior could she decide how often she would want to do it.

Sometimes, then, you will not know your ultimate goal until you reach it. Then you will realize that you have gone as far as you want. This is a normal process.

Imagine two students, both of whom start out to increase the amount of time they study each day. At the beginning, each is studying very little, an average of half an hour per week. Each succeeds in increasing his study time to five hours per week, and both find their ultimate goals of mastery coming closer. At this point, student A may conclude "Well, that's my upper limit. I could keep on shaping myself up to higher levels, but I don't really want to. That is a good balance with other activities I value, and improving my grades further is not worth sacrificing my other interests."

Student B, on the other hand, might well decide to continue further. At five hours, he might say to himself "Well, that's pretty good. But I would like to go higher, maybe up to eight hours per week. I'm still idle a lot, and the satisfactions from learning are greater than I thought they would be."

Both of these decisions are reasonable. But neither of them could have been made until each person had experienced his new level of attainment.

In this sense, *a decision to terminate an intervention plan is a value decision.* Your values shift and evolve as you interact with your environments. These value changes are changes in attitudes and emotions. This is a part of self-modification, because changes in attitudes are a component of new reinforcement contingencies. The girl who desensitized herself to birds should *expect* that she will have a different attitude toward the library, where the steps are crowded with pigeons.

Furthermore, as you change yourself, you often change your environment. Changing your social behavior, for example, will change the reactions of other people to you, for your behavior is a stimulus for their behavior and, as you change, you change the stimulus. A student who increases her interactions with professors will find that they begin to react differently to her. This is, after all, *the major point of self-modification: to change the reaction of the natural environment to your behaviors so that you receive a more positive pattern of reinforcement for the behaviors that you value.* These changes in environmental responses can rarely be programmed perfectly, because the behavior of other people is being influenced by other sources too. Thus, you must always expect to find your goals shifting as a changing environment teaches you new alternatives.

In summary, your goals do, and should, change as a part of self-modification. Therefore, it is often unrealistic to decide far in advance on a termination point.

Formal termination

Nevertheless, you may reach a point when your data match your goals. You decide that you still do not like cockroaches, but you are well enough desensitized that you no longer fear going into strange houses. When your graphed data are at the level where you currently place your goal, you could certainly say that you are finished—at least with this, at least for now. This seems like such an obvious point that it really needs no discussion. *In fact, the interesting point about formal termination is that it is so rare.*

Most successful intervention plans are not officially ended on a particular day. They seem to die a natural, though happy, death because the desired behavior continues without the use of formal self-reinforcement.

In talking with students some months after they have completed the course, we often ask about their modification programs. A quite common reaction is the embarrassed confession that they really aren't keeping data any longer, and they're not really using self-reinforcement either. But the problem? Oh no, it's not really of much concern anymore

—the studying or the dating or getting up late in the morning isn't really a hassle now; in fact, they haven't thought about that for a long time.

From our point of view, this is an excellent "termination" outcome. We do not advocate formal self-modification as a life-style. Rather, we urge the contrary: we see formal reinforcement contracts as a temporary expedient, a device to use when you are trapped in a behavioral-environmental bind that requires particular planning to break. Therefore, the fact that self-controlled reinforcement is no longer necessary means that you have really succeeded—succeeded in achieving an adjustment so that you and the environment are mutually supporting a pattern that you endorse.

This achievement of adjustment is also a dynamic thing, made up of modifying behaviors, evolving goals, and shifting environmental responses. The "petering out" of a self-modification program can be a desirable outcome of this gradual dynamic adjustment. In short, formal self-modification becomes less and less necessary, so you gradually do it less and less. When it is unnecessary, you have reached an adjustment of the behavior to its environmental situation.

Such an outcome is desirable. In fact, a good intervention program can even foster its development. *The best self-modification program will include plans for its own gradual obsolescence.* This can be done by planning for naturally occurring reinforcement to supplant your contrived reinforcement. You can gradually "fade out" the programmed or special supports for your behaviors.

Evolving natural contingencies

The contingent relationship between the behavior and the reinforcements gained for it keeps behavior going in the natural environment. *It will be most possible to stop your self-modification plan while keeping the target behavior at the level it has gained under the impact of the self-modification by arranging ongoing environmental contingencies to reinforce the newly developed behavior.*

Suppose you have successfully increased your study time and improved your study habits after a lifetime of being a bad student. Where in the natural environment can studying be reinforced? Not in a relatively advanced course that has several prerequisites, because that course will draw upon the background that you may not have. There will be other courses, however, that do not draw upon such a background; they let you start from the beginning. In this second kind of course you are much more likely to be reinforced for new, good study habits than you would be in the first.

The point is this: you should plan for natural-environmental situations that will reinforce your new competence *without simultaneously punishing you for skills you still lack.*

In a way, this is a continuation of shaping procedures. But a good intervention plan will move the source of reinforcement gradually away from tokens and contracts into real-life situations.

Here is an example of this process. A young man, early in the semester, was assigned in one of his courses to a small-group team project. The team of six met regularly and was required to complete a major project together. This man had always felt awkward in small peer groups, and he alternated between strained silence and sarcastic remarks. He took this opportunity to improve himself by reinforcing the frequency of friendly or task-related statements in the group. His reinforcement was time spent surfing, the amount depending on the frequencies of the target behavior achieved each week. He greatly improved his performance and his comfort. Because he was still not completely satisfied when the course was over, he regretted the end of the semester. He wanted another situation in which to practice but felt that the reinforcement of surfing was no longer necessary. From among several possibilities, he chose to start attending evening meetings of the Poetry Club. This was a good choice because he was very interested in writing poetry and he had much to say on the subject. Furthermore, any lapses into his more aggressive behavior would not be punished too severely, since criticism of the members' poems was a part of the club function. In short, this group was one into which he could bring his newly modified abilities and from which he could expect enjoyment and relative lack of punishment. These natural reinforcements would solidify and increase the kind of participation he valued.

New behaviors, if they are really adjustive, should find natural support, natural reinforcements. In early stages of termination, though, it is often helpful to remind yourself of the chain of events that bolsters your behavior. A woman who had succeeded in losing many pounds through self-reinforcement for reduced eating was delighted to discover that other people found her more attractive too. She was having many more dates. She stopped the reinforcement but posted a sign on the refrigerator door: "Dieting keeps the telephone ringing!"

When your new target behavior has become well established through your self-intervention plan, you will want to search for opportunities to practice the new behavior, and gain the reinforcements that the world has to offer for that behavior. *You should make a list of the kinds of situations in which you are likely to be able to perform the behavior and be reinforced for it.* Performing the behavior in each of these situations will allow you to move toward natural reinforcement and simultaneously increase generalization.

The girl who had set out to increase her smiling with eye contact when she met strangers initially required herself to perform this behavior only to people who wore sunglasses. That way, she could look into their sunglasses but wouldn't know whether they were looking back or not. After she had established this behavior firmly, she began to make eye contact with people who did not wear sunglasses. Over a period of weeks, she was able to learn this new behavior as well.

She realized that the reaction of other people to her new skill would matter to her, something that had already been demonstrated. Therefore, it was important that she be reinforced and not punished for the behavior. So she made a list of the kinds of people who would probably reinforce her for smiling. At the top were people who seemed very friendly. At the bottom were people she thought were "stuck-up" or so shy themselves that they wouldn't respond or too busy to smile back.

Programming for stimulus generalization

In Chapter Nine, we discussed the strategy of programming for stimulus generalization. After a behavior has been solidified in relation to one antecedent condition, you can make the behavior even more frequent by gradually increasing the range of situations in which you are reinforced for it.

As you consider termination, you should test for generalization. This rule applies, of course, only when your target behavior is one that you wish to perform in a variety of situations. This is often the case with social behaviors—listening, talking, smiling, making eye contact, asserting, encouraging, and so on. It is also the case with any behavior that is not situation bound: making-the-bed behaviors should only occur in the one situation of an unmade bed, for example. But you may wish to be able to study or smile in more than one room or to more than one person or on more than one street.

As you begin to consider termination, then, observe yourself to see if you perform your new behaviors in a wide variety of appropriate situations. Count these frequencies, and compare their rates with those in the original situation. If you see that your newly achieved improvement is situation-specific, then you should add a generalization phase to your program before terminating. The techniques for this have been discussed on pages 163–164.

Thinning: Building in resistance to extinction

In the unprogrammed environment, you do not get reinforcement every time you perform some behavior. In your self-modification plans, conversely, you may have been doing just that in order to produce the fastest change. Once it is time to start thinking about transfer to naturally occurring reinforcers, it is necessary to take steps to ensure that your newly gained behaviors are not lost due to extinction. Taking such steps is necessary because a behavior that has been reinforced continuously is one most likely to extinguish in the natural environment, where reinforcements do not occur every time.

The best way to ensure that this extinction does not happen is to place your target behavior on an intermittent reinforcement schedule. Don't stop your self-modification plan abruptly. Once you have established an acceptable upper level for your target behavior, you can cut down the ratio of its reinforcement.

A wife had been working to increase the number of times she communicated really warm and affectionate feelings to her husband. He had complained that she seemed cold and disinterested. She knew that this was a reflection of her overt behavior but not of her feelings. She did achieve a sharp increase by using a token system.

She was reinforcing herself every time that she performed the desired behavior. She gave herself a point, a token, which, at a more convenient time could be turned in for selections from a menu of very desirable foods. A piece of cake, for example, cost one token, a pizza cost two, a beer cost one, a glass of champagne, four.

However, she reached a desirable upper limit. Even her husband would soon tire of a constant stream of "I love you. I love you! You are wonderful."

At this point, instead of stopping her reinforcement system straight away, she *thinned* the reinforcement schedule. She was preparing for the fact that her husband did not reinforce her new behavior every time: sometimes he was preoccupied or in the wrong mood.

She began to thin (moving to an intermittent schedule of reinforcement) in the most simple way: by not getting a token every time. She cut down so that she got tokens only 75% of the time. She then reduced further—to every other time, 50%; then only 25%, and so on. She did not do this too rapidly, for a slow thinning process guards against extinction. Using this procedure, it would take an increasingly large number of statements to gain one token.

In thinning, you must be careful to continue to count the frequency of the target behavior. There is some danger that it will decline. You might be able to stand some drop from your upper goal, but you will want to know if there has been a drop and how much. *Alternating between periods of thinning and 100% reinforcement can keep your frequency at an acceptably high level,* if the natural contingencies are slow to evolve.

Practice

Evolving natural contingencies, programming for generalization, and thinning are designed to increase the chances of holding your gains after termination. Another such strategy is to ensure that adequate *practice* has occurred during intervention. In general, behaviors are made more probable by providing some optimum number of trials on a reinforcement schedule. At some point, a behavior will "take hold." This take-hold point is a complicated function of schedules of reinforcement and antecedents, but it also has something to do with the number of times the behavior has occurred. *Practice is important.*

Think about learning to drive a car. When you first begin, you have to concentrate fully on every aspect of your driving behavior. You dare not take your mind off it for a second. After several years' driving experience, on the other hand, you can drive long distances without this concentrated attention.

This need for practice implies that you will not want to terminate just as soon as you reach your goal. Instead, it would be wise to continue the plan for a time—a week or two or perhaps more, depending on the frequency of your opportunities to practice. We can give no rule for the precise number of times required; this depends on every other aspect of the intervention plan. But a trial at thinning is a good test of the degree to which you can maintain behavior after termination. *If, as soon as you begin to thin*—dropping perhaps to 75% reinforcement instead of 100% *—the frequency of your target behavior drops alarmingly, it means that you have not practiced it enough.* In this case, you should return to the 100% reinforcement schedule and gain more practice.

The risks involved in stopping too soon

There does not seem to be much of a risk that you will continue the plan too long. The only risk is that you will become bored or just tired of the thing. This is no great problem; it probably means that you were past the time when you could have stopped. On the other hand, there is a risk in stopping too soon. You may lose your gains.

If you have gradually been increasing some desired behavior and stop too soon, you will find that obvious. You will fall below the termination level. *For this reason, we recommend continuing frequency counts after termination of self-reinforcement until the rate has stabilized.* A significant decrease would mean that you should reinstitute a reinforcement program. It's best to be conservative in the matter of termination: whenever you are in doubt about whether to continue the plan, continue it but thin it. The worst thing that can happen is that you'll get a bit bored.

Never-ending projects

Some problems may require a lifelong contract. Consummatory responses, which we have mentioned several times before, are the most likely candidates. Once you are a heavy smoker, you will have to maintain lifelong vigilance to stay off cigarettes, and you may have to reinstate active self-modification plans several times if you slip back into smoking. The same applies to the other consummatory problems. It is best to reinstate a self-modification plan as soon as the old problem reappears. If you once smoked forty cigarettes per day and succeeded in quitting, only to find yourself back at three cigarettes per day five months later, institute a new plan immediately. Don't wait until you are back up to forty. It's much better to quit at three. The same idea applies to other consummatory behaviors and any behavior that has produced a physiological addiction. It may be that some day the permanent treatment for these problems will be invented. Today, that universal permanent solution does not exist (Lichtenstein, 1971). It is certainly true that some people have stopped smoking forever or have permanently stopped overeating. By far the wisest expectation, though, is that this kind of problem will recur. You are more likely to rapidly reinstitute a self-modification program if you remain aware that it may be necessary.

Unsuccessful self-modification

There is one further time at which you may terminate self-modification: if it is not working at all. In such a case, you must consider the alternatives. Should you abandon your goals? Should you seek professional assistance? In order to answer these questions, you need to examine the place of self-modification in the full spectrum of techniques for behavior change. Are there theoretical limits to the effectiveness of self-help? If so, what are they? How can you tell if they have been reached?

In Chapters Thirteen and Fourteen, we turn to a discussion of these issues.

Your own self-modification project: Step twelve

As you consider termination, there is a series of procedures you should follow.

1. Make a list of the opportunities in the natural environment in which you can practice your newly learned behavior.
2. Rate these in terms of how likely you are to be naturally reinforced for the new behavior.
3. Test for stimulus generalization. Perform the new behavior in a variety of situations. (If stimulus generalization has not occurred, you should program it into your plan.)
4. Program for resistance to extinction by instituting intermittent reinforcement.
5. Continue counting the target behavior during the above procedures.

Chapter Thirteen
Professional Help

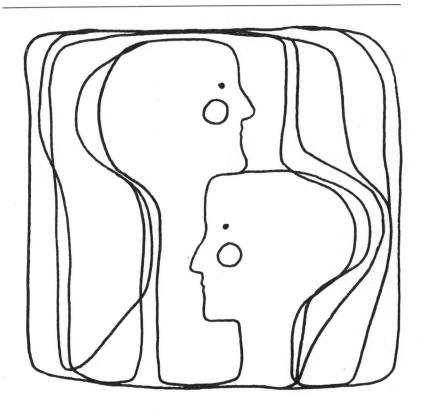

1. There are limits on self-modification: unclear goals, insufficient skill in designing an intervention plan, insufficient control over the natural environment.
2. Professional help establishes new situations that encourage the development of new behaviors and emotions.
3. A brief description of the various types of professional help that are likely to be available is presented:
   a. Nondirective counseling.
   b. Psychoanalysis.
   c. Psychotherapy.
   d. Group therapy.
   e. Sensitivity and encounter groups.
   f. Behavior therapy and behavior modification.
4. Seeking help in order to be able to help others.
5. Limits on the ability to help others.
6. Procedures for choosing a professional helper.

The aim of this chapter is to place self-modification in its proper perspective in relation to other procedures for achieving personal adjustment. Self-directed behavior change is not always possible, and there are many techniques for providing assistance. You may encounter obstacles in self-modification that you cannot overcome alone; for some of these obstacles, professional help is desirable and effective. There are so many forms of help, however, that it is often difficult to choose the appropriate one. In this chapter, we will review the major schools of thought on helping so that you can better judge the available alternatives.

The limits of self-modification

There are times when self-modification procedures are ineffective. Throughout this book, we have described points of potential difficulty. We have been optimistic in suggesting ways to correct these problems as they arise, but *there are conditions in which self-modification will not be effective.* Under these conditions, some kind of help is necessary. After a period of professional help, self-modification *can* begin, and the learning of self-determined behavior can proceed.

There are at least three conditions limiting the feasibility of a self-modification project. They are: (1) unclear goals, (2) insufficient skill in the design of the intervention, and (3) not enough control over the natural environment. We will discuss each of these in order.

Unclear goals

This limitation is an obvious and logical one. Setting specific goals in terms of behavior-in-a-situation is the first step in the mechanics of self-modification. It is also the first requirement for an effective plan. You cannot set shaping steps unless they are steps to somewhere. You cannot reward behavior unless there is some criterion for determining when the reward is earned. Think of the simplest example we have discussed: increasing study behavior. Very few students are unconcerned with doing their academic work well. But a very common kind of concern is not *how* to increase studying but *whether* to make that change. A student may have asked himself "Do I really want to? Is school that important to me? Is this really me who wants it? Maybe I should drop out for a while, maybe forever. On the other hand, my future requires college. But what future? Do I really want that future? What do I need to know? What do I want to know?" This kind of questioning can take place when considering *any* prospective self-change, from becoming less socially anxious to becoming an early riser.

So long as you are not able to formulate clear, here-and-now goals, it is useless to undertake a self-modification program. There is nothing particularly wrong with being in this condition. In fact, times of self-questioning are often very creative, and the tension is worth feeling because it will help in the task of genuine self-examination. But for some people, at some times, this uncertainty persists and intensifies. It may be emotionally upsetting. It may interfere with doing the things you want, and you may be unable to break out of the conflict into a decision. Some readers may truly want a change from this state. But self-modification, as we have outlined it in this book, is not the appropriate first step. For this problem, personal counseling (or psychotherapy) is probably the best *first* step though, as we shall see, not the last one.

Insufficient skill in designing intervention

It is perfectly clear that some efforts at self-change work better than others. There are technical differences in strategies that make a real difference in outcome. Self-directedness involves a set of skills and knowledge. If one does not have enough skill to design a solution to a particular problem, then self-change is not very likely to occur. Familiarity with the principles of behavior is one way to facilitate skill building. Study of the techniques discussed in this book is another. Actual performance of self-modification projects is the best. Some people learn the skills without ever considering them abstractly. No matter how they are learned, skill and knowledge must be acquired somehow. Without adequate learning, self-modification cannot be expected to succeed.

Competence for dealing with any problem is always a matter of two things: your skill and the difficulty of the problem. So "adequate skill" is not an absolute concept: your skills may be adequate for some problems but not for others. Increasing skill means expanding the range of problems and difficulty with which you can deal. But even experts in self-modification, who could reasonably be expected to be proficient in these matters, find situations in which consulting other professionals is useful. Any individual who is engaged in behavior modification will encounter *some* technical problems that challenge his immediate capacity to analyze. This is a situation in which help from others is appropriate. Professional help would be particularly appropriate, since professional, technical expertise is often exactly the missing ingredient.

At any point in a self-modification program, some particularly knotty problem can arise: establishing appropriate categories, understanding complicated and obscure chains of events, observing highly subtle antecedents to emotional reactions, analyzing paradoxical *suds* ratings, and so on. Professional experts can be very useful consultants who can assist you back to the route of self-directedness.

Often, for the careful reader of this book, a quite brief professional consultation is enough to spark the ideas for a problem solution. Even our beginning students at the university have rarely needed more than two or three "professional consultations" during their first self-modification projects. These consultations usually take the form of chatting with us for fifteen minutes or so about a particular shaping or category or reinforcement problem. Most students have required no such assistance, and fewer than 5% have required continuous professional guidance for their projects. Nevertheless, even though the typical reader is not likely to need professional consultation, *any* reader very well might profit from such assistance at some time.

Insufficient control over the natural environment

There are circumstances in which problems are not ones of technical analysis. Rather, they require for their solution situations that simply cannot be arranged. The natural environment is often stubborn, and it is always complex. The small steps required by some *in vivo* management programs may not be arrangeable in a bustling and unpredictable world.

We can illustrate this problem by comparing two actual cases, one that was manageable and one that was not. It is interesting that the manageable one was an extremely severe problem, while the unmanageable one was much less extreme.

A career navy officer was responsible for training naval recruits in beach landings. For several years, he had not faltered in the performance of this duty, even though it required truly extraordinary personal cour-

age. This courage was required because he had developed a nearly
overwhelming fear of water. The history of his fear was easily traceable
to a series of terrifying beach landings during earlier combat years. This
fear had become conditioned to the surf itself. For days before each new
beach-landing exercise, he would be in a state of dread, sleeplessness,
and shame. His extraordinary courage cannot be overemphasized, as
anyone will realize who has consistently forced himself into fearful
situations. But courage will not suffice to remove the fear itself.

This officer designed a totally effective *in vivo* self-desensitization
program. He correctly outlined a series of gradual approaches to the
surf, starting from a distance of fifty yards and ending by splashing in
breakers over his head. The relaxation needed for reconditioning was
achieved in two ways. First, he conducted the program in a maximally
relaxed atmosphere—on a public beach, on the weekend, on picnics
with his family. Second, and most important, he used the relaxed and
secure feelings that being with his wife brought him. He made each of
his approaches to the water while holding her hand. Because she was
a patient and understanding wife, she helped by providing rich cues for
relaxation—smiling, attentiveness, patience, and affection. In a matter
of two months, they were enjoying swimming together, and his fear
during landing exercises had disappeared.

Although this was a severe problem, it yielded easily to self-modification because the natural environment of the officer was manageable
in two important ways. The first was that the surf is a relatively stationary thing. *When a feared object is stationary, you can regulate your distance
from it.* If the feared object moves around unpredictably, as birds do, it
is much more difficult to carefully regulate approach steps.

The second important way in which the officer's environment was
manageable was in his wife's sensitive willingness to cooperate. Recall
the opposite situation in Chapter Ten when the boy friend pushed the
girl into the flock of pigeons. *When a self-modification program requires
certain behaviors by other people, you must be able to induce those behaviors.*

Our second case illustrates the problem of lack of control over the
environment. A very shy girl found herself suffering from increasing
loneliness during her second year in college. She had always been very
quiet and did not really mind that, but now she had become almost
completely isolated socially. Because she lived at home and took a city
bus to her campus each day, she saw her classmates only on campus.
A careful analysis revealed that she felt reasonably comfortable talking
to just one person at a time, but her discomfort increased sharply when
there were more people in a group. At those times, her rate of speaking
fell to almost zero.

She attempted to increase her conversations by carefully shaping the time spent with one other person and by requiring herself to increase the number of sentences exchanged in conversation. The plan was not successful, because this small college had only one main building and the students were always together in a small space. The opportunities to talk to one person at a time almost never occurred. The discomfort she felt when others joined her two-person group was too great for her to overcome. The social mixing was too continuous and uncontrolled for her to get the gradual practice opportunities she needed. In this case, the natural social environment could not be organized in the way that her shaping program required.

We suggested that she use the help of her professional school counselor, who did provide the initial assistance she needed. After growing more comfortable in her conversations with him, the girl was enrolled into a counseling group. This small group provided an artificial but well-controlled social environment. She was able to practice many conversational behaviors in that setting and gained reduction of her anxieties. She was then better equipped to continue her self-improvement program in the more difficult natural environment.

The general principle of professional psychological help

In the next section, we will discuss some of the many forms of professional psychological help. There is one general strategy that they all employ. It is this: *the help is in establishing new situations that encourage the development of new behaviors and emotions.* This help toward new situations can take many forms: sometimes it will be direct consultation in self-modification design; sometimes the helper himself *is* the new situation.* Thus, a psychotherapist (or a sensitivity group) may provide the regulated social environment that allows careful shaping and that, at its best, can also provide reinforcement.

The principles governing professional help are not different from those by which self-modification operates. The helping professions do not force behaviors and experiences out of people against their wills. Unless the self-guiding, self-directing functions of the individual are engaged in the process, behavioral and emotional changes simply do not

---

*There is one exception to this principle, which is the use of medicines that have a direct chemical effect on the physiological correlates of behavior and emotions (for example, tranquilizers). These tactics are temporary ones and must be supplemented by new situational supports to the new behaviors. Tranquilizers can reduce anxieties, but new learning still requires the readjustment of antecedents and consequences.

occur during psychological treatment. For this reason, counselors and psychotherapists have always warned that their help is effective only if the client is motivated to change. Behavior-modification psychologists are prone to emphasize the professional helper's responsibility for arranging incentives and reinforcers, but even behavior-modification helpers enlist the active participation of the client in establishing criteria, negotiating reinforcers, writing contracts, and so on. (The only exceptions might be with extremely young children, severe retardates, court-committed mental-hospital patients, and the like.)

So the reader who chooses professional help will find himself still engaged in building his own self-modification skills. What you will find is professional assistance in the creation of an environment that will foster your own efforts to change.

There are many techniques used by psychological helpers for creating these new environmental supports. Some procedures have been developed into "schools" of treatment, and there is much dispute among practitioners over preferred methods. Ideally, *different methods should be selected according to the particular problem facing a particular client.* The criterion for selection should be how well a method may be expected to establish an environment that will best foster the goal, since the general principles that determine change are the same for each method.* These environments are not "better" or "worse" than one another, but one may certainly be preferred over another for a given goal. The next section is designed to give the reader an overview of the helping environments created by several of the techniques.

Summary

There are three reasons why self-modification may not work: (1) unclear goals, (2) insufficient skill in designing the modification plan, and (3) insufficient control over the natural environment. For these situations, professional help can be sought. The professional helps by establishing new situations that encourage the development of new behaviors and emotions.

The helping environments

The title of this section, "The helping environments," has been chosen to emphasize the one element of professional treatment on

---

*Several authors—Ullmann and Krasner (1969), Bandura (1969), and Kanfer and Phillips (1970)—have described how different forms of treatment, when they are successful, have *correctly applied principles of learning in their various treatment tactics.*

which we focus. Each of the positions we will discuss has an elaborate theoretical justification and an extensive literature; proponents of every position discussed here may find our necessarily brief discussion frustrating. The list of recommended readings at the end of the chapter contains at least one thorough and sympathetic work on each technique.

This section is written for the consumer, not the provider, of services. The niceties of theory are of less interest to the prospective client than are *the simple issues: What will be done with me? Will it help? How can I tell to whom I should go?* Our discussion focuses on these issues. It is an effort to create an informed clientele, one that can judge the intentions and qualities of professional help.

Nondirective counseling

Nondirective (or "client-centered") counseling is the technique most likely to be used in college counseling centers. The technique involves regular, private conversations between the counselor and the client. The counselor creates a special environment by his noncritical acceptance of whatever the client says. The counselor must signal by speech or gesture his acceptance of a very broad range of statements about thoughts and feelings. The counselor's speech is mostly limited to brief questions or restatements of the client's statements, especially those about feelings, in order to clarify exactly what the client means. This extremely simple technique is much harder to manage than it sounds. It is also surprisingly powerful.

A moment's thought will suggest that this is indeed a new (and almost unique) interpersonal environment. Because of the wide range of statements that are reinforced by the counselor, more statements about more subjects *will* be made than ever before. Thus, this is an excellent environment for self-exploration, since the client becomes more and more free to verbalize his feelings and to think aloud about many alternatives. Unlike usual conversations, the client is not punished by being scolded, laughed at, mocked, argued with, reasoned with, or subjected to the listener's own hangups. The typical outcome of nondirective counseling is a greater degree of self-acceptance and a clarification of goals and values. For this reason, we suggested early in the chapter that *counseling can be helpful in clarifying goals for self-directedness.* Nondirective counseling may also be helpful in increasing feelings of self-esteem (Rogers and Dymond, 1954). However, nondirective counseling would not be the most effective environment for the treatment of a specific problem or for a difficulty in a self-modification design.

Psychoanalysis

The intellectual history of the western world has been profoundly affected by the work of Sigmund Freud and his followers. Psychoanalysis, the movement originated by Freud, is actually composed of several theories—theories of the organization of the mind, the development of human personality, the organization of society, the development of abnormal behavior, and the treatment of psychological problems. We will deal only with the theory of treatment itself. As a treatment technique, psychoanalysis involves regular, sometimes daily, hour-long private sessions between the psychoanalyst and the patient, in which the patient's task is to say whatever comes into his mind (free association). In the early stages, the analyst says almost nothing, except what is required to build and maintain rapport. Later, he may offer explanations (interpretations) of the patient's thoughts and behaviors. This simple technique is extraordinarily difficult for both the analyst and the patient, because it requires the analyst to gain a strong emotional investment from the patient, while the patient is being "frustrated" by the analyst's relative inactivity. This is truly a unique interpersonal environment, because both positive reinforcement and punishment are virtually absent.

In learning-theory terms, nondirective counseling operates by broadly reinforcing the client's behavior, while psychoanalysis operates by *extinguishing* his usual behaviors. As would be expected, as the patient's usual interpersonal behaviors extinguish, new ones are tried. Those newer ones extinguish and so on, until the patient's responses are reduced to rather childish ones. (This process is called therapeutic "regression.") From that point, the analyst attempts to help the patient rebuild his repertoire into a more effective, mature set of behaviors and emotions. At this time, the analyst may become more active in verbal reinforcement. However, the actual analysis of thoughts and behaviors is carried out largely by the patient himself. In this sense, psychoanalysis is a self-help technique.

Because of the extinction and regression during treatment, the patient experiences considerable emotionality, frustration, and uncertainty. Analysts suggest that their patients delay any major life decision (marriage, divorce, career change, and so on) until treatment has ended. This may be a period of years.

Psychoanalysis requires that the client possess verbal skill, an introspective bent, an intellectual personality, and great patience. These limitations, plus the fact that psychoanalysis is expensive, have caused public and professional disenchantment with this once-favorite technique. However, psychoanalysis does create a very powerful environment for change. These changes are likely to cross a wide range of behaviors (at least at a verbal level), and the outcome of treatment is hard to anticipate. The use of this treatment in correcting specific problems is also rather limited, as would be expected from an environment that does not differentially reinforce specific behaviors.

In our opinion, psychoanalysis may soon be of primarily historical interest. Its impact on current techniques is likely to be felt indirectly through its profound affect on the history of ideas and through the influence it has had on *psychotherapy.*

Psychotherapy

"Dynamic" *psychotherapy* is the technique used by most psychiatrists, clinical psychologists, and psychiatric social workers in public institutions and private practice. It often draws from the theory of psychoanalysis but less from psychoanalytic technique. Actually, in the private weekly or semiweekly conversations, the therapist uses "client-centered" reinforcement and psychoanalytic "extinction" quite liberally. He is also apt to make specific suggestions for behaviors, to use medicines as aids, to consult with family members or friends, and generally to be more directive and active.

The psychotherapist self-consciously *uses the environment of the therapist-patient relationship* as the arena for the patient's learning. Many therapists do not consciously use behavior theory, but all reward or do not reward certain behaviors (usually verbally) and all use the patient's behaviors toward the therapist as examples of real-life habits. Hopefully, the serious problems *will* occur in interaction with the therapist (fear or shyness or suspicion or whatever) and they can be modified by the therapist's reactions. The newly learned behaviors and emotions can then, it is hoped, be transferred or generalized by the patient outside the therapy hour.

The use of the therapeutic relationship as an *example* of real life is psychotherapy's strength and its weakness. It is a weakness because generalization to real life does not occur automatically. Behavior is often quite specific to situations, and a patient can become very well adjusted to his therapist but still experience great difficulty in the real world. For this reason, Kanfer and Phillips (1970) have advocated that psychotherapy pay much more attention to teaching self-modification skills. Thus, the therapist would suggest various patient behaviors and would help him design effective real-life plans simultaneously with the psychotherapy. Good psychotherapists do this, of course, but Kanfer and Phillips argue that it should become a more self-conscious and central intervention technique. We completely agree.

Using the therapy relationship as an example, or sample, of real life is also the great strength of psychotherapy. This is one relationship that can be regulated and controlled for the patient's welfare. The therapist will not push the patient into a flock of pigeons or push him into unduly frightening conversations or allow the patient to get in over his head by shaping too rapidly toward greater skill. This special relationship is valuable precisely *because* it is not like the restless, often unpredictable real world.

For this reason, psychotherapy can be very useful when self-modification fails due to the impossibility of controlling other people's behavior. Through psychotherapy, enough competence may be gained by the patient so that he can continue his self-direction efforts in the more difficult world outside the therapy sessions.

Like nondirective counseling and psychoanalysis, ordinary psychotherapy is more appropriate for general problems than for specific ones, because the therapy relationship itself tends to become complicated and involve many issues. For this reason, too, psychotherapy is appropriate for severe emotional problems, which often cause disruption of a wide range of behaviors including self-modification efforts. Thus, psychotherapy can help in efforts toward self-modification when (1) the general social world cannot be adequately controlled in self-modification; (2) emotional problems are severe enough to interfere with self-modification behaviors themselves; and (3) so many separate problems exist that the nonprofessional cannot analyze and understand them. Ideally, psychotherapy should contain strong elements of assistance from the therapist in designing extratherapy, self-directed behaviors.

Group therapy

We will use the term *group therapy* to refer to regular, continuing meetings with a professional psychotherapist by a group of approximately eight people whose purpose is to modify general or specific problems of adjustment. (Sensitivity and encounter groups will be discussed next.) Therapy groups meet for an hour or more, one or more times a week. This technique is prevalent in college counseling centers, mental health centers, hospitals, and in private practice. The patients in a group are usually similar to one another in age and types of problems. The activity of the therapist is very much like that in psychotherapy, and the strategy is the same: to consider the behavior in the group as an example of general life behaviors.

Group therapy has advantages and disadvantages, and these grow out of the characteristics of this helping environment. Because there are more people present, the relationships among group members are more varied. *This makes the therapy environment a more accurate and representative sample of real life.* But this is also the disadvantage: the group is necessarily a less controlled social environment than one with only the therapist and one patient present.

Everyone in the group speaks, and clients' comments to one another can be extremely helpful. On the other hand, sometimes they aren't helpful at all. The therapist's task is to teach good helping behaviors and to protect individuals from nonhelpful group interactions. A "good" therapy group—one that has been working together for a time and that has developed effective mutual helping behaviors—can be a most powerful environment for change because the group members become very important to one another and their interactions become powerful positive and negative reinforcers.

Group therapy provides an excellent "artificial" environment for a person who has limited social relationships. If you have few friends to depend on for helping with self-modification programs, or if your friendships are such that you can't count on them to help organize the natural environment, the therapy group is appropriate as a first step in training for self-directedness. This is especially true if the problematic behaviors and feelings involve relationships with other people.

Actually, the group-therapy environment can be an excellent one with which to coordinate a self-modification program. It is an appropriate arena for shaping steps of social behaviors, and it gives a good limited environment for self-observation.

Unfortunately, few group therapists at this time are accustomed to focusing on specific goals. Group discussions are naturally wide ranging, and the technique easily results in diffuse attention to a whole variety of relationship issues. No doubt because of this, group therapy has not been remarkably successful in modifying specific patient problems. But active and motivated patients largely agree that general emotional and social-adjustment changes do occur, and these are usually reported as beneficial and pleasant ones. As with other forms of psychotherapy, we recommend group treatment for a reader who has failed in self-modification because of broad emotional problems or because of a limited flexibility in his social world. Ideally, group therapy could be considered after the failure of one attempt at self-modification and before another attempt is made.

Sensitivity and encounter groups

Although they began as shorter and more intense adaptations of group therapy, *sensitivity* and *encounter* (S and E) groups have now developed techniques and a rationale of their own. It is difficult to describe the exact nature of the techniques because new variations are offered frequently. Basically, a group of individuals meet together with a group leader, sometimes called a "facilitator" or "convener." The group may be much larger than the therapy group. Meetings may be for one time only, or they may continue for a period of months. They may be two or three hours long or last for entire continuous weekends. A popular variation of this "marathon" length is the twelve- or twenty-four-hour meeting.

The press has paid much attention to the nude-group variation, and all manner of exotic environments are offered by competing encounter "retreats" or resorts: nude-swimming groups, sulfur-bath groups, encounter groups with instant replay television facilities, groups engaging in quasi-sexual or actual sexual activities, groups designed specifically for verbally attacking one another, tramping-through-the-woods groups, and so on, with these activities occurring in many combinations.

S and E groups are usually held in far less sensational settings, however, and nudity and sexuality are not typical components. Currently, most groups are conducted on college campuses or in churches and by leaders in private practice. The basic aim of these environments is to increase interpersonal sensitivity, to foster honest and direct self-expression, and to encourage "authentic" encounters among people.

Advocates of S and E see these environments as an antidote to our currently dehumanized lives and to the lack of real contact in this depersonalized, overpopulated world. Leaders of the groups have developed many techniques for fostering instant relationships, heightened emotionality, and unusually direct speech. Marathon groups also depend upon exhaustion and sleeplessness to produce unusual behaviors and experiences. Continuing sensitivity groups, popular now in many college courses, concentrate more on encouraging accurate perceptions of what people communicate to one another.

Scientific evidence that S and E groups provide any long-term behavior or emotional change is *totally* lacking. This certainly is not because "nothing happens" in S and E. The main reason for lack of evidence has been the antiscientific attitudes of most S and E leaders. Research into the group activities is said to be a part of what the group is trying to get away from: excessive rationality and the impersonality of science.

Nevertheless, anyone who has participated fully in an S and E experience knows that *something* has happened. And of course it has. New behaviors have been tried out, new patterns of social reinforcement have been received, strong and unusual emotional experiences have reconditioned many stimuli. There is no reason to expect that these changes will last, of course, unless the general environment is modified to support the changes. If enduring change is to occur, it must be through self-directed activity *after* the S and E experience. However, some people do report that their group experience has given them ideas for new self-goals.

At the present time, we consider S and E groups as an adventure. *Like all adventures, the outcome is uncertain.* There are several reasons why people go adventuring. One is for the flash, the rush, the excitement of rapid action and novelty. Another is to make discoveries. S and E groups can serve both of these motives. The individual who wants his life shaken up in some unspecified way, almost any way, might better look to S and E than to systematic self-modification. The latter is appropriate only when goals are clear.

One word of caution. S and E, like any adventure, has its dangers. People whose emotional balance is rather precarious have had extremely bad experiences in S and E. Intense marathon sessions are especially likely to precipitate major emotional disorders in some few individuals. Unfortunately, to identify these individuals beforehand is difficult, even for the person himself. *The best protection against misfortune is an experienced and competent leader.* We are rather conservative in this position and recommend that *the reader avoid any S and E group that is not led by a professional psychologist or psychiatrist or an experienced social worker or counselor.* The credentials and experience of the leader should be carefully evaluated before enrolling. There are many itinerant S and E facilitators these days who are not trained to assume any responsibility for the welfare of their customers and who do not remain in the community to help anyone adversely affected.

Behavior therapy and behavior modification

The current practice of behavioral treatment involves a combination of all principles of learning, just as self-modification does. Behavioral-treatment professionals are likely to be expert in the analysis of chains of events, in the arrangement of antecedents, and in the design and management of contingencies. One major example of behavioral treatment is *clinical desensitization,* which we have already detailed on pp. 171–189.

Another important technique is *assertive training,* in which clients are taught to be more socially assertive. This strategy is designed to reduce frustration and fear by making clients more effective in achieving their goals.

Assertive training is of special interest because it is typically achieved in the real world through a series of gradual steps. The therapist and client work out the shaping schedule together in the office, and between appointments the patient looks for opportunities to practice— for example, telling a waitress to take back a bowl of cold soup, insisting on correct change, speaking to a strange girl, and so on. These are *in vivo* methods. Since generalization opportunities are greater, *in vivo* methods are always the best methods if the technical problems of environmental control can be solved.

Behavior therapists are flexible in moving back and forth between clinical (office) methods and *in vivo* ones. When a client cannot manage to control his natural environment, the therapist may begin *imaginative assertive* training, in which the client *imagines* demanding correct change or sending back the soup, and, as the therapist verbally guides the fantasy, the client also imagines pleasant outcomes. These clinical imagination techniques are useful. They do have some learning effect, although less than that accompanying *in vivo* experiences, and the imagination can be controlled when the real world cannot. When these imaginative events have produced initial steps of learning, the therapist begins to move back to *in vivo* settings as the client's adjustment evolves.

This meshing of action and fantasy techniques is the great strength of behavior therapy. In both processes, the client is actively involved and so gains self-determination skills and confidence during the treatment itself.

Behavioral treatment is consistent with the overall strategy suggested in this book. Behavior therapy is appropriate as a helping environment whenever you encounter difficulties in analyzing problems, in designing self-modification plans, or in controlling the natural environment.

The research evidence for the effectiveness of behavior modification is persuasive. In fact, *higher success rates are reported than for any other form of psychological therapy.*

The behavior therapist is likely to focus on specific behavioral or emotional problems and design relearning experiences for them. Critics of behavior therapy, however, object that it is *too* specific. They argue that behavior therapists focus on such specific problems that they ignore the ways in which different problems are connected to each other. Behavior therapy is said to ignore the "whole" person. This criticism is likely to come from psychotherapists who have the rather different goals of overall self-discovery and self-realization. Behavior therapists counter that behavior and emotion *are* rather specific and that few clients need or want a total reorganization. It is true that behavior therapy began with a tight focus on individual behaviors and emotions. At the present time the field is changing toward a broad-spectrum focus in which the client's entire set of abilities is considered and evaluated (Lazarus, 1971; Bandura, 1969).

The professional behavioral consultant—one who offers his services to the public, either privately or through a mental health or counseling center—is likely to be a professional psychologist, though some psychiatrists, social workers, and counselors also have behavioral consultation as a specialty. These helpers are the most appropriate *technical* advisors for correcting a self-modification system.

Earlier we warned against inadequately trained sensitivity-group leaders. The same caution must be exercised in selecting a behavior-modification professional. The successes of behavioral treatment have brought about an increase in their popularity and a corresponding increase in self-styled behavioral "experts." Declaring oneself an expert does not make it so. The potential client should satisfy himself as to the genuine qualifications and experience of the professional whom he consults.

Seeking help in order to help others

When you want to help someone else, it is also appropriate to seek professional assistance. Although many helpers—psychotherapists, psychodynamically oriented counselors or psychiatrists, and so on—may be expected to offer advice, the professional behavior-modification consultant is more likely to offer direct advice that will facilitate your helping others. The consultant must determine the appropriate reinforcers and the appropriate target behavior for the person with the problem. Often you may be the best individual to dispense his reinforcement, and the consultant can help you to evaluate this issue.

For behavior-modification programs designed to help others in the natural environment, the intervention technique is highly similar to that for self-modification. That is, the problem must be behaviorally specified, observations and baseline data collected, an intervention plan designed, a contract specified, and reinforcement made contingent on the desired behavior. The same principles must be considered: avoiding punishment, using immediate reinforcement, shaping carefully, selecting incompatible responses, and so on. The difference between self-modification and the helping of others is in *who dispenses the reinforcers.*

In self-modification, you ordinarily control your own reinforcement. When someone else is being helped, the reinforcers may be dispensed and withheld by a second person, called the "mediator." The mediator is often active in collecting observations and frequency data and in generally supervising the maintenance of the intervention plan.

When should you seek professional assistance in helping someone else? The answer is a simple one: when you have decided to help someone and are unable to do it successfully. This situation will most often happen when you have responsibility for someone else. If you are a parent, you have responsibility for your young child. If you are a teacher, you are responsible for your pupils. If you are a resident counselor, you are responsible for the delinquent girls who live in your cottage. Cases like this are clear and, if you are unable to help your charges achieve the behavioral goals that have been set for them, it would seem appropriate to seek expert help.

But what if your concern is for a friend, a fiancé, a spouse, or a roommate? To what extent should you intervene in someone else's life and behavior?

The value judgment

The values of our society are such that if the person himself requests your help, few would think that helping is unethical. If a friend asks you to help him develop good study habits, many would applaud this request. But suppose your friend asks your help in increasing the number of homosexual contacts he makes. Some would consider this goal worth your assistance, but most would not. Helping is much more than just a bag of technical tricks. Whenever you make the decision to aid in devising an intervention for someone else's behavior, you must ask yourself two value questions: (1) Do I feel that it is ethical to increase this behavior? (2) Do I feel that it is ethical to intervene in this person's life?

Our personal values lie with self-determination—that is, we feel that each person can best choose and determine his own behaviors. That is why the largest part of this book deals with techniques that you can use to gain greater control over your own life. But it is unrealistic to simply say "Don't intervene in other people's lives." Some people are important to us, and we do want to help them; some others, we *must* try to help. The question is *when is your "help" helpful?*

Is your "help" helpful?

In considering whether or not to agree to help someone who is asking for your assistance in designing an intervention, the primary question to answer is: *Do you know enough to help someone else?* If your help is requested for washing the car or listening patiently to a distraught friend or sharing some of your experiences in handling a similar crisis, of course you probably do. But if your help is requested in specifically designing some form of behavior-modification intervention, the answer is probably no. Certainly *reading this book,* if that is your sole preparation, *is not sufficient to prepare you for designing interventions for other people for any but the simplest problems.*

This may seem inconsistent with our general encouragement to attempt *self*-modification in quite complex situations. However, it is not inconsistent: you are probably the best judge of your own feelings, your own reinforcers, your own current behavior capacities, your own relative values, and all the complexities of your personal life. But making these judgments for someone else is just as difficult as it would be for someone else to know all of this information about you.

There is a second reason for this caution. Intervention plans often involve people other than the target person himself. Mediators may be involved, or the target behaviors may be directed toward other people. This requires knowledge and ability to make judgments about people whom you may not know. Furthermore, the technical problems of involving mediators in a plan are considerable. For example, each mediator must also be reinforced for continuing his correct behaviors. It is often necessary to create a complex system of interlocking reinforcements when a group of people are involved.

Of course, the behavioral principles are the same when the target is someone else as they are in self-modification, but the effects of a plan on yourself can be judged immediately and sensitively by you. The effects of a plan on someone else are much more difficult to perceive. Emotional effects are especially subtle and difficult to judge in other people. Frequency data on behavior changes are available, of course, and effectiveness can be judged in this way. But the more subtle feeling reactions occur long before frequency data can be evaluated. In self-modification, your plan will be continuously guided by your own judgments and emotional reactions. It is difficult to be this sensitive to *other* people's concerns. It is even difficult to be present often enough to try to understand.

That is not to say that these skills cannot be learned. Of course they can be, because that is what professional training for expert consultants involves. Fortunately, there is an increasing number of excellent references. Careful study of these materials will increase your knowledge of how to help others. This further preparation is highly desirable. For example, if you are thinking of designing a behavior-modification program for your own child, you should master a source such as Patterson and Guillon's *Living with Children* (1968) before proceeding.

There is no reason, however, why you may not attempt to help others, if you have adequate access to the amount of knowledge needed. Your own study may be sufficient for some issues; at other times you should seek consultation for yourself in order to make yourself a more effective consultant to others. In all cases, we suggest a conservative estimate of your own skills. Behavioral techniques are powerful ones, and they can go awry with unfortunate but still powerful results.

Choosing a professional helper

The ideal helper possesses the full range of techniques and can vary them according to the changing needs of the client. As we have seen, some helping environments are more appropriate than others in the learning of different behaviors. The principles that describe the relationship of behavior to the environment are general ones and apply to all.

It is unfortunate that the potential client cannot depend on encountering this ideal helper. We fervently hope that the next decades will see this ideal realized. In the meantime, the reader who has decided to seek professional assistance should, like all consumers, carefully evaluate the products offered.

Where are professional helpers located? They are found in college counseling centers, student health services, psychological clinics in departments of psychology, psychiatric clinics in schools of medicine; in community mental health centers, family service agencies, guidance clinics; in the private practice of psychology, psychiatry, or social work; in community centers, church counseling centers; and in specialized clinics, such as those for drug abuse or alcoholism.

Are professional degrees a reliable guide to competence? They are reliable to some extent, but not totally. The Ph.D. is generally the minimum degree for independent professional practice of psychology, but the degree should have been obtained in the area of practice. The M.D. is the minimum degree for the practice of psychiatry, but the field of psychiatry ethically requires an additional residency training in that specialty: the M.D. alone is not a guarantee of professional psychological competence. The same issue is present in the practice of social work, in which the M.S.W. is the minimum degree. But there are several specialties in this profession also, not all of which equip the social worker to professionally consult on psychological problems. For pastoral, vocational, and educational counselors, the degree requirements are even less standardized.

Is a legal license or certificate to practice a reliable guide to competence? The *absence* of the required license or certification in your state is a reliable guide to below-minimum qualifications. But holding such a license or certificate ensures only a minimum of training and experience: all licensed individuals are not equally competent. Furthermore, few states require licensing or certification for many helping professions—social work, pastoral counseling, and so on. In addition, professionals working in institutions are often excused from legal requirements, so that a lack of licensing in that case does not indicate low qualifications.

How do you choose, then? A beginning step in choosing a satisfactory professional helper is to assess his general reputation. This information may be sought from other professionals, from people whose opinion generally can be trusted, or from previous clients of the individual in question. Obviously, this is not totally reliable.

The more important step is to determine the training and experience of the professional. This is not difficult to do, because the professional himself can be asked to detail these matters for you. The prospective client should not be embarrassed about making inquiries. Direct questions about schools attended, degrees obtained, location of internship or residency training, years of experience, theoretical orientation, and so on, will *not* offend the competent practitioner. A prospective client is very wise to get this information, directly or indirectly.

The third step is also highly important but is rarely taken by prospective clients. Ask the professional to determine exactly what procedures he intends to follow in your case. The *goals* of treatment should be clearly understood by both you and the professional. It is also reasonable to discuss how his intended procedures relate to achieving the goal.

In this way, the process of self-determination can proceed during any phase in which professional help is used. The helping professions are just that—*helping;* this implies a responsibility for you, the client, in the continuing process of achieving self-determination.

Summary

If you think that you need to consult a professional, you should be able to state why. Is it because your goals are unclear: you're not sure what you want? Is it because you do not have the experience to design a successful intervention plan or because the problem is complicated? Is it because you do not have adequate control over the natural environment? Is it because you cannot carry out the intervention plan as it should be done?

The professional can provide new situations in which new behaviors can be developed. Thus, you can better select a professional if you have an idea of the kind of situation he is likely to provide—nondirective, psychoanalytic, psychotherapeutic, group, S and E, behavior modifying—and the kind of situation you think would be best for you. You should feel free to question the professional about his training and qualifications and about how he proposes to work with you.

Recommended readings

Nondirective counseling

Rogers, C. R. *Client-centered therapy, its current practice, implications, and theory.* Boston: Houghton Mifflin, 1951.

Rogers, C. R. *On becoming a person; a therapist's view of psychotherapy.* Boston: Houghton Mifflin, 1961.

Psychoanalysis

Brenner, C. *An elementary textbook of psychoanalysis.* New York: International Universities Press, 1955.

Menninger, K. A. *Theory of psychoanalytic technique.* New York: Basic Books, 1958.

Psychotherapy

Ford, D. H., and Urban, H. B. *Systems of psychotherapy: A comparative study.* New York: Wiley and Sons, 1963.

Group psychotherapy

Bach, G. R. *Intensive group psychotherapy.* New York: Ronald Press, 1954.

Sensitivity and encounter groups

Burton, A. (Ed.) *Encounter: The theory and practise of encounter groups.* San Francisco: Jossey-Bass, 1969.

Behavior therapy and behavior modification

Franks, C. M. (Ed.) *Behavior therapy: Appraisal and status.* New York: McGraw-Hill, 1969.

Bandura, A. *Principles of behavior modification.* New York: Holt, Rinehart & Winston, 1969.

Tharp, R. G., & Wetzel, R. W. *Behavior modification in the natural environment.* New York: Academic Press, 1969.

Chapter Fourteen
Self-Modification and Willpower

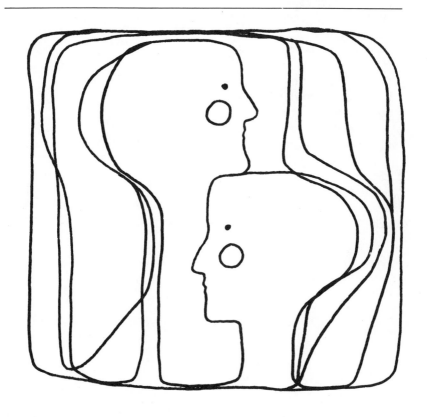

1. This chapter raises the general issue of how much willpower is required to perform the behaviors of self-modification.
2. Does self-modification really work? Responses to the following series of questions provide an answer.
   a. Is self-reinforcement reinforcing?
   b. Is self-reinforcement learnable?
   c. How does setting a rule for oneself affect one's behavior?
   d. How does knowledge of results affect one's behavior?
3. Shaping, immediate reinforcement, and the incentive value of the reinforcement reduce the amount of willpower necessary.
4. Will *is* the act of self-determination.

Does self-reinforcement *really* work? Even the reader who has completed a successful project may ask this question: was it the self-reinforcement or was it the willpower that made the difference?

This is a worthy issue, that raises a whole series of questions. First, what does "willpower" mean? Defining willpower is the real purpose of this entire chapter, so we would like to hold our answer to that question. For the time being, use the ordinary dictionary definition of willpower.

The second question that arises pertains to the theory itself: *is self-reinforcement reinforcing*? That is, does it affect behavior in the same way that other reinforcers do: does it strengthen the behavior that it follows?

Is self-reinforcement reinforcing?

The answer to this question is *yes*. Research in self-reinforcement began years ago, and by now there are laboratory studies that demonstrate that reinforcers, dispensed by the self, do increase the reinforced behaviors. The work of Kanfer, Marston, Bandura, and their associates is especially important here, and a decade of this investigation has recently been summarized by Kanfer (1970a). For example, Kanfer and Duerfeldt (1967) demonstrated that individuals will recognize geometric designs more accurately if they have self-reinforced accurate recognitions during training. Marston and Kanfer (1963) reported that instituting self-reinforcement for recognizing syllables results in greater accuracy than does an extinction condition, although less accuracy than continued external reinforcement. Bandura and Perloff (1967) found that self-reinforcement will maintain manual work behavior in children in a way that is comparable to external reinforcement and superior to noncontingent reinforcement or no reinforcement at all.

So reinforcement *is* reinforcement, even when administered by the self.

241

Can one learn to engage in
self-reinforcement?

To ask "Does it really work?" raises a third question: can one learn the *act* of self-reinforcement in the same way that one learns other acts?

Again, the answer is *yes.* Self-reinforcing behavior can itself be modified by reinforcement, as demonstrated by Kanfer and Marston (1963a).

Self-reinforcement can also be learned by imitation. When subjects are exposed to models who demonstrate self-reinforcing behavior, they learn new standards for self-reinforcement and self-evaluative responses and apply these to their behavior (Bandura and Kupers, 1964; Bandura and Whalen, 1966; Bandura, Grusec, and Menlove, 1967; McMains and Liebert, 1968). This vicarious learning of self-reinforcement appears to follow principles involved in other imitative learning. (That is, it is affected by the nature of the model, the past history with the task, and so on.) The point is this: self-reinforcement is a behavior that can be learned just as other behaviors are learned.

But, the reader may still object, one must *learn* to self-reinforce. And can one use self-reinforcement to learn self-reinforcing behavior? Isn't this just putting the issue back one step—at *some* point, isn't self-modification inevitably a question of willpower?

No, not necessarily. Note that there are techniques involved in self-modification other than self-reinforcement—for example, *rule setting, knowledge of results, shaping, immediate reinforcement,* and *incentives.* Before continuing with the direct question of whether willpower is necessary, we will examine these other techniques, for each of them reduces the amount of willpower that will be necessary.

Additional techniques involved in
self-modification

Rule setting

An important part of self-modification is the *contract,* which specifies the details of the intervention plan. The contract is the *set of rules* to follow in self-modification. By rules we mean guides to behavior, statements of what one should or should not do, independent of any positive or negative reinforcements that are attached to the rules. As it turns out, *setting* rules makes it more likely that the self-modifier will follow the rules.

Skinner (1963) has pointed out that rules and plans serve as discriminative stimuli. They become cues to behavior. Of course, their cue function is acquired or lost according to the same principles that determine the learning of any other cue: the behavior that is stimulated by the cue must be followed by reinforcement.

Rule setting does not operate independently of incentives or reinforcement. Rather, rule setting increases the chances that learning will occur when the incentive to engage in the behavior is sufficient and when the behavior is reinforced. If a man wanted to begin jogging, he would have to provide some reinforcement for that behavior, and he would have to have some incentive for wanting to increase that behavior. But it would also help if he set a rule to perform the behavior. In spite of these limitations on the power of rules, rule setting does have an effect on learning to self-reinforce one's behavior.

This topic of rule setting has been reviewed by Cheyne and Walters (1970). In addition, there are several laboratory studies that have analyzed the process. For example, O'Leary (1968) demonstrated that the simple act of *stating the rule aloud* increased the rule-following behavior. He taught first-grade boys to press a telegraph key. Whenever the key was pressed, the boy received a marble. The *rule* was this: the key should be pressed only when a certain cue (a signal or discriminative stimulus) was present. (This procedure is similar to the rules of any self-modification project.) O'Leary then left the boys alone and observed their behavior from behind a one-way mirror. Before leaving the room, half of the boys were told to state the rule aloud: they had to say when pressing the key was "fair" and when it wasn't. The other half did not have to state the rule aloud. The experimenter then simply counted the number of times each boy pressed the key and got a marble when he should not have done so—that is, in violation of the rule. The boys who had said the rule aloud deviated from the rule *four times less often* than the boys who did not have to state the rule.

Making a rule "one's own," then, by stating it instead of simply having it imposed by someone else does increase one's conformity to the rule, even when the motivation is the same.

This is true not only of first-graders. The ability, or tendency, to regulate one's behavior by verbal statements about that behavior appears to increase with age and for a variety of tasks (see Cheyne and Walters, 1970; Birch, 1966; Lovaas, 1964; Luria, 1961).

The explicitness and detail of a rule also affect learning. Liebert, Hanratty, and Hill (1969) had children observe a model playing a bowling game and rewarding himself for good scores. The children were then asked to do the same. The experimenters used three levels of rule detail, which varied from (1) having the model announce his score, "15," and take a chip, through (2) adding "that's (not) a good score," to (3) "that deserves (does not deserve) a chip!" They found that the greater the degree of rule specification, the less the children rewarded themselves inappropriately.

A precise, self-constructed contract is very important in the self-modification of behavior, because making a rule one's own and stating it explicitly affect the chance that the behavior will be performed.

To summarize, we have been discussing why willpower is not the only issue in self-modification. So far, we have considered: (1) the self-reinforcement itself and (2) the way one learns to self-reinforce. In addition, we have begun a discussion of the other techniques involved in self-modification that reduce the need for willpower. The first of these was rule setting. The next is knowledge of results.

Knowledge of results

For decades, psychology has studied the contribution of knowledge of results to learning. Hundreds of studies have been performed. A good summary source for this field may be found in W. K. Estes (1970). The basic question in the field has been this: does knowing whether one is correct or incorrect, in and of itself, improve learning?

Various forms and levels of information feedback have been studied: the experimenter has simply announced "right" or "wrong" after each of the subject's actions; the experimental subject has been signaled right or wrong by a light; the subject has been rewarded and not rewarded. Actually, the basic question has not been answered to everyone's satisfaction. Not all psychologists agree on whether or not knowledge of results alone (without any reinforcement) is sufficient to cause learning. This is because it is so difficult—perhaps actually impossible —to disentangle the simple *information* in a message from the *reinforcement* in the message. For example, saying "right" gives the subject information, but "right" is probably a social reinforcement also.

Fortunately, we do not have to face that issue here. Self-modification programs do not typically rely solely on either knowledge of results or reinforcement. The research evidence (see Estes, 1970) is very clear: all else being equal, *the more knowledge of results a person receives about his performance, the greater is his learning.*

This is one reason why we emphasize that data collection *is* a form of self-modification. Most people do not observe themselves carefully. Undertaking the task of collecting data increases the carefulness of self-observation. Increased self-observation produces greater knowledge about one's behavior. Behavioral records provide feedback and guidance, and thus one is more likely to learn (Kolb, 1971; Kolb, Winter, and Berlew, 1968).

This feedback is often enough for behavior change to occur. In working with the behavior modification of problems more severe than most of those discussed in this book, Tharp and Wetzel (1969) report that the collection of baseline data alone brought about modification of 7% of their cases' problems, and no "contracted" intervention program was required. Those cases were able to adjust their natural interactions, producing new learning, once they had adequate information feedback.

This intervention effect of gathering the baseline data sometimes works in self-modification as well. You may start out to count how many times per day some act is performed and find that the frequency changes greatly just because you are so carefully observing each occurrence.

In summary, the strongest will might be insufficient if the contingencies are wrong, if one has never learned to self-reinforce, if there are no explicit rules set, and if there is no feedback. Conversely, attention to these issues can sharply reduce the strength of will needed to establish self-determination. But is there still some minimum amount of willpower required to change ourselves? Perhaps not, because the next two techniques to be discussed, *shaping* and *immediate reinforcement*, go even further toward whittling away willpower as a principal explanation for success.

Shaping and immediate reinforcement

The logic of shaping is very simple: one is much more likely to take a small step than a giant one. People who give up their self-change programs as failures are almost always neglecting the principle of shaping. This is true whether one is working with an *in vivo* desensitization or a contingency-reinforcement program. Theoretically, it is possible to reduce the size of each next step to such a small increment that it becomes virtually "painless" to take that step.

The logic of immediate reinforcement is equally simple: one is much more likely to perform some behavior if the reinforcement comes immediately after performance than if one has to wait a long time. The trouble with New Year's resolutions is that they so often rely on a very delayed reinforcer. "If I could only lose twenty pounds this year, how much better I would look and feel at the end of the year!" It takes a long time to accomplish many of the things one wants to accomplish, and there are many opportunities to go astray before reaching that ultimate goal. It takes more willpower to stay on a diet when the reward will come only after weeks of effort than it does to stay on it when the rewards are daily. A common reason for failure in self-modification comes from relying on the ultimate, intrinsic reinforcement rather than providing immediate reinforcement for each step toward the final goal.

You can see, then, that by using shaping and immediate reinforcement along with the other helpful techniques, *you can even self-regulate the amount of willpower that you will demand of yourself.*

This does not mean that every human problem can be solved by self-modification. Sometimes other people cannot be controlled well enough for you to achieve a successful program. Sometimes immediate, sufficient reinforcers cannot be marshaled. But these are not willpower problems, *they are technical problems.*

At any moment, each of us has a given amount of self-control over a particular behavior. Shaping brings behavioral steps down to the level where self-control can be maintained. After performing at that level and being reinforced for it, you not only have made a behavioral improvement, but *you also have brought self-control (or willpower) up another step.* This increased willpower will then make it possible to move to the next step.

Thus, it does not make sense to talk about any minimum of required willpower unless it is in reference to a particular shaping step and to the amount of delay of the reinforcer.

Willpower and incentives

There is another way in which self-modification programs balance the existing level of self-control against one's behavioral requirements. That is through the use of *incentives.* Specifying in a contract that one will reward a first step with a given reinforcer provides greater incentive to take that step. Jogging a mile to pick up a penny requires a lot of "willpower." Jogging a mile to pick up a hundred-dollar bill requires almost none. Some theoreticians of human learning believe that the incentive value of rewards is much greater than their reinforcing value. This issue is not important in self-modification, because the reward is both incentive and reinforcement.

If you were able to use a strong enough incentive, the majority of your willpower problems would vanish. (Perhaps not all—we are still not done with that question.) For the moment, though, we may conclude that the willpower issue is further reduced by considering the incentives you offer yourself.

The will to self-modify

The person considering a first self-modification program will often wonder "Do I have the willpower to carry it through successfully?" At the beginning, it almost always seems that a separate act of the will must be performed each time some self-reinforcement is withheld until the required behavior has been performed. It may seem that a strong act of will is required just to launch the program in the first place.

In our terms, these questions become issues of whether or not one has, at a given moment, previously learned enough self-determining behavior to undertake the plan. Therefore, the real question is: how much ability at self-determination must one already have in order to successfully modify some behavior?

The answer is: some. But the amount needed and the point at which it is needed are rather surprising.

First let us consider the problem of withholding self-reinforcement, according to a contract, until the specified criterion is met. Readers usually anticipate this as the crucial issue. "Won't I really listen to the radio in the morning anyway, even if I haven't earned it by making up the bed?" "Won't I go to the party on Saturday night, even if I haven't earned all thirty-two points?"

The answer is: probably not. Startling as this may be, self-modification programs rarely break down over this issue. We have discussed this point earlier, under "cheating," in Chapter Eight. Most people who are seriously into their self-modification programs can step back down the shaping ladder when this problem arises and reestablish the contracted contingency. Withholding reinforcement until a reasonable shaping step has been reached is one of the easier tasks in self-modification. It requires relatively little ability at self-determination. Actually, this should not be surprising because it is to be expected logically. The whole technique of self-modification is to juggle incentives and shaping until the contingency *will* be possible to perform.

In addition to this logical point, our experience with self-modifiers indicates that the real problem with self-determination occurs much earlier in the process. If the self-modifier has the technical knowledge required to readjust his shaping schedule, withholding reinforcement will not be a large problem. The point at which the problem arises most keenly is in the earliest stages of the self-modification process.

Ordinarily, we say that in order to change, one must *want* to change. This formulation is not inconsistent with behavior analysis—it is merely incomplete. That is, one must also know *how* to change. Deciding "how" is where the real problems arise. The reader of this book has gained some knowledge of how to change through management of environmental supports. Furthermore, performing the self-determining behaviors of self-modification does make one more skillful *at* performing them. As one acquires greater self-determination skills, the second and the third projects will require fewer and fewer contrived incentives. The individual who has achieved a high level of self-determination rarely needs to formalize each of the steps outlined in this book. He already has a storehouse of self-observation and analysis abilities, and he understands the things in the environment that must be adjusted to help him achieve his goals.

But even such a person—perhaps especially such a person—will not self-direct a change that he does not want. So the desire to change is certainly a necessary component of self-directed change. A strict learning analysis would point out that *what you want is also largely learned* and that you can teach yourself to want different things. But the practical problems of self-modification face a simple question: for a project to succeed, *how much must you want that change?*

At this point in our knowledge, the answer appears to be this: *enough to do the work of the self-modification program.* Arranging self-rewards for each stage—such as self-reinforcing recording behaviors or manipulating antecedents to make behaviors less effortful (for example, by locking the refrigerator door between meals)—minimizes the efforts required by a program. But there is no way to altogether eliminate the effort factor: the energy expenditure required by the mechanics of taking notes, of formulating categories, of designing recording sheets, of counting, graphing, and analyzing. That is the willpower that is necessary. The expected benefits from change must outweigh the expected cost of effort in the project.

What is will?

In everyday language, willpower often means self-restraint: "I had the willpower not to eat too much!" Sometimes willpower means a force that enables one to pass up some immediate gratification in favor of a long-range goal or in favor of personal values. Sometimes willpower is used to explain doing something one expects to be unpleasant. At other times the word is used to explain doing something that is very difficult or that requires a long wait for positive reinforcement.

The philosophical conception of human will is more general. In this sense, the *will* refers to an aspect of the human spirit by which one guides, directs, and determines one's own destiny. A behavioral conception of the will can be very similar to the philosophical one. B. F. Skinner has written "When a man controls himself, chooses a course of action, thinks out a solution to a problem, or strives toward an increase in self-knowledge, he is *behaving*" (Skinner, 1953, p. 228). This behavior can be learned by the same principles as any other.

Scientific principles of behavior can be used to increase your range of self-determination. Self-determination can be strengthened by managing the environmental conditions that affect it. Therefore willpower *is not something separate* that must be invoked to explain self-modification. It *is* self-modification. Learning to increase self-determined behavior is learning will.

Bibliography

Ayllon, T., & Azrin, N. *The token economy: A motivational system for therapy and rehabilitation.* New York: Appleton-Century-Crofts, 1968.

Annon, J. The extension of learning principles to the analysis and treatment of sexual problems. Unpublished doctoral dissertation, University of Hawaii, 1971.

Bandura, A. *Principles of behavior modification.* New York: Holt, Rinehart & Winston, 1969.

Bandura, A., Grusec, J. E., & Menlove, F. L. Some social determinants of self-monitoring reinforcement systems. *Journal of Personality and Social Psychology,* 1967, **5,** 449–455.

Bandura, A., & Kupers, C. J. Transmission of patterns of self-reinforcement through modelling. *Journal of Abnormal and Social Psychology,* 1964, **69,** 1–9.

Bandura, A., & Perloff, B. Relative efficacy of self-monitored and externally imposed reinforcement systems. *Journal of Personality and Social Psychology,* 1967, **7,** 111–116.

Bandura, A., & Whalen, C. K. The influence of antecedent reinforcement and divergent modeling cues on patterns of self-reward. *Journal of Personality and Social Psychology,* 1966, **3,** 373–382.

Bergin, A. E. A self-regulation technique for impulse control disorders. *Psychotherapy: Theory, Research, & Practice,* 1969, **6,** 113–118.

Birch, D. Verbal control of nonverbal behavior. *Journal of Experimental Child Psychology,* 1966, **4,** 266–275.

Bringman, W. G., Kirchev, A., & Balance, W. Goethe as behavior therapist. South-Eastern Psychological Association, New Orleans, February 28 to March 1, 1969.

Cautela, J. R. Treatment of compulsive behavior by covert sensitization. *Psychological Record,* 1966, **16,** 33–41.

Cautela, J. R. Behavior therapy and self-control: Techniques and implications. In C. M. Franks (Ed.), *Behavior therapy: Appraisal and status.* New York: McGraw-Hill, 1969.

Cheyne, J. A., & Walters, R. H. Punishment and prohibition: Some origins of self-control. In T. M. Newcomb (Ed.), *New directions in psychology 4.* New York: Holt, Rinehart & Winston, 1970. Pp. 281–366.

Davison, G. C. The elimination of a sadistic fantasy by a client-controlled counter-conditioning technique: A case study. *Journal of Abnormal Psychology,* 1968, **73,** 84–90.

Di Cara, L. V. Learning in the autonomic nervous system. *Scientific American,* 1970, **222,** 30–39.

Estes, W. K. *Learning theory and mental development.* New York: Academic Press, 1970.

Ferster, C. B. Classification of behavioral pathology. In L. Krasner & L. P. Ullmann (Eds.), *Research in behavior modification.* New York: Holt, Rinehart & Winston, 1965.

Ferster, C. B., Nurnberger, J. I., & Levitt, E. G. The control of eating. *Journal of Mathetics,* 1962, **1,** 87–109.

Fox, L. Effecting the use of efficient study habits. In R. Ulrich, T. Stachnik, & J. Mabry (Eds.), *Control of human behavior.* Glenview, Ill.: Scott, Foresman, 1966. Pp. 85–93.

Freud, S. *New introductory lectures in psychoanalysis.* New York: Norton, 1933.

Goldiamond, I. Self-control procedures in personal behavior problems. *Psychological Reports,* 1965, **17,** 851–868.

Hall, V. R., Axelrod, S., Weiss, L., & Rohrer, S. Use of self-imposed contingencies to reduce the frequency of smoking behavior. Association for the Advancement of Behavior Therapy, Washington, D.C., September 5-6, 1971.

Harris, M. B. A self-directed program for weight control: A pilot study. *Journal of Abnormal Psychology,* 1969, **74,** 263–270.

Homme, L. E. Perspectives in psychology: XXIV. Control of coverants, the operants of the mind. *Psychological Record,* 1965, **15,** 501–511.

Homme, L. E., de Baca, P. C., Devine, J. V., Steinhorst, R., & Rickert, E. J. Use of the Premack principle in controlling the behavior of nursery school children. *Journal of the Experimental Analysis of Behavior,* 1963, **6,** 544.

Kahn, M., & Baker, B. Desensitization with minimal therapist contact. *Journal of Abnormal Psychology,* 1968, **73,** 198–200.

Kahn, M., & Sandler, A. A manual for self-desensitization. Unpublished manuscript, 1966.

Kanfer, F. H. Self-regulation: Research, issues, and speculations. In C. Neuringer & J. L. Michael (Eds.), *Behavior modification in clinical psychology.* New York: Appleton-Century-Crofts, 1970a. Pp. 178–220.

Kanfer, F. H. Self-monitoring: Methodological limitations and clinical applications. *Journal of Consulting and Clinical Psychology,* 1970b, **35,** 148–152.

Kanfer, F. H., & Duerfeldt, P. H. Motivational properties of self-reinforcement. *Perceptual and Motor Skills,* 1967, **25,** 237–246.

Kanfer, F. H., & Marston, A. R. Conditioning of self-reinforcing responses: An analogue to self-confidence training. *Psychological Reports,* 1963a, **13,** 63–70.

Kanfer, F. H., & Marston, A. R. Determinants of self-reinforcement in human learning. *Journal of Experimental Psychology,* 1963b, **66,** 245–254.

Kanfer, F. H., & Phillips, J. S. Behavior therapy: A panacea for all ills or a passing fancy? *Archives of General Psychiatry,* 1966, **15,** 114–128.

Kanfer, F. H., & Phillips, J. S. *Learning foundations of behavior therapy.* New York: John Wiley, 1970.

Kolb, D. A. Self-directed behavior change. In D. A. Kolb & R. Schwitzgebel (Eds.), *Behavior change.* New York: McGraw-Hill, 1972.

Kolb, D. A., Winter, S. K., & Berlew, D. E. Self-directed change: Two studies. *Journal of Applied Behavioral Science,* 1968, **4,** 453–471.

Lazarus, A. A. *Behavior therapy and beyond.* New York: McGraw-Hill, 1971.

Lichtenstein, E. Modification of smoking behavior: Good designs—ineffective treatments. *Journal of Consulting and Clinical Psychology,* 1971, **36,** 163–166.

Liebert, R. M., Hanratty, M., & Hill, J. H. Effects of rule structure and training method on the adoption of a self-imposed standard. *Child Development,* 1969, **40,** 93–101.

Lovaas, O. I. Cue properties of words: The control of operant responding by rate and content of verbal operants. *Child Development,* 1964, **35,** 245–256.

Luria, A. R. The genesis of voluntary movements. In N. O'Conner (Ed.), *Recent soviet psychology.* New York: Liverwright, 1961. Pp. 273–289.

Mahoe, L. Personality characteristics and record-keeping behavior in self-modification projects. Unpublished study, University of Hawaii, 1970.

Marston, A. R. Personality variables related to self-reinforcement. *Journal of Psychology,* 1964, **58,** 169–175.

Marston, A. R., & Kanfer, F. H. Human reinforcement: Experimenter and subject controlled. *Journal of Experimental Psychology,* 1963, **66,** 91–94.

Marston, A. R., & McFall, R. M. Comparison of behavior modification approaches to smoking reduction. *Journal of Consulting and Clinical Psychology,* 1971, **36,** 153–162.

McFall, R. M. Effects of self-monitoring on normal smoking behavior. *Journal of Consulting and Clinical Psychology,* 1970, **35,** 135–142.

McGuire, R. J., & Vallance, M. Aversion therapy by electric shock: A simple technique. *British Medical Journal,* 1964, **1,** 151–153.

McMains, M. J., & Liebert, R. M. Influence of discrepancies between successively modeled self-reward criteria on the adoption of a self-imposed standard. *Journal of Personality and Social Psychology,* 1968, **8,** 166–171.

Melamed, B., & Lang, P. J. Study of the automated desensitization of fear. Paper presented at the meeting of the Midwestern Psychological Association, Chicago, 1967.

Menninger, K. *Theory of psychoanalytic technique.* New York: Basic Books, 1958.

Migler, B. A supplementary note on automated self-desensitization. *Behavior Research and Therapy,* 1968, **6,** 243.

Migler, B., & Wolpe, J. Automated self-desensitization: A case report. *Behavior Research and Therapy,* 1967, **5,** 133–135.

Miller, N. E. Learning of visceral and glandular responses. *Science,* 1969, **163,** 434–445.

Munroe, R. L. *Schools of psychoanalytic thought.* New York: Dryden Press, 1955.

Nolan, J. D. Self-control procedures in the modification of smoking behavior. *Journal of Consulting and Clinical Psychology,* 1968, **32,** 92–93.

Nurnberger, S. I., & Zimmerman, J. Applied analysis of human behavior: An alternative to conventional motivational inferences and unconscious determination in therapeutic programming. *Behavior Therapy,* 1970, **1,** 59–69.

O'Leary, K. D. The effects of self-instruction on immoral behavior. *Journal of Experimental Child Psychology,* 1968, **6,** 297–301.

Orne, M. T. From the subject's point of view, when is behavior private and when is it public: Problems of inference. *Journal of Consulting and Clinical Psychology,* 1970, **35,** 143–147.

Patterson, G. R., & Guillon, M. E. *Living with children: New methods for parents and teachers.* Champaign, Illinois: Research Press, 1968.

Paul, G. *Insight vs desensitization in psychotherapy.* Stanford, California: Stanford University Press, 1966.

Rardin, M. Treatment of a phobia by partial self-desensitization. *Journal of Consulting and Clinical Psychology,* 1969, **33,** 125–126.

Rehm, L. P. & Marston, A. R. Reduction of social anxiety through modification of self-reinforcement: An instigation therapy technique. *Journal of Consulting Psychology*, 1968, **32**, 565–574.

Reppucci, N. D., & Baker, B. L. Self-desensitization: Implications for treatment and teaching. In R. D. Rubin & C. M. Franks (Eds.), *Advances in behavior therapy.* New York: Academic Press, 1969. Pp. 151–159.

Rogers, C. R. & Dymond, R. F. (Eds.) *Psychotherapy and personality change.* Chicago: University of Chicago Press, 1954.

Rutner, I. T. The modification of smoking behavior through techniques of self-control. Unpublished masters thesis, Wichita State University, 1967.

Rutner, I. T., & Bugle, C. An experimental procedure for the modification of psychotic behavior. *Journal of Consulting and Clinical Psychology*, 1969, **33**, 651–653.

Schachter, S. Cognitive effects on bodily functioning: Studies of obesity and eating. In D. C. Glass (Ed.), *Neurophysiology and emotion.* New York: Rockefeller University Press and Russel Sage Foundation, 1967. Pp. 117–144.

Skinner, B. F. *Science and human behavior.* New York: Macmillan, 1953.

Skinner, B. F. Operant behavior. *American Psychologist*, 1963, **18**, 503–515.

Staats, A. *Learning, language, and cognition.* New York: Holt, Reinhart & Winston, 1968.

Staats, A. W. Social behaviorism, human motivation, and conditioning therapies. In B. A. Maher (Ed.), *Progress in experimental personality research.* New York: Academic Press, 1970.

Staats, A., & Staats, C. *Complex human behavior.* New York: Holt, Rinehart & Winston, 1963.

Stuart, R. B. Behavioral control of overeating. *Behavior Research and Therapy*, 1967, **5**, 357–365.

Stuart, R. B. Situational versus self control of problematic behaviors. In R. D. Rubin (Ed.), *Advances in behavior therapy, 1970.* New York: Academic Press, 1971.

Tharp, R., & Wetzel, R. *Behavior modification in the natural environment.* New York: Academic Press, 1969.

Tooley, J. T., & Pratt, S. An experimental procedure for the extinction of smoking behavior. *Psychological Record*, 1967, **17**, 209–218.

Ullmann, L. P., & Krasner, L. *A psychological approach to abnormal behavior.* Englewood Cliffs, N.J.: Prentice-Hall, 1969.

Ullmann, L., & Krasner, L. (Eds.) *Case studies in behavior modification.* New York: Holt, Rinehart & Winston, 1965.

Ulrich, R., Stachnik, T., & Mabry, J. (Eds.) *Control of human behavior,* Glenville, Ill.: Scott, Foresman, 1966–70. 2 vols.

Watson, J. B., & Rayner, R. Conditioned emotional reactions. *Journal of Experimental Psychology,* 1920, **3**, 1–14.

Wolpe, J. *The practice of behavior therapy.* New York: Pergamon Press, 1969.

Wolpe, J., & Lazarus, A. A. *Behavior therapy techniques: A guide to the treatment of neuroses.* New York: Pergamon Press, 1966.

Name Index

Subject Index